Policing the 2012 London Olympics

The summer Olympic Games are renowned for producing the world's biggest single-city cultural event. While the Olympics and other sport mega-events have received growing levels of academic investigation from a variety of disciplinary approaches, relatively little is known about how such occasions are experienced directly by local host communities and publics.

This ethnography examines the everyday policing of the London Borough of Newham in relation to the London 2012 Olympics. It explains how police defined, monitored, prioritized, contained and investigated 'Olympic-related' crime, and how 'Olympic-related' policing connected to the policing of Newham. The authors examine how the threat of terrorism impacted on the everyday policing of the 2012 Olympics, as well as the exaggeration of other threats to the Games – such as youth gangs – for political reasons. The book also explores local resistance to Olympic policing, and the legacy of the Games with regard to policing, local housing, demographics and social exclusion.

Discussing the lessons that can be learned for the future staging of sporting mega-events, this book will appeal to scholars and students with interests in sport, policing, crime and criminology, mega-events, event management, urban studies, global studies and sociology.

Gary Armstrong is Reader in the Department of Sociology at Brunel University, London, UK.

Richard Giulianotti is Professor of Sociology at Loughborough University, and also Professor II at Telemark University College, Norway.

Dick Hobbs is Professor of Sociology at University Western Sydney University, Australia, Professor Emeritus at the University of Essex, UK, Visiting Professor of Sociology at Goldsmiths College, University of London, UK, and an Associate Fellow of the Royal United Services Institute.

Routledge Advances in Ethnography
Edited by Dick Hobbs
University of Essex
and Les Back
Goldsmiths College, University of London

Ethnography is a celebrated, if contested, research methodology that offers unprecedented access to people's intimate lives, their often hidden social worlds and the meanings they attach to these. The intensity of ethnographic fieldwork often makes considerable personal and emotional demands on the researcher, while the final product is a vivid human document with personal resonance impossible to recreate by the application of any other social science methodology. This series aims to highlight the best, most innovative ethnographic work available from both new and established scholars.

Policing the 2012 London Olympics

Legacy and social exclusion

Gary Armstrong, Richard Giulianotti and Dick Hobbs

Routledge
Taylor & Francis Group

LONDON AND NEW YORK

First published 2017
by Routledge
711 Third Avenue, New York, NY 10017

and by Routledge
2 Park Square, Milton Park, Abingdon, Oxon OX14 4RN

Routledge is an imprint of the Taylor & Francis Group, an informa business

Library of Congress Cataloging in Publication Data
Names: Armstrong, Gary, 1960- author. | Giulianotti, Richard, 1966- author.
    | Hobbs, Dick, 1951- author.
Title: Policing the 2012 London Olympics : legacy and social exclusion /
    Gary Armstrong, Richard Giulianotti and Dick Hobbs.
Description: New York, NY : Routledge, 2017. | Series: Routledge advances
    in ethnography
Identifiers: LCCN 2016009840| ISBN 9781138013377 (hardback) | ISBN
    9781315795270 (e-book)
Subjects: LCSH: Police—England—London—Case studies. | Olympic
    Games (30th : 2012 : London, England) | Olympics—Security measures.
    | Crime prevention—England—London—Case studies. | Public safety—
    England—London—Case studies.
Classification: LCC HV8196.L6 A76 2017 | DDC 363.2/3209421090512—
    dc23
LC record available at https://lccn.loc.gov/2016009840

ISBN: 978-1-138-01337-7 (hbk)
ISBN: 978-1-315-79527-0 (ebk)

Typeset in Times New Roman
by Swales & Willis Ltd, Exeter, Devon, UK

Printed and bound by CPI Group (UK) Ltd, Croydon, CR0 4YY

Contents

Contributors

Dr. Gary Armstrong is Reader in the Department of Sociology, Brunel University, London. His research has primarily focused on the sociology of deviance and the sociology of sport using ethnographic methodology. His books include: *Images of Control: The Rise of the Maximum Surveillance Society* (co-authored with Clive Norris), *Football Hooligans: Knowing the Score,* 'Global and Local Football' (co-authored with Jon Mitchell), *and Football, Fascism and Fandom: The UltraS of Italian Football* (co-authored with Alberto Testa). More recently, an interest in the London 2012 Olympics led to the publication of *Securing and Sustaining the 2012 Olympic City,* co-authored with Pete Fussey, Jon Coaffee and Dick Hobbs.

Richard Giulianotti is Professor of Sociology at Loughborough University, and also Professor II at Telemark University College, Norway. His main research interests are in the fields of sport, globalization, development and peace, sport mega-events, crime and deviance, cultural identities, and qualitative methods. He has headed several projects on these subjects, funded by the UK ESRC, European Commission, and Nuffield Foundation. He is author of *Football: A Sociology of the Global Game* (1999), *Sport: A Critical Sociology* (2005, revised 2015), *Ethics, Money and Sport* (with A.J. Walsh, 2007), and *Globalization and Football* (with R. Robertson, 2009). He has guest co-edited special issues of *British Journal of Sociology, Global Networks,* and *Urban Studies,* edited a further twelve books, and published numerous articles in international journals and edited collections. His work has been translated and published in a dozen languages.

Dick Hobbs is Professor of Sociology at the University of Western Sydney, Professor Emeritus at the University of Essex, Visiting Professor of Sociology at Goldsmiths College University of London, and an Associate Fellow of the Royal United Services Institute. He previously held Chairs at the University of Durham, the London School of Economics, and the University of Essex. He is an ethnographer, and has published widely on deviance, professional and organized crime, illegal markets, the night-time economy, the sociology of London, and research methodology. He is the author of *Lush Life: Constructing Organised Crime in the UK,* winner of the 2014 International Association for the Study of Organized Crime Outstanding Publication Award.

Acknowledgements

In the 112 years since the foundation of the modern Olympics there has been no study examining how this sporting mega-event impacts upon the policing of the host city. This book is an attempt to fill that gap.

In researching and writing this book we have many people and organisations to thank:

We wish to acknowledge the ESRC who funded this project. We thank Gavin Hales for his contribution as research associate to the project. Nick Bracken first had the idea for the research on which this book is based, and remained a valuable source of knowledge throughout. Professor Betsy Stanko was a great supporter of our project and helped us enormously in opening doors to the Metropolitan Police. Thanks to Lisa Tucker for her mapwork. We greatly appreciate the time, knowledge and insights of the many residents, police officers, business people, council officials, local politicians, various faith group leaders, volunteers, and all of those who live or work in Newham and who gave us their precious time. Particular thanks are due to the staff and volunteers at the Newham Monitoring Project. Thanks to Victoria Stonebridge and Laura Parker of the *London Legacy Development Corporation* for their assistance in answering our queries regarding the Queen Elizabeth Olympic Park. Copyright for Map 2 is owned by the Queen Elizabeth Olympic Park.

GA wishes to acknowledge at Brunel University: Prof Geoff Rogers and Prof Ian Rivers, Coral Hankins, Gary Dear and Julie Bradshaw. The masses of research notes were converted into something resembling coherence by the sterling efforts of Karen Kinnaird and Christine Preston. Those who lived the project also include Hani, Lennie and Phoebe Armstrong. Thanks for tolerating my various enthusiasms, fatigues, despairs and euphoria around the research and writing up.

RG wishes to acknowledge: for sharing their expertise on Olympism and sport mega-events, Ian Henry, Barrie Houlihan, and David Howe (Loughborough University), and Atle Hansen, Hans Hognestad, and Jan Ove Tangen (Telemark University College). At Loughborough, we also thank Gail Matthews for transcribing many interviews; Jenny Sutton and Alicia Davies for managing project finances; and David O'Byrne for thorough assistance with the references. Thanks are also due to Donna, Gabbie and Livvy for my multiple physical and mental disappearances into London's Olympic-land, while doing fieldwork and interviews, typing up the notes, scanning through the literature, and writing up for publication.

DH would like to acknowledge at Essex University: Eamonn Carrabine, Pete Fussey, Kenny Monrose and Nigel South. In Stratford: Terry Sylvie and Marshall Jackson. In Sydney: Michael Kennedy, David Rowe, and Stephen Tomsen. DH would also like to acknowledge the long suffering citizens of E6, E7, E12, E13, E15 and E16. The incredible Len Hoffman, who has dedicated his life to sport in East London, and the enduring criminal practice of Adrian Maxwell. Most importantly Sue, Nik, Pat, Lisa, the Bump and the Bruise, who all were put through the mill in various ways during the period of this research.

Abbreviations/glossary

ACPO	Association of Chief Police Officers
BOA	British Olympic Association
DCMS	Department of Culture, Media and Sport
GLA	Greater London Authority
GFU	Gangs and Firearms Unit
HMRC	Her Majesty's Revenue and Customs
IOC	International Olympic Committee
LBN	London Borough of Newham
LDA	London Development Agency
LDDC	London Dockland Development Corporation
LLDC	London Legacy Development Corporation
LOCOG	London Organising Committee of the Olympic and Paralympic Games
LTGDC	London Thames Gateway Development Corporation
MOPAC	Mayor's Office for Policing and Communities
MPD	Metropolitan Police District
MPS	Metropolitan Police Service
MUTUAL AID	the provision of policing assistance from one force to another, usually in response to or in anticipation of a major incident or event
NOC	National Olympic Committee
OCD	Olympic Policing Command and Special Crime and Operations Directorate

OCZ	Olympic Command Zone
ODA	Olympic Delivery Authority
ORN	Olympic Route Network
OSSU	Olympic Site Security Unit
PCSO	Police Community Support Officer
PRN	Paralympic Route Network
PSU	Police Support Units – a public order unit consisting of one inspector, three sergeants and 21 constables
TSG	Territorial Support Group – a flexible policing unit frequently deployed to public order duties
UKBA	United Kingdom Borders Agency

Figures

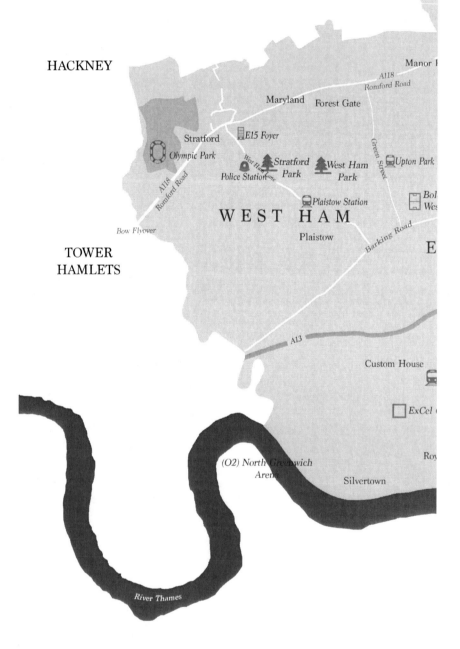

WALTHAM FOREST

HACKNEY

Manor P

A118
Romford Road

Maryland   Forest Gate

E15 Foyer

Stratford
Olympic Park

West Ham Lane

Police Station   Stratford
Park

West Ham
Park

Green Street

Upton Park

Plaistow Station

Bol
Wes

WEST HAM

Bow Flyover

Plaistow

Barking Road

E

A118
Romford Road

TOWER
HAMLETS

A13

Custom House

ExCel

Roy

(O2) North Greenwich
Arena

Silvertown

River Thames

London Borough of Newham

REDBRIDGE

Park

High Street Nth

East Ham Station

BARKING &
DAGENHAM

Station

eyn Ground
t Ham Utd
FC

AST HAM

A13

Beckton

River Thames

Canning Town
Station

Centre

Newham Town Hall

UEL Campus

al Docks

London City Airport

GREENWICH

QUEEN ELIZABETH OLYMPIC PARK MAP AND GUIDE

Use our map to find your favourite spots to explore, play, relax or just simply eat your lunch!

Walking distance (approx.)

0 mins   5 mins   10 mins   15 mins

TRAVEL KEY

- ENTRANCE
- LONDON UNDERGROUND
- LONDON OVERGROUND
- DOCKLANDS LIGHT RAILWAY
- NATIONAL RAIL SERVICES
- LONDON BUSES
- PARKING
- DISABLED PARKING
- BUS STOP

FACILITIES

- INFORMATION POINT
- TOILETS AND ACCESSIBLE TOILETS
- ATM
- REFRESHMENTS
- PLAYGROUND
- CHANGING PLACES TOILET FACILITY
- VENUE SPECIFIC PARKING
- WALKWAYS / CYCLE ROUTES
- IN DEVELOPMENT

SEE & DO

1. THE STADIUM (fully open 2016)
2. ARCELORMITTAL ORBIT
3. SOUTH LAWN
4. EASTTWENTY BAR & KITCHEN
5. THE PODIUM
6. LONDON AQUATICS CENTRE
7. FOUNTAINS
8. OUTDOOR ROOMS
9. CARPENTERS LOCK

SEE & DO

10. COPPER BOX ARENA
11. AGITOS
12. WETLANDS
13. TIMBER LODGE CAFÉ
14. TUMBLING BAY PLAYGROUND
15. OLYMPIC RINGS
16. LEE VALLEY VELOPARK
17. LEE VALLEY HOCKEY AND TENNIS CENTRE
18. MULTI-STOREY CARPARK

Queen Elizabeth Olympic Park
© Queen Elizabeth Olympic Park

1   Policing and Olympic Newham

The 2012 London Olympics had no precedent in UK policing. Although they knew that they faced a scenario where high expectations demanded unprecedented preparation and mobilization, there was no script to which the London and wider UK police could turn. Police strategies, tactics and operations were required to take full account of the diverse risks surrounding the Games: some of those risks were based in London, while other policing challenges emanated from further afield.

The main focus of Olympic police activity was Stratford in the London borough of Newham. Stratford hosted the 560 acre Olympic Park (OP) which contained within its boundaries the Olympic Stadium and various other Olympic structures: namely, the Aquatics Centre, Basketball Arena, Copperbox, Riverbank Arena, Velopark, Water Polo Arena, Athletes' Village, and Media Centre. The other Olympic venue in Newham, located three miles from the Olympic Park in the south of the borough, was the ExCel Arena, which hosted a large number of indoor events including: boxing, fencing, judo, taekwondo, table tennis, weight-lifting and wrestling. Another site integral to the Olympics, but not an Olympic venue, was the Westfield Mall, located adjacent to the Olympic Park, which, when it opened in September 2011, held the status of Europe's largest retail shopping mall.

The summer Olympic and Paralympic Games is the world's largest single-city sporting and cultural event, attracting an audience of millions of spectators, and billions of television viewers. The 2012 Games was seven years in preparation, and was delivered at a cost estimated somewhere between the official figure of £9 billion and the media quoted figure of £24 billion. The chosen location, Newham, was an economically under-privileged and highly diverse location for staging the Olympics: the sixth poorest local authority in England, with just over half of its adult population (aged 16–74) in work. Newham, along with the neighbouring borough of Tower Hamlets, has been identified as the UK's most ethnically diverse borough, with over 70 per cent of residents classified as 'non-white', and London's highest number of recent UK residents (defined as living in the UK for two years or less). Newham was also London's youngest borough (the average age was around 32), with the highest national levels of resident overcrowding (over 25 per cent of households).[1] Yet much of the borough's poverty was submerged by its own marginality, and its scale could only be approximated. In part this is due to the fact that the borough featured hundreds of illegal 'supersheds', typically located in back-gardens, housing migrant workers and others too poor to afford more orthodox accommodation. Newham was particularly characterized by high levels of 'churn' (annual household moves), in part a consequence of its large stock of rented accommodation; some parts of the borough were estimated to experience an annual population churn of up to 30 per cent. Clearly, for the police, and for social scientists undertaking research, Newham was a highly complex social setting for the 2012 Olympics.

Researching Newham and the police: the 2012 Games

In this book we examine the everyday policing of Newham in relation to the London 2012 Olympics. Although our research began in 2008, our main focus was on the period from January 2011 to December 2012; covering the build-up to the Olympics, the actual Games in July and August 2012, and the immediate post-Olympic context. We discuss how police defined, monitored, prioritized, contained and investigated 'Olympic-related' crime, and how 'Olympic-related' policing connected to the policing of Newham. The research focused on the policies and practices of both specialist Olympic police personnel, and local (i.e. borough) policing. Our study provides uniquely rich data and subsequent analysis in two main senses: first, with respect to the everyday policing of the Olympic mega-event; and second, more widely, with respect to the contemporary policing of highly diverse populations within global cities.

We explore in particular how the Olympics impacted on local policing in Newham, and how both the routine and the extraordinary were managed and policed at a time of exceptional organizational change within the Metropolitan Police Service (MPS). Our study builds heavily upon our extensive prior personal knowledge and research experience both in East London and in relation to sport mega-events (see Armstrong et al. 2011; Fussey et al. 2011; Giulianotti 1991; Hobbs 1988), and is based upon unprecedented access to personnel, meetings, sites and documentary evidence at a variety of levels within the MPS, Newham Council (the 'London Borough of Newham', or LBN), and across the wider borough population.

The origins of this project are to be found in the relationship between one member of the research team and a former student, then a serving Newham police officer, who suggested that the policing challenge of hosting of the 2012 Games could provide an interesting research topic. A second member of the team specialized in researching various aspects of the sociology of sport, in particular sporting mega-events. The third, a native of Newham, has undertaken a considerable body of ethnographic work in the borough over a 30-year period. Some tentative informal meetings and tours of the borough convinced us that the research was viable, but we needed a 'badge' that would literally and metaphorically open doors to the Newham police. Accreditation was obtained via the then MPS Head of Strategic Analysis, who in the interim had also contacted one of the authors with regard to the possibility of carrying out some Olympic-based police research. Eventually we obtained a grant from the UK Economic and Social Research Council (ESRC) which provided funding for 30 months of research, including the employment of a full-time researcher over that period.[2]

Our project consisted of extensive qualitative research. Semi-structured interviews were conducted with LBN council employees, with MPS officers of all ranks, particularly those in specific Olympic-related roles, and with staff from other Olympic-related security and emergency services. Ethnographic data was collected by attending strategic meetings of senior officers, sitting amidst desk-based staff in the four MPS stations in Newham, and working shifts with mobile patrol officers of the borough. No doors were closed to us. At times we asked permission – no request was ever refused, and on other occasions we simply sat in on meetings, hoping that we would not be thrown out. The confusion, never resolved throughout the research, as to whom we 'belonged', was an asset. In terms of responsibility we were 'someone else's problem', we knew someone in Scotland Yard, we had security access and a laminated identity card, and so we went largely unchallenged.

We attended Olympic security meetings featuring local businesses and community representatives, sat in on numerous LBN, police and Olympic agency forums, and both made and renewed acquaintances with a wide range of individuals in the local community – often utilizing the familiar empirical technique of 'hanging around'. The latter method was used in the streets, cafes and pubs of Newham, but was also a strategy for researching the police, who generally enjoyed the novel presence of interested outsiders. Importantly, by virtue of the staggering levels of pre-Olympic re-deployment of police officers, we sometimes found ourselves as the most knowledgeable attendees at meetings with regard to both the borough and its policing. At times we alone could explain to relevant newcomers the historical backdrop to the events or issues under discussion.

We wish to be clear that researching the police does not equate to being 'pro-police'. Through our extensive experience and critical reflection there was never any chance of us 'going native', and notwithstanding the good relationships that we developed with a number of individual officers, we approached this research in much the same way as our previous research on subjects such as football hooligans, robbers, thieves, bouncers and drug dealers. Similarly, just because we were conducting research into the London Olympics, it should not be assumed that we are cheerleaders for the event. Nonetheless, we did consider that the award of the 2012 Games to London afforded a remarkable opportunity to analyse policing in a highly diverse location that was about to be struck by waves of post-industrial 'regeneration'.

Hosting the Olympics, bidding for legacy

Although the other designated Olympic boroughs in London were Hackney, Tower Hamlets, and Waltham Forest (which all adjoin the Olympic Park), as well as Greenwich (to the south of the River Thames and hosting a number of Olympic events), and Barking and Dagenham (which was named as a sixth 'Olympic Borough' in April 2010), in recognition of its 'Olympic-related' regeneration plans, the 2012 Games were mostly played out in Newham.

Hosting the Olympics is often portrayed as a once in a lifetime opportunity for the large-scale redevelopment, regeneration and rebranding of a city (Burbank et al. 2001). Encapsulating this belief, the term 'legacy', as employed by various individuals and organisations embedded in the Olympic project, represents a means of justifying and legitimizing the costs of both bidding for and hosting the Games. Accordingly, 'legacy' is often used as a catch-all buzzword to depict a panacea which will address any and all shortfalls within a host city – economic, social, political, and everything in between. For some, this has resulted in an over-emphasis on spatial form at the expense of social processes (Chalkley & Essex 1999). For others, the less visible 'community-oriented' benefits of hosting are consistently forfeited in order to secure more spectacular, globally-focused transformations, such as new shopping complexes and cosmopolitan apartment blocks (Coaffee & Johnston 2007). Wherever it finds itself, the Olympic event is wrapped in narratives of human development, bound up in the Olympic Charter,[3] which emphasises dignity and harmonious human development. This contrasts with those investigative journalists and critical social scientists who view the Games as synonymous with bribery, elitism and remarkable levels of *realpolitik* (Jennings 2000; Lenskyj, 2000, 2002). The Olympics are seductive, but contested.

The process of bidding for the Games is extensive and expensive, necessitating the assiduous cultivation of political capital both within and beyond the International Olympic Committee (IOC). The Olympic bidding process begins with the submission of a city's application by its National Olympic Committee (NOC) to the IOC, and costs an initial total of $500,000 in fees. The IOC Executive Board selects cities qualified to proceed to the next phase, which involves candidate cities being studied by the IOC Evaluation Commission composed of IOC members, representatives of sport federations, NOCs, athletes, the International Paralympic Committee and experts in various fields. The Commission members then make inspection visits whilst being briefed on details covered in the Candidature File, and during this period the candidate city must guarantee that it will be able to fund the Games. The choice of host city is made by the assembled IOC members and the successful bid delegation signs the 'Host City Contract', leaving a lead-up time of seven years to actually staging the mega-event.

The promotion of former Olympic gold medallist and twice world record-holder Lord Coe to Head of the London Organising Committee for the Olympic Games (LOCOG) led to a specific focus in the London Olympic bid. For Coe, the 2012 Games were intended to 'inspire a generation' to participate in sport, and to be of holistic benefit to the nation's youth. Mike Lee, Director of Communications and Public Affairs for the 2012 bid explained: 'We also set about developing key themes that we could reinforce through presentations and communications events. The core elements were regeneration of the East End of London, the diversity of London, the legacy of the Games, use of London's landmark iconic sites and what the Olympics could offer British and world sport' (Lee, 2006: 35).

On 6 June 2005 the 117th IOC Session, at which the host city for the 2012 Games was to be announced, was held in Singapore. Paris was widely considered to be the favourite; London had scored poorly on criteria for transportation and public support, but received good feedback on accommodation, facilities and promised sporting legacy. In the one-hour final presentations of the candidate cities, London's Olympic pitch was delivered by an ensemble of the British Prime Minister, a member of the British royal family, the British Olympic Association (BOA) Chairman, former Olympic gold medallists, the London Mayor, the Olympic Minister and, perhaps most conspicuously, a group of 40 children drawn from Newham schools. The diplomatic overtures and glamourous presentations did the trick; London won the 2012 Games, and entered 'banana republic mode' (Jenkins, 2015: 10). The Olympic host borough of Newham now awaited its transformation.

Legacy: some notes on a buzzword

'London's bid was built on a special Olympic vision. A vision of an Olympic Games that would not only be a celebration of sport but a force for regeneration. The Games will transform one of the poorest and most deprived areas of London. They will create thousands of jobs and homes. They will offer new opportunities for business in the immediate area and throughout London' (Home Secretary Jack Straw, House of Commons, 6 July 2005).

The promise of Olympic legacy is used by the host cities' bidding teams as a vehicle to transform Olympic host neighbourhoods and create a unique place identity.[4] However, as Gratton & Preuss (2008) explain there is no exact definition of what constitutes 'Olympic legacy'; there is instead an immense variety of apparent 'legacies'. Therefore it might be best to conceptualize legacy 'as a cube with three dimensions: positive and negative; planned and unplanned; and tangible and intangible' (2008: 41). As Cashman (2006: 15) states, the term 'is often assumed to be self-evident, there is no need to define precisely what it is', and it is clear that legacies from hosting the Games are multifarious, making the term easily appropriated, and in the case of negative Olympic-related effects, just as easily abandoned. Legacy can include physical elements, most obviously sporting infrastructure, as well as wider urban and environmental developments, through to socio-economic improvements to an Olympic hosting area, which are intended to bring with it 'skills and work-force development, community relations and social capital' (Davies, 2012: 310).

During the 2005 voting process, the stated legacy aims of the London bid with regard to young people were highly influential in swaying IOC members. The *Report of the IOC Evaluation Commission for the Games of the XXX Olympiad in 2012* recognized that: 'A new Olympic dimension would be introduced into existing educational programmes for 400,000 school children' (International Olympic Committee, 2012: 79). A particular feature of this educational programme was to be an education pack for schools to be developed in association with the British Olympic Foundation.[5] The idea of Olympic-related change drew its inspiration from the example of Barcelona 1992, typically presented as the ideal model to follow for a successful Games legacy (Barney et al. 2002: 280).

The post-2012 meta-evaluation by the DCMS (2012) considered legacy to be all that has and will happen over the period 2007–2020. Yet, external economic and political forces are apt to reshape legacy objectives for sport mega-events. In the UK, the impacts of the global economic downturn from 2007 onwards were followed by the forming of a Conservative-led coalition government in 2010 committed to economic and social austerity.

Legacy: the local perspective

In 2009 the six boroughs published their own legacy plans, entitled: *A Strategic Regeneration Framework: An Olympic Legacy for the Host Boroughs* (Host Boroughs, 2009). The document set out plans for how, within 20 years, the communities set to host the 2012 Games, which included some of the poorest parts of England, would benefit from the same social and economic opportunities, amenities and standards of living as their civic neighbours in more affluent West London. In addition, the government and the Department of Culture, Media and Sport (DCMS) sought to measure the success of London 2012 in terms of urban 'regeneration', notably around the Olympic Village and wider Olympic Park area, and infrastructural developments in Stratford.

The Olympic Delivery Authority (ODA), the prime body responsible for the Games infrastructure, was gifted some £7 billion of public monies to be directed towards major construction works on what was portrayed as a largely derelict and polluted post-industrial site in Stratford. The ODA funding was intended to pursue the objectives set out by the London Olympic Games and Paralympic Games Act (2006), which included planning and building new sporting venues and transport infrastructure for the Games, securing their long-term use after 2012, and setting new standards for sustainable development. Previous Games, notably Athens 2004, had been heavily criticized for wasteful legacy failures, particularly in building facilities that had no post-Games usage. Conversely, the stated aims of London 2012 'fitted in with the idea of a compact, non-wasteful Games, with several temporary venues to be relocated elsewhere in the UK. There would be no white elephants' (Keogh & Fraser, 2005: 1).

Legacy promises were to be achieved through effective 'leveraging', another 2012 Olympic buzzword, which by definition refers to 'strategic approaches to event planning and management' to maximize long-term benefits (Chalip, 2004: 245 Bramwell, 1997; Chalip & Leyns, 2002). Olympic leveraging aims are manifold, and include stimulating economic development, encouraging change in social and environmental agendas, boosting cultural work, providing employment, attracting tourists, and generating a cohesive 'vibe' locally and beyond.[6] The long-term dimension of Olympic legacies means that their evaluation must be similarly patient. As Gratton & Preuss (2008: 1926) indicate: 'In order to identify if legacies have a lasting effect on the host cities, a study needs to be conducted 15–20 years after the event has occurred'.

We have argued elsewhere that, like other contemporary sport mega-events, the London Games provided a case study in 'festival capitalism' (Giulianotti et al. 2015). By festival capitalism, we are referring to how public events are structured to promote free-market and broader commercial interests, with important backing from public authorities through, for example, the sale of public land for private development, or public spending on transport and security infrastructures that particularly assist business interests. Long before the Olympics were scheduled, neo-liberal urban development policies were well established in East London. Most notably, billions of pounds had been spent by the State on pro-business regeneration projects during the 1980s and 1990s, such as a new financial centre at Canary Wharf, which was built on the site of what had once been the West India Docks. (Hamnet, 2003: 222–226). Canary Wharf was not only the first post-industrial East End site to pursue the myth of trickle-down economics (Cohen, 2013: 110–135), and significantly, post-2005, hosted the headquarters of both the London Organising Committee of the Olympic and Paralympic Games (LOCOG), and the Olympic Delivery Authority. Canary Wharf was, both pragmatically and symbolically, an ideal venue to plot the next stage of market incursion into East London.

In Newham, festival capitalism was associated with a variety of Olympic-related developments. For example, the Westfield Stratford City shopping mall, opened in September 2011 and featuring over 250 retail units typically filled by international companies and high-end brands. During the Games, the majority of visitors would arrive at Stratford train and underground station, and pass through the mall en route to the Olympic Park. Inside the park itself, after the Games, the main sporting tenant at the Olympic Stadium was to be West Ham United FC. The Olympics were the flagship project of the Stratford 'Metropolitan Masterplan' which capsulated the local council's long-term strategy to create almost 50,000 jobs, and to construct 20,000 homes: processes which would be fuelled by new retail, transport, educational and cultural opportunities and provisions. In addition to the Olympics, Newham was experiencing a construction programme on a scale not seen in the capital since the aftermath of the Second World War. The Thames Gateway project and developments around the Royal Docks scheduled 40,000 new homes by the end of the current decade (LBN, 2011a: 7–8). Against a backdrop of rapidly declining owner-occupation in the borough (half the rate of London as a whole) and mortgage repossession rates that stood amongst the highest in London, compounded by the 2008 global recession, the Olympic legacy promised 'the regeneration of an entire community for the direct benefit of everyone who lives there'.[7]

Not everyone believed the hype. Some local residents and Council employees were concerned that these aims would produce a classic case study in the downside of urban regeneration, with poorer populations squeezed out by incomers, such as wealthier new residents or businesses. Indeed, we argue in this book that Newham's principle Olympic legacy is E20, a new postcode covering the Westfield Mall and the post-Olympic rebranded Queen Elizabeth Olympic Park (QEOP). Before the 2012 Olympics E20 had only existed in the long running

BBC soap opera, *EastEnders* as the postcode for the programme's fictional neighbourhood of Walford. However, by the end of our research in 2015 truth had indeed become stranger than fiction.

The policing context for London 2012

However, between the award of the Games and the Opening Ceremony there were to be many challenges. On the 6th of July 2005 London was awarded the right to host the 2012 Olympics. The next day, suicide bombers attacked London's public transport network, killing 52 and injuring 700. The convergence of global sporting mega-events and security systems, required to respond to all possible eventualities, was laid bare. As the agency with primary responsibility for keeping London safe, the MPS was also required to ensure that, as their Olympic motto stated, 'the Games remained the story'.

Subsequently, the Games witnessed the largest peacetime mobilization of security and policing personnel in the UK. There were 34 Olympic venues, and on peak days 89,000 police officers and 13,000 military personnel were deployed, while missile defence systems were positioned in public locations adjacent to the Olympic Park. The policing and security budget was set officially at £480 million, although a further estimate put overall security costs at £1.265 billion during a period of fiscal austerity that entailed significant cuts being made to public service provision, including policing. For the MPS the Olympics were a 105 day interruption (late June to early September) of routine borough policing.

In 2006, just one year after London was awarded the Games, Newham was labelled as a failing borough in terms of its police performance. The report by Her Majesty's Inspectorate of Constabulary (HMIC), stated that: 'the fact that every category of Newham's performance sits within the bottom quartile of its MSBCU [Most Similar Basic Command Unit] group, recent declines in performance in all categories except one (robbery reduction) and its under-performance over the past three years, indicates a pressing need to review and significantly improve upon many fundamental BCU business processes' (Bainbridge, 2006: 1). The borough's local government ward of Stratford returned some of the highest levels of knife crime in the MPS remit, and according to MPS crime data Newham as a whole had the fourth highest level of serious violence in London in 2009/10 (accessed March 2011).

Newham police worked out of aged and shabby police stations, and there were limited interactions between the various squads and units; the one exception was the designated smoking locations – invariably the station car-park. This atomisation of policing was aided and abetted by the demise of two canteens in the borough's four stations in 2011. The two that remained operated with reduced hours, and whilst their dining areas saw the Borough Commanders eating in the same room as the lower ranks, the everyday job of policing remained stubbornly deferential, discouraging any 'showing out', or coming to the attention of those of senior rank, whether for positive or negative reasons. The same hierarchical structures produced an apparent lack of appetite for reflection or deliberation when implementing changes requested by senior commanders. Although there was a shared sense of risk particularly amongst the lower ranks (cf. Skolnick & Fyfe 1993; Chan et al. 2003), we found that commitment to the job was consistently moderated across all ranks by an insistence that officers were not 'looked after' either by the police organization or by their political leaders, be it at local or national level. It did not surprise us that a 2012 MPS-wide staff survey revealed that Newham's police officers had among the lowest levels of job satisfaction across the London force.

Meanwhile, and in common with previous research on policing in the UK, geographical forms of policing (in other words, 'Safer Neighbourhood' and other 'Ward' policing) were viewed with low-level disdain by the specialist teams in particular. There remained, as ever, praise for old-fashioned 'coppering' and 'thief taking' based around notions of craftsman-like perception and carefully-honed instinct. However, one bedrock of the craftsman era, drinking culture (Hobbs, 1988), was now long gone. Daytime drinking had been replaced in some specialist squads with celebratory breakfasts, notably when arrests had resulted in custodial sentences. What drinking remained was confined to 'leaving' and 'promotion do's', and usually took place outside of the borough, away from prying eyes.

Busy not dangerous

The most potentially dangerous individuals in the borough did not routinely trouble day-to-day policing. We were constantly told by officers of all ranks that Newham contained more people involved in and suspected of involvement in Islamic terrorism than anywhere else in the UK (see Pantazis & Pemberton, 2009). We saw no evidence of this alleged terrorist 'footprint', and indeed terrorism had little impact on everyday policing. Similarly, violent youth in the shape of 'gangs' rarely impacted on daily police working practices, and as we discuss in Chapter 3, the policing of violent youth became a specialism in the period leading up to the Games. Further, these youths were not a source of fear for police, such that officers rarely wore stab vests when visiting the homes of suspected gang members. Despite examples of excellent work with individual gang members and their families, uniformed policing had a tendency to fall back on adversarial relationships with these young men, reflected in how regularly police resorted to 'getting hands in pockets'; that is, searching suspects on the slightest pretext. This inevitably produced hostility towards the police, particularly regarding the legitimacy of being stopped and searched. The preference in Newham for using public order police units – specifically the MPS-wide Territorial Support Group (or TSG), who were considered more 'robust' in their approach – was key to understanding local youth–police relations. A confrontational young man pinned to the ground by a police unit was regarded as a victory by uniformed ranks. However, while this 'result' meant that the police might consider that they had won an individual battle, an increasingly attritional war continued with a somewhat monotonous sense of certainty.

Centralization was a major characteristic of policing in Newham, and strategies were created far from the 'shop floor' of everyday policing, with its routine compromises and negotiations. Strategy was reduced to identifying and resourcing the policing of priority crime types, and both the needs of victims and notions of police-community consent were all but abandoned in the pursuit of favourable crime statistics. Briefings rarely called on the local knowledge of officers with decades of service, and the contributions of other agencies (for example, probation and drug treatment providers) were routinely ignored. Decisions on the deployment of resources depended in part on the analysis and input of civilian staff, who were themselves at constant risk of redundancy as budget cuts were implemented; indeed their numbers were decimated in the course of the research. Profound questions around legitimacy and public confidence were routinely side-stepped; such issues were too abstract and not compatible with management models that were pre-occupied with an organizational culture centred on tactics and case-by-case contingencies. In the words of the Acting Commander for Territorial Policing: 'tactics deliver, strategy delays'. Tactics rather than strategies were the preferred measure of quality police work, largely due to the ease with which they could be linked to the actions of individual officers and therefore were career-enabling.

The numbers game: Olympic add-ons

The MPS operated within a culture reliant on metrics which could define police practice and make or break a policing career. In addition to numbers, there was an ongoing requirement to develop a credible narrative around the relationship between policing activity and levels of crime and disorder. Beyond these metrics and their accompanying narratives, we found that contemporary London policing relied upon two correlates: the first concerned the management of *risk* (the threat of damage or loss occurring at personal and institutional level), and in particular its relationship to *reputation* (again, personal and institutional levels of positive status and standing, which can be won, lost or maintained), which governed every rank from constable to commissioner; the second correlate concerned *resources,* (such as personnel, equipment, technologies, finances, and the ability to mobilize these material entities) and *resilience* (understood broadly as the capacity to maintain competence under pressure, unwillingness to fragment, and the ability to respond to any eventuality). Personal and institutional concerns about reputation dominated risk assessments, and led to a series of consequences including an emphasis on short- over long-term risks, and the prioritization of the regional and national over local risks, which resulted in resourcing decisions that could leave local policing overstretched. These realities were magnified by the arrival of the 2012 Olympics and by subsequent global risks to reputations; the result was that policing further prioritized MPS and 'UK PLC'[8] over local policing issues that were typified as 'business as usual'.

Institutionally, the police present themselves as operating through privileged powers, information and expertise, and the notion of 'Intelligence' (Intel), was heavily fetishized both in the build up to the Games, and during Games Time itself. However, a critical analysis must question the privileged knowledge that defines so much of policing, including Olympic policing. In the case of the Olympics, the role of the police 'Centre', the intensely hierarchical managerial core of the MPS, located away from Newham in a number of central London locations, was of major importance. The Centre came to take a particular interest in local issues concerning how information was produced, assessed and filtered, and we were particularly well placed to observe how competing versions of the 'true' picture on Newham's crime and policing were generated and privileged. Our research raises questions as to how such information is manipulated to serve the interests of particular parts of the policing organization, notably in capturing scarce resources. Integral to these processes were notions of police performance, jurisdiction, and accountability, and the way that classifications of crime, specifically the notion of 'Olympic-related crime', may be manipulated in order to manage official knowledge concerning the extent of crime and subsequent responses to criminal activity. Thus, embedded within our analysis was the notion of institutional 'truths' (cf. Douglas, 1987) and the privileging of institutional sources over all others.

A troubled force: protest, death and reorganization

The years immediately preceding the Olympic Games were challenging, as exemplified by a number of high-profile incidents. In November and December 2010 protests were staged across the country by university students angered by the Conservative–Liberal Democrat Coalition government's decision to raise the cap on tuition fees from £3,290 to £9,000.[9] A mass protest was organized jointly by the National Union of Students (NUS) and the University and College Union (UCU), and on the 10th November 2010 more than 30,000 demonstrators marched on central London along a route approved by the MPS. As the march passed the Houses of Parliament en route to Tate Britain, where the demonstration was due to end with a rally, a large group of marchers broke away and converged upon the headquarters of the Conservative Party at 30 Millbank. The relatively modest police presence there was unable to cope with a group of protesters who occupied the building, a number of whom made their way onto the roof. The TSG arrived around an hour later, and were pelted with eggs, banners and rotten fruits while removing the protesters. Police attempts to 'calm' the crowd involved the controversial method of 'kettling', with protesters surrounded by police cordons and prevented from leaving the scene for hours until officers were satisfied that the protest had died down and after arrests had been made. This method was deployed at another protest over tuition fees on 24th November 2010 and during subsequent protests on 30th November and 9th December, at Trafalgar Square and Parliament Square respectively. By the end of the protests over 150 young people had been arrested, and the Independent Police Complaints Commission (IPCC) received nearly 50 complaints about police conduct during the demonstrations. In the aftermath of the protests, footage emerged online of one protestor with cerebral palsy being pulled out of his wheelchair and dragged across the ground by MPS officers.

The then MPS Commissioner Sir Paul Stephenson admitted that he was embarrassed by his force's inability to control the protesters, whilst describing the actions of some demonstrators as 'thuggery' (Camber, 2010). His colleague, Chief Inspector Jane Collins, defended the practice of 'kettling', stating that it was only used as 'a last resort' after her officers came under attack (Gabbatt & Batty, 2010). Jenny Jones, Green Party member of the London Assembly, accused Stephenson of 'punishing people for going on a protest' (Gabbatt et al., 2010).[10]

In May 2011 an inquest jury found that newspaper vendor Ian Tomlinson had been unlawfully killed by a constable from the MPS' Territorial Support Group. The incident in question had occurred in 2009 during the G20 summit protests. Tomlinson was working on a newspaper stand situated outside Monument tube station. At around 07.00 hours, he had left work and headed to the Lindsey Hotel (a homeless shelter) where he was staying. His normal route had been blocked by a series of police cordons. Footage filmed by an American hedge fund manager showed Tomlinson walking slowly away from a group of police officers, one of whom lunged at Tomlinson striking the back of his legs with a baton, and pushing him to the floor. After being helped to his feet by a protester, he walked around 60 metres then collapsed. Attended to by police medics, he was pronounced dead on arrival at hospital. Post-mortems found that he had fallen on his elbow which, in turn, impacted on his liver causing internal bleeding that led to his death a few minutes later (see Gammell, 2010).

Eventually a TSG officer was suspended on suspicion of manslaughter. More than a year later the Crown Prosecution Service (CPS) stated that there would be no criminal charges against the officer as the discrepancy between the findings in respective post-mortems meant that no causal link could be demonstrated between the fatality and the alleged assault. However, the CPS reversed its decision in May 2011 after an inquest jury ruled that Tomlinson had died unlawfully. The officer was later found not guilty of manslaughter by a jury at Southwark Crown Court.[11]

As a response to the policing of the G20 demonstration, Chief Inspector of Constabulary Denis O'Connor produced a two- part report, which among its many features criticized the routine deployment of riot gear in response to lawful protest, the use of shields as a weapon, variations in public order training across the 44 forces, and ignorance of the law, particularly in relation to the Public Order Act. The report also recommended a set of national principles emphasizing the minimum use of force, and stressed that privacy and human rights concerns about police surveillance teams (known in the MPS as Forward Intelligence Teams) and their use of data be taken seriously. The report also recommended making the display of police ID a legal requirement (Her Majesty's Chief Inspector of Constabulary, 2009a, 2009b). *The Guardian* newspaper hailed O'Connor's report as a return to consent-based policing.[12]

However, there was little consent evident in August 2011 when, with less than a year before the opening ceremony, four days of rioting and looting broke out on the streets of London and in other cities across England. The disorder followed the fatal shooting in North London of 29-year-old Mark Duggan as he stepped out of a mini-cab on the instructions of armed police.[13] What followed made global headlines and called into question the ability of the MPS to anticipate and respond to events on the ground. In London, almost 4,000 crimes, including two deaths, were recorded by the police, there was £200–300 million in damage to property, and more than 4,000 arrests were made. The final policing bill was estimated at £34 million. The Prime Minister made clear his assessment that the MPS had failed in their duty, and made a specific link to the international reputation of Britain less than a year away from the Olympics.[14]

In March 2011, Her Majesty's Chief Inspector of Constabulary Tom Winsor published the first part of his wide-ranging review of the conditions of service of police officers in England and Wales. Part One of the reports[15]recommended that the police pay bill be cut by £1.1 billion over three years, and although its recommendations were endorsed by the Association of Chief Police Officers, the Police Federation saw the report as an unprecedented attack on police pay and conditions. Part Two, published in March 2012,[16] set out a battery of longer-term recommendations which included linking pay to performance rather than length of service, legislating for the capacity of forces to make officers redundant regardless of whether they had attained full pensionable service, establishing a new retirement age of 60, a fast track to Inspector rank for promising entrants, and compulsory fitness tests.[17] Particularly aggrieved at a three year pay freeze and increased pension contributions, the Police Federation responded to the report's recommendations with 'utter dismay, consternation and disillusion', and called on UK Home Secretary, Theresa May, to reject it 'outright' (Heffer, 2012). The federation declared that 'full industrial rights' for its officers would be sought, including the right to strike over pay and conditions, and staged a march of 32,000 officers past the Home Office and the Houses of Parliament in protest. The protest did not result in any unsavoury 'kettling' incidents, but the Police Arbitration Tribunal (PAT) successfully challenged the report's recommendation of compulsory severance for officers with under 30 years' service, with May deciding not to proceed with it 'at this time'.

In 2011, the Police Reform and Social Responsibility Act was passed which established a Police and Crime Commissioner (PCC) for each police force area across England and Wales. In London, the equivalent to the PCC was the elected Mayor of London, and the Mayor's Office for Policing and Crime (MOPAC) became the strategic body, setting the direction and budget for the MPS on the Mayor's behalf, and thus becoming a powerful centralizing influence on the policing of London.

In September 2011, and less than a year before the London Games commenced, the MPS acquired a new boss, with two commissioners resigning in the space of less than three years. First, Sir Ian Blair was forced out in October 2008 by the newly elected Mayor Boris Johnson, followed in July 2011 by Sir Paul Stephenson's resignation in the wake of a media phone-hacking scandal. Headed by Commissioner Sir Bernard Hogan-Howe, for the MPS' new leadership team the Games were a potential distraction from the more immediate matters. It was against this backdrop of public disorder, widespread criticism, violence, scandal, managerial churn and impending organizational upheaval that we undertook our research. Unsurprisingly, the workforce which we encountered at this juncture could not be considered as enjoying high morale.

While the governance of the entire public sphere is synonymous with risk assessment, management and reduction (Beck, 1992, Giddens, 1999), the Olympic Games operate with a set of specifications requiring a balance to be struck between economic and corporate entities and other multiple stakeholders. The IOC (as 'brand owners') requires the host city to agree to implement the Olympic Charter in its entirety, and Rule 51, s.3 of the Charter explicitly forbids public protest near Olympic venues, thereby overriding enshrined domestic rights and freedoms. International sponsors and regulatory bodies and their accompanying values threaten the democratic local realm, demanding a safe and secure Games at all costs. Typically the State's response is to pass bespoke legislation, so that for the 2012 event the London Olympic Games and Paralympic Games Act 2006 was passed including (section 19) provisions to curb unauthorized advertising, sales of counterfeit goods, and 'over-commercialization' near Olympic venues. This meant, for example, event authorities were permitted to demand the covering of placards, while the police (as 'enforcement officers') were empowered to 'enter land or premises on which they reasonably believe a contravention of regulations under section 19 is occurring'. Crucially, the wording of the Act meant such measures could extend beyond commercial endeavours to encompass political activity.

The announcement of the London Olympic bid provoked a series of protests. One protest sought to preserve full access to Leyton Marshes, which were under the protection of a 'Lammas Land' covenant, designating the area as a public space offering anyone unfettered access. The Manor Garden Allotments at the Hackney side of the Olympic Park protested against their forced eviction, and considered the alternative site offered to them as both inferior and inadequate. The '*London 2012 Killing Local Business*' campaign reached its zenith when its banner was unfurled before an IOC delegate visit in 2005. Most importantly, compulsory purchase orders were imposed on local residents and businesses, as 'the Olympics . . . acted like a tidal wave crashing over local businesses and clearing them away in the first stage of a longer regeneration process' (Raco & Tunney, 2010: 14). In the north of Newham, residents of the Clays Lane Estate protested against the loss of their homes and community to compulsory purchase orders, however as residents gradually left the estate, the campaign eroded (Armstrong et al. 2011; Lindsay, 2014). The plans for the Olympic Village required the destruction of two 'permanent' sites for Travellers[18] – one on Clays Lane, Newham, and a second on Waterden Crescent, Hackney; these plans were unsuccessfully challenged in the High Court in May 2007.[19] In total, approximately 450 people lost their homes.

Despite the informal 'business as usual' mantra of Newham's senior police officers, policing in the borough would change fundamentally for the 64 days designated as Olympic Policing Time. 'Olympic issues' and their impact on local policing were manifold and, as we discuss through this book, they required negotiations over details and the envisioning of possible scenarios that harboured potential local, national and global risks (see Jennings, 2008, 2010). While responsibilities were shared or open to negotiation, the police were assumed to be the primary holders of Olympic risk, and the potential for reputations to be ruined was ever-present. Formally, the big Olympic issue for Newham's policing related to the Last Mile around Newham's two Olympic venues at the Olympic Park and the ExCel Centre. At ground level, however, as we explain, the focus was more commonly on the policing of gangs and street crime.

About this book

Although its focus is the policing of the London 2012 Olympics, this book is more generally concerned with post-industrial class relations and their relevance to governance and social control. Our discussion requires a full understanding of the social context for Olympic policing and Games-centred regeneration plans, hence in Chapter 2 we set out the social and economic history of Newham, the rise and decline of its industries and labour, the making and breaking of communities and social networks, and different epochs of migration and dislocation.

In Chapter 3, we examine the position of youth in relation to crime and policing in Newham. While the borough has played host to diverse youth subcultures over the years, a major police focus in recent times has been on the perceived 'gang problem' and its connection to serious violence, robbery, theft, and delinquency. We consider in particular the gang *bête noire* of Newham police, the 'Portuguese Mafia', who were the subjects of much activity both in the prelude to the Olympics, and during Games Time. We then turn to the case of the Westfield shopping mall in Chapter 4, and specifically the diverse ways in which policing and overall security responsibilities were contested, negotiated, and managed by a fluid assemblage of organizations and units of social control. In such circumstances, the notion of policing 'partnerships' and the dominant institutional ideology of 'total policing' within the MPS proved highly problematic to put into effective practice.

In Chapter 5, we discuss one Olympic-focused policing strategy which was in part intended to deal with potential problems in partnership work: a set of 'Table Top' meetings staged prior to the Games, which presented key decision-makers within the police and other emergency services with possible problem scenarios. In Chapter 6 we examine the Olympic-related planning, preparations and activities of Newham police with particular reference to Stratford. In particular, we look at the manner in which responsibilities were negotiated and managed.

In Chapter 7, we look at policing strategies at the Opening Ceremony, particularly in relation to Meridian Square, just outside the Westfield Mall and Stratford station, and in Chapter 8, we turn to the policing of the Games in and around the Olympic Command Zone (OCZ). In Chapter 9, we examine the policing of the wider Newham area during Games Time, in addition to considering how the police themselves were subject to close examination by a long-established local community group. We conclude in Chapters 10 and 11 by looking at post-Games Newham, its Olympic legacy, and the future for both the borough and its policing.

Notes

1 As we report in Giulianotti et al. (2015).
2 ESRC award number ES/I/0005424/1.
3 The Olympic Charter is available at: http://www.olympic.org/Documents/olympic_charter_en.pdf.
4 See Boukas, Ziakas & Boustras (2012: 204); Weed, (2008: 60); Essex & Chalkley, (1998: 192); Garcia-Ramon & Degen, (2006: 187).
5 The British Olympic Foundation is a charity concerned with the promotion and advancement of the Olympic movement. http://opencharities.org/charities/1122080#sthash.cot4soRe.dpuf.
6 See, for example, Kellett et al., (2008); O'Brien & Chalip, (2007), Hiller, (1989), Smith (2010), Horne, (2007), Malfas et al., (2004).
7 http://www.london2012.com/documents/candidate-files/theme-1-olympic-games-concept-and-legacy.pdf.
8 This intensely irritating term was used extensively by a wide range of institutions and agencies during the Olympics as a smug shorthand for British commercial interests. See for example: https://www.gov.uk/government/uploads/system/uploads/attachment_data/file/77430/John_Armitt_Report.pdf.
9 The Browne Report into the funding of Higher Education was published in October 2010, only five months after the new coalition government had taken office. Browne had in fact suggested that the cap on university tuition fees be lifted altogether. However, the coalition, led by Prime Minister David Cameron, opted to raise the cap to £9,000. Unsurprisingly, the decision of the fledging government met with the ire of both current and prospective university students. Their outrage was heightened by a pre-election promise made by Liberal Democrat leader and coalition partner Nick Clegg that his party would oppose any hike in fees.
10 Perhaps the most poignant critique of MPS methods came from author Lara Pawson (writing in the *Guardian*), who pointed out that the German equivalent of the term 'kettle', *Kessel*, referred to the rounding up of the Jews in the Warsaw Ghetto (Pawson, 2010).
11 However, in September 2012 the MPS dismissed the officer on the grounds of gross misconduct, and a year later settled a civil action brought by Tomlinson's family by paying an undisclosed sum in compensation and formally apologising for its 'use of excessive and unlawful force' (Taylor, 2013).
12 See 'G20 Report Lays Down the Law to Police on Use of Force', the *Guardian*, 25 November 2009.
13 A jury concluded that although he was not in possession of a firearm at the time that he was shot, Mark Duggan was killed lawfully (the *Guardian*, 8 January 2014).
14 See http://www.bbc.co.uk/news/uk-politics-14492789.
15 http://webarchive.nationalarchives.gov.uk/20130312170833/http://www.review.police.uk/part-one-report/.
16 http://webarchive.nationalarchives.gov.uk/20130312170833/http://review.police.uk/publications/part-2-report/.
17 Writing in the *Guardian*, crossbench member of the House of Lords and former Chief Constable of West Midlands Police, Lord Geoffrey Dear, hailed the report as 'bold and brave in its vision for the future of policing' (Dear, 2012).
18 In this context Travellers denotes a generic term referring to Gypsy, Roma, and other communities defined by their itinerant cultures.
19 See' Gypsies lose Olympic site battle', *BBC News*, 3 May 2007.

References

Armstrong, G., Hobbs, D. & Lindsay, I. (2011) 'Calling the Shots: The Pre-2012 London Olympic Contest', *Urban Studies, 15*: 3176–3184.

Bainbridge, J. (2006) *Inspection of Newham BCU Metropolitan Police Service (MPS)*. London: Her Majesty's Inspectorate of Constabulary London and the British Transport Police Office.

Barney, R.K., Wenn, S.R., & Martyn, S.G. (2002) *Selling the Five Rings: The International Olympic Committee and the Rise of Olympics Commercialism*. Salt Lake City, UT: University of Utah Press.

Beck, U. (1992) *Risk Society*. London: Sage.

Boukas, N., Ziakas, V. & Boustras, G. (2012) 'Olympic Legacy and Cultural Tourism: Exploring the Facets of Athens' Olympic Heritage', *International Journal of Heritage Studies, 19*(2): 203–228.

Bramwell, B. (1997) 'Strategic Planning Before and After a Mega-Event', *Tourism Management, 18*: 167–176.

Burbank, M., Andranovich, C., & Heying, C.H. (2001) *Olympic Dreams: The Impact of Mega-Events on Local Politics*. Boulder, CO. Lynne Reiner.

Camber, R. (2010) 'Top Police Chief Warns of New Era of Violence And Lawless Riots as Students Gear Up for Third Week of Protest Action', *Daily Mail*, November 25. Retrieved on 14 February 2015 (online: http://www.dailymail.co.uk/news/article-1333087/Student-protests-prompt-police-chief-warn-new-era-violence-lawless-riots-students-gear-week-protest-action.html.)

Cashman, R. (2006) *The Bitter-Sweet Awakening: The Legacy of the Sydney 2000 Olympic Games*. Sydney: Walla Walla Press.

Chalip, L. (2004) 'Beyond Impact: A General Model for Host Community Event Leverage', in Ritchie, B. W., Adair, D. (eds) *Sport Tourism: Interrelationships, Impacts and Issues*. Clevedon: Channel View.

Chalip, L., & Leyns, A. (2002) 'Local Business Leveraging of a Sport Event: Managing an Event for Economic Benefit', *Journal of Sport Management, 16:* 132–158.

Chalkley, B. & Essex, S. (1999) 'Urban Development through Hosting International Events: A History of the Olympics Games', *Planning Perspectives, 14:* 369–394.

Chan, J., Devery, C. & Doran, S. (2003) *Fair Cop: Learning the Art of Policing*. Toronto: University of Toronto Press.

Coaffee,J. & Johnston, L. (2007) 'Accommodating the Spectacle', in J. Gold & M.Gold (eds) *Olympic Cities*. London: Routledge.

Cohen, P. (2013) *On the Wrong Side of the Track?: East London and the Post Olympics*. London: Lawrence and Wishart.

Davies, L. (2012) 'Beyond the Games: Regeneration Legacies and London 2012', *Leisure Studies, 31*(3): 309–337.

DCMS (2012) *Meta-Evaluation of the Impacts of the Legacy of the London 2012 Olympics and Paralympic Games. Report 4: Interim Evaluation*. London: Department for Culture, Media and Sport. Retrieved from: http://www.culture.gov.uk/images/pulications/2012_Meta_Evaluation_Report_4_Summary.pdf.

Dear, G. (2012) 'The Winsor Report is Bold and Brave in its Vision for the Future of the Police', the *Guardian*, March 15.

Douglas, M. (1987) *How Institutions Think*. London: Routledge.

Essex, S.J., & Chalkley, B.S. (1998) 'The Olympics as a Catalyst of Urban Renewal: A Review', *Leisure Studies, 17*(3): 187–206.

Fussey, P., Coaffee, J., Armstrong, G. & Hobbs, D. (2011) *Securing and Sustaining the Olympic City: Reconfiguring London for 2012 and Beyond*. Aldershot, UK: Ashgate.

Gabbatt, A. & Batty, D. (2010) 'Second Day of Student Protests – how the Demonstrations Happened', the *Guardian*, November 24.

Gabbatt, A., Lewis, P., Taylor, M. & Williams, R. (2010) 'Student Protests: Met Under Fire for Charging at Demonstrators', the *Guardian*, November 26.

Gammell, C. (2010) 'G20 Pathologist Dr Freddy Patel Guilty of Blunders in Other Post-Mortems', the *Telegraph*, August 25.

Garcia-Ramon, M. and Degen, M. (2006) 'Barcelona – The Breakdown of a Virtuous Model?'. Paper presented at XVI ISA World Congress of Sociology, Durban.

Giddens, A. (1999) *Runaway World.* London: Profile.

Giulianotti, R. (1991) 'Scotland's Tartan Army in Italy: The Case for the Carnivalesque', *Sociological Review*, *39*(3): 503–527.

Giulianotti, R., Armstrong, G., Hales, G. & Hobbs, D. (2015) 'Global Sports Mega-Events and the Politics of Mobility: The Case of the London 2012 Olympics', *British Journal of Sociology*, *66*(1): 118–140.

Gratton, C. & Preuss, H (2008) 'Maximising Olympic Impacts by Building up Legacies', *The International Journal of the History of Sport*, *25*(14): 1922–1938.

Hamnet, C. (2003) *Unequal City: London in the Global Arena.* London: Routledge.

Heffer, S. (2012) 'The Battle Between the Police Federation and the Government on Police Reform Rages on', the *Daily Mail*, October 26.

Her Majesty's Chief Inspector of Constabulary (2009a, July) *Adapting to Protest.* London: Central Office of Information.

Her Majesty's Chief Inspector of Constabulary (2009b, Nov) *Adapting to Protest – Nurturing the British Model of Policing.* London: Central Office of Information.

Hiller, H. (1989) 'Impact and Image: The Convergence of Urban Factors in Preparing for the 1988 Calgary Winter Olympics', in Syme, G., Shaw, B., Fenton, D. & Mueller, W. (eds) *The Planning and Evaluation of Hallmark Events.* Aldershot: Avebury.

Hobbs, D. (1988) *Doing the Business.* Oxford: Oxford University Press.

Horne, J. (2007) 'The Four "Knowns" of Sports Mega-Events', *Leisure Studies, 26*(1): 81–96.

Host Boroughs (2009) *A Strategic Regeneration Framework: An Olympic Legacy for the Host Boroughs.* London: London 2012 Host Boroughs.

International Olympic Committee (2012) *Report of the IOC Evaluation Commission for the Games of the XXX Olympiad in 2012.* Lausanne, Switzerland: IOC.

Jenkins, S. (2015) 'Review of *Circus Maximus* by Andrew Zimblast', the *Guardian*, 23 May.

Jennings, A. (2000) *The Great Olympic Swindle.* London: Simon & Schuster.

Jennings, W. (2008) 'London 2012: Olympic Risk, Risk Management and Olymponomics', *John Liner Review, 22*(2): 39–45.

Jennings, W. (2010) 'Governing the Games in an Age of Uncertainty: The Olympics and Organisational Responses to Risk', in Richards, A., Fussey, P. & Silke, A. (eds) *Terrorism and the Olympics. Major Event Security and Lessons for the Future.* Oxford: Routledge.

Kellett, P., Hede, A., & Chalip, L. (2008) 'Social Policy for Sport Events: Leveraging (Relationships with) Teams from Other Nations for Community Benefit', *European Sport Management Quarterly, 8:* 101–121.

Keogh, F. & Fraser, A. (2005) 'Why London Won the Olympics', *BBC News*, July 6.

Lee, M. (2006) *The Race for the 2012 Olympics: The Inside Story of How London Won the Bid.* London: Virgin.

Lenskyj, H. (2002) *The Best Olympics Ever? The Social Impacts of Sydney 2000.* Albany, NY: SUNY Press.

Lenskyj, H.J. (2000) *Inside the Olympic Industry: Power, Politics, and Activism.* New York: SUNY Press.

Lindsey, I. (2014) *Living with London's Olympics.* Basingstoke: Palgrave.

London Borough of Newham (LBN) (2011a) 'Curbs on "Shanty" Dwellings', *The Newham Mag*, Issue 227, 19 August–2 September, p. 5.

London Borough of Newham and NHS Newham (LBN) (2011b) *Joint Strategic Needs Assessment 2010: The London Borough of Newham.* London: London Borough of Newham.

Malfas, M., Theodoraki, E. & Houlihan, B. (2004) 'Impacts of the Olympic Games as Mega-Events', *Proceedings of the Institute of Civil Engineers, Municipal Engineer*, *157*: 209–220.

O'Brien, D. & Chalip, L. (2007) 'Sport Events and Strategic Leveraging: Pushing towards the Triple Bottom Line', in Woodside, A. G., & Martin, D. (eds) *Tourism Management: Analysis, Behaviour and Strategy.* Oxfordshire: CAB International.

Pantazis, C. & Pemberton, S. (2009) 'From the "Old" to the "New" Suspect Community', *British Journal of Criminology 49*(5): 646–666.

Pawson, L. (2010) 'The Student Protests are Important and Brave. But This is Not War', the *Guardian*, December 2.

Raco, M. & Tunney, E. (2012) 'Visibilities and Invisibilities in Urban Development: Small Business Communities and the London Olympics 2012', *Urban Studies*, *47*(10): 243–263.

Skolnick, J.H. & Fyfe, J.J. (1993) *Above the Law: Police and the Excessive Use of Force.* New York: Free Press.

Smith, A. (2010) 'Leveraging Benefits from Major Events: Maximizing Opportunities for Peripheral Urban Areas', *Managing Leisure*, *15*(3): 161–180.

Taylor, M. (2013) 'Ian Tomlinson's Family Win Apology from Met Police Over Death in 2009', the *Guardian*, August 6.

Weed, M. (2008) *Olympic Tourism.* Oxford: Elsevier.

2   Newham

A brief history of 'the Gash'

Progress with the People.

(Motto of the London Borough of Newham)

When Olympic Park Legacy Delivery Company Chief Executive, Andrew Altman, claimed at the London School of Economics in 2009 that Newham constituted 'London's Gash', he was doing little more than confirming an opinion long held by writers, politicians and activists that the East End was damaged and needed mending, healing or, perhaps eliminating all together (Armstrong et al. 2011). Altman's comment, grounded upon a common perception of the area, was based upon an imagery of poverty and chaos that is little different from the 'awful east' (London, 1903) of the 'old' East End of Whitechapel, Stepney and Bethnal Green. This was the East End of Jack the Ripper, the Jewish ghetto, and later the Kray twins: an iconic terrain of assimilation, refuge and asylum perpetually shadowed by gothic poverty and violence. Scholars such as Bill Fishman, Raphael Samuel and Gareth Stedman-Jones have documented the vibrant history of these areas that are now part of the London Borough of Tower Hamlets, and whose easterly boundaries are marked by the putrid banks of the River Lea, and a largely uncelebrated landscape with its roots firmly placed in the industrial era.

While the very concept of a definable identifiable territory of East London is highly problematic, the 2012 Olympics were never London's or even East London's. They belonged to the marshy polluted flatlands oozing eastwards into the self-congratulatory haven of suburban Essex, a territory with a socio-economic history all of its own. Until the Olympics arrived, this vast area remained strangely ignored by politicians, urban *flâneurs* or Olympic *apparatchiks*. Few bothered to distinguish the peculiarities and particularities of space and place contained within the borough of Newham.

Formed in 1965 via a governmental convenience which merged two quite distinct boroughs, West Ham and East Ham, Newham stands in stark contrast to the tawdry Dickensian glamour, stylized cosmopolitanism and cutting-edge gentrification of the contemporary inner East End (Hobbs, 2006). The borough is geographically bounded by the rivers Thames, Lea and Roding, and by the common lands of Wanstead Flats to the north. Cut off from the heart of London by the meandering course of the River Lea and the north-south axis of the A12 trunk road, Newham is increasingly economically marginalized and has defied the gentrification of post-industrial service-sector London. This chapter will try to provide a context, not only for Altman's outburst, but for the contemporary culture and economy of the borough that was to bear the majority of the 2012 Olympic burden. The emphasis will be upon Newham's industrial era, specifi-cally the post-Second World War golden age of high employment and stability that preceded the borough's pre-Olympic status as a 'gash', and this will hope-fully bring some light and shade to an area that has for too long been crudely labelled a 'dreadful enclosure' (Damer, 1976).

Our discussion will also contribute substantial original empirical detail and analysis to the extensive prior literature on the staging of sport mega-events, particularly in urban locales that are deemed to be impoverished and a suitable target for regeneration. In what follows, we outline Newham's pre-history, up to 1965, focusing on the boroughs of West Ham and East Ham; we then discuss the changing demography and economy of Newham, particularly the impact of post-industrialism; and we set out the key features of Newham today, notably its highly mobile and diverse population. What emerges is a portrait of an old borough that has endured generations of painful economic and political 'restructuring' as well as major demographic shifts.

Pre-Newham to 1965: West Ham and East Ham

West Ham

A City Ordinance of 1371 declared that; 'all oxen, sheep, swine or other large animals for the sustenance of our City aforesaid to be slaughtered, should be taken to the village of Stretford on the one side, and the village of Knytterbrigge on the other side of the said city and there be slaughtered' (Hobbs, 1988: 91). As Bermant notes, while Knightsbridge was to become part of fashionable London, Stratford continued to be a 'depository of nuisances' (1975: 42). However, it was the Metropolitan Building Act of 1844 that defined the character of industrial era West Ham. The Act banned toxic and noxious industry within the boundary of London; consequently the County Borough of West Ham, sitting just outside the metropolitan area on the eastern bank of the River Lea, boomed as manufacturing relocated there. The subsequent population growth was astonishing. In 1841 the borough had less than 13,000 residents, yet by 1901 there were 267,000, making West Ham the ninth most populous town in England.

The building of the railways in the nineteenth century led to Stratford developing as an important transport hub. North of Stratford Broadway, where the Olympic Park was to be subsequently built was the Stratford Engineering Works, originally the manufacturing works of the Great Eastern Railway, which by the time of its closure in 1991 had built 1,682 locomotives, 5,500 passenger vehicles and 33,000 goods wagons (Larkin, 2009: 88–92).

The Northern Outfall Sewer, designed by Joseph Bazalgette after an outbreak of cholera in 1853 and 'The Big Stink' of 1858 (Trench & Hillman, 1984: 72–75), is a vast pipe standing 40 feet high, cloaked with grass and known to locals as the 'sewer bank'. Officially renamed in the mid-1990s as the more fragrant 'Greenway', it runs 4.5 miles from Wick Lane in Hackney through Stratford and Plaistow to Royal Docks Road in Beckton. Until the late twentieth century's decimation of the noxious trades, upon which much of West Ham was founded, the stink wafting up from the iron gratings on the surface of the sewer bank merged with the stench from the ribbon of abattoirs, ink factories, chemical works, a processed meat plant, a perfume factory and much more. Consequently, the back gardens of local residents and the playgrounds of several primary schools, particularly in the north of the borough, were often enveloped in choking yellow acrid emissions. Walking southwards from Stratford through Plaistow, the disinfectant factory in Plaistow Road added the distinct aroma of Jeyes Fluid to the borough's industrial miasma (Newton, 2008).[1] The borough's noxious heritage also goes a long way to explaining why, when work began on Stratford's Olympic Park in 2005, the detoxification of the earth proved to be such a major task.

The southern area of West Ham is worthy of particular examination. South West Ham owed its very existence to the construction, between 1855 and 1921, of the Royal Docks – the Royal Albert Dock, the Royal Victoria Dock – where the future Olympic venue the ExCel Centre was first opened in 2000 – and the King George V Dock. Casual dock workers needed to reside in proximity to the dock gates, and a series of neighbourhoods were formed, clinging to the world's largest enclosed docks. As Besant noted, the building of the Victoria and Albert Docks in 1855 and 1880 respectively, resulted in East Ham and West Ham boasting a joint population of 360,000 by 1901 (Besant, 1901: 213–214). Generally, the housing stock was poor, particularly in the districts of Silvertown, Canning Town and Custom House, where dwellings were built quickly on marshland in order to accommodate the new population, many of whom were Irish who had arrived in East London to build the docks, and stayed to engage in unpleasant manual occupations to which the English were deemed to be no longer suited, either physically or temperamentally (Hobbs, 1988: 96). The Irish filled crucial niches in the labour market that did not require 'steady methodological application, inner motivations of sobriety, forethought, and punctilious observation of contracts' (Thompson, 1974: 473). Their experience of agricultural subsistence labour was easily replicated in the casualized employment market that dominated dock work (Hobbs, 1988: 94–98).

For Dickens, South West Ham rapidly evolved as a poor, dirty and dangerous place:

> A place of refuge for offensive trades . . . Canning Town is the child of the Victoria Docks. The condition of this place and of its neighbour prevents the steadier class of mechanics from residing in it. They go from their work to Stratford or to Plaistow. Many select such a dwelling place because they

are already debased below the point of enmity to filth; poorer labourers live there, because they cannot afford to go farther, and there become debased.

(Dickens, 1857)

Even local leisure was fraught with toxic danger. In September 1878 the *Princess Alice* left Gravesend in Kent intending to return to Woolwich, East London laden with 750 passengers. The 200-foot-long pleasure cruiser was the pride of the London Steamboat Company's fleet. Built in 1865, it was tasked with transporting Londoners to the pleasure gardens that thrived on the banks of the Thames between London and Gravesend. At Gallions Reach, Woolwich, the *Princess Alice* sunk after colliding with the *Bywell Castle*, an 890-ton vessel transporting coal. Close to the point where sewage from the Northern Outfall Sewer was pumped into the Thames, 640 passengers lost their lives (White, 2007: 264; Lock, 2013; Foley, 2011: 69–84), constituting the largest loss of life on a British waterway.

Amongst those companies locating to West Ham as a result of the Metropolitan Building Act of 1844 was the Thames Ironworks and Shipbuilding and Engineering Company Ltd. Incorporated in 1857, the company blossomed during the Ironclad Era, building warships for the Italian, Japanese, Romanian and Peruvian navies, as well as for the British Admiralty. Increasing competition both from foreign shipyards, and the lower-cost northern yards, who lobbied against the Ironworks as a result of the eight-hour day that was introduced by the London firm,[2] led to the Ironworks going out of business in 1912, preceding the commercial bonanza of militarization that was to arise from the Great War. However, from the Ironworks emerged the social institution for which the borough became most readily identifiable: West Ham United Football Club (Korr, 1986).

Many noxious trades and businesses, including paint and varnish manufacturers, soap factories, disinfectant, glue and fertilizer works, and several large oil, petrol and chemical plants were also based in the area. Of crucial importance was Beckton Gas Works, an industrial site of 600 acres that processed 1,000 tons of coal per day. Many of the by-products from gas production, such as coke (iron production), coal tar (disinfectants) and sulphur (sulphuric acid), were utilized in local processing and manufacture, particularly in Silvertown (Townsend, 2003). Danger was an everyday fact of life for local residents, and on the 19th January 1916 an explosion at the Brunner Mond munitions factory in Silvertown destroyed the plant, killing 73 and injuring over 400. Nine hundred nearby buildings were either destroyed or irrevocably damaged. In total over 70,000 properties were damaged including buildings eight miles away in the West End of London. The blast was heard 100 miles away (Hill & Bloch, 2003).

Flour and sugar mills, rubber processing, cable plants, ship repair and marine engineering workshops all congregated in this busy, vibrant corner of London. Full employment, however, was half a century away due largely to the preponderance of casual work in the docks. Statistics indicate the depths of poverty: West Ham was the first borough to introduce the Unemployed Workers Act in 1905 and by 1925 70,000 people in West Ham were being supported by poor relief.[3]

The importation of sugar into the Royal Docks led to the area becoming a centre of sugar processing and the manufacture of sugar-based products: an industrial sector dominated by female labour. The two factories of Tate and Lyle at the south of the borough in Silvertown were the most important sugar-based workplaces in Newham, sharing the 'sugar mile' with jam manufacturers Keiller, Crosse and Blackwell pickles, Sharps Toffee, and Trebor. The Thames Refinery of Tate's became the largest cane sugar refinery in the world and operated with a patriarchal ethic that overshadowed all other local employers. The firm paid relatively high wages, gave profit-sharing related bonuses and provided an onsite surgery, chiropodist and hairdresser. Social and sports facilities were outstanding, Lyle Park was financed by the Lyle Family, and the Christmas and New Year parties held in the firms social club, the 'Tate Institute' were legendary (see Barrett & Calvi, 2012).[4]

As an offshoot of the 'sugar mile', female labour boomed in local sugar dependent workplaces such as Trebor in Forest Gate (Crampton, 2012),[5] and Clarnico, which was initially situated in Hackney Wick and ideally situated for deliveries of sugar on the banks of the River Lee. Clarnico was once the largest sweet manufacturer in the country, which at its peak in the 1900s employed 1,500 people, and had their own fire brigade, ambulance, a 100-strong choral society, and a brass band that toured abroad. The factory moved across the Lea to Waterden Road, Stratford in 1955 where it survived for another 20 years (Crampton, 2012). Eventually the factory buildings were demolished in 2007 to make way for the 2012 Olympic International Broadcast Centre and the Basketball Arena.

East Ham

During the industrial era, East Ham was a distinctively separate place from West Ham. While being a less industrial, greener, and more desirable place to live than its grubby neighbour, crucially, residence in East Ham did not require bourgeois affiliation and so remained politically and culturally proletarian. East Ham's growth between 1880 and 1914 was unmatched by any other place of equivalent size in England, and was made possible by a rapidly improved transport system and a decent housing stock which together attracted clerks and skilled workers.

Most of East Ham's neighbourhoods developed a longstanding prosperous skilled blue collar identity that stood in contrast to many of the neighbourhoods in West Ham that were dominated by the smaller 'two up, two down' houses built for casual dock labourers. East Ham's slum areas were limited to the poorly built Cyprus estate adjacent to Beckton and to Manor Park, where some shabby construction took place between 1895 and 1899 on the Little Ilford Manor Farm estate that was redeveloped in the 1960s (Powell, 1973a). Although the Royal Victoria Dock, which opened in 1855, was in East Ham and the Royal Albert Dock (1880) and the King George V Dock (1921) were mainly in East Ham, in common with Beckton Gas Works, most workers commuted from the adjacent West Ham. With the exception of a large coke works on Manor Way, employment outside of East Ham's southern industrial zone was largely limited to comparatively small industrial units in chemicals, engineering, timber, food and drink, clothing and footwear (Ashworth, 1964: 84). In addition, with five cemeteries in the borough, specialist craft-based industries such as monumental masons thrived, especially in the north of the borough in Manor Park (Powell, 1973b: 14–18). East Ham's highest official population of 143,246, was recorded in 1921, and partly as a result of wartime bombing and subsequent redevelopment, the population decreased to 120,836 in 1951 and 105,682 in 1961.

Compared to West Ham, much of East Ham's housing stock was superior, and the borough lacked the longstanding pollution, overcrowding and poverty that were a feature of its western neighbour. With marshes in the south and north of West Ham, land was cheap and housing poor quality. However, at the north east of West Ham the artisan cottages of Stratford and Maryland gradually gave way to a housing stock which in parts of Forest Gate (E7) resembled the villas of East Ham (E6) and Manor Park (E12), and within these streets a remarkable estate was constructed for middle-class commuters. Built between 1877 and 1892, the 1,160 houses on Balmoral, Claremont, Hampton, Osborne and Windsor roads that made up the Woodgrange Estate were predominantly double-fronted three and four bedroomed houses. The estate, along with much of the housing that bordered the green swathes of Wanstead Flats, had little in common with the grimy industrialism and visceral cultures of West Ham and south East Ham. Well built and spacious, some of the larger houses had servants' quarters and featured front gardens and ornamental iron work. Trees were planted, and shops on Woodgrange and Romford Roads thrived as this part of Forest Gate evolved into a middle-class commuter suburb with good rail links to the City of London.

Compared to other nearby areas, East Ham was less industrial. There were trees in the streets, and its High Street had developed into a fine shopping centre matched only by the affluent West End of London. Boasting an ornate town hall and a cluster of fine parks and playing fields, East Ham was a step up the ladder of working-class respectability from its grubbier relative, and closer in cultural flavour to its eastern neighbour Barking, with its suburban pretentions and aspirational Essex identity.

The war: blitz and its consequences

The two boroughs of East and West Ham suffered massive damage during the blitz of the Second World War. West Ham in particular was heavily bombed, and much of the area between North Woolwich Road and the Thames was destroyed, while one night in September 1940 Silvertown was, for a time, encircled by fire (Idle, 1943). On September 10th 1940, Hallsville Junior School in Canning Town became the site of Britain's worst civilian tragedy of the Second World War when 600 people, after sheltering in the school for three days and nights with very little food and water, were killed. The fatalities were mainly women and children waiting for evacuation after being bombed out of their homes. Locally it was rumoured that the evacuation buses had gone to Camden Town rather than Canning Town by virtue of someone mishearing the instruction, and the subsequent delay in transport meant that the school was full when it suffered a direct hit. Most of the dead were never recovered, and the crater was filled in while the official death toll was given as 77 by a government keen to cover up the extent of the tragedy. The bodies that were recovered were identified and buried in a mass grave at East London Cemetery. The full extent of the death toll did not enter the public realm until 2010.[6]

By 1945, as a result of bombs, flying bombs and rockets, over 27 per cent of the houses in West Ham had been destroyed. In the southern wards adjacent to the docks, structural damage was even more extreme, rising to some 85 per cent in Tidal Basin, and 49 per cent in Beckton Road (Idle, 1943). By 1945, 14,000 houses in West Ham alone had been destroyed by Nazi bombing. The war damage made it possible to undertake large-scale redevelopment, especially in the south of the borough, and between 1945 and 1965 the council built over 9,500 dwellings, of which 8,000 were permanent. To meet the demand for housing destroyed and damaged, East Ham and West Ham councils built homes in neighbouring Essex at Ingrave, Hutton, and in particular Stanford-le-Hope, establishing the foundations for subsequent eastward migration in future decades.[7]

The making and unmaking of Newham

Housing and direct labour

The post-war boom years saw both councils develop large fixed labour forces to rebuild and refurbish entire neighbourhoods affected by bombing. When the two boroughs were combined in 1965, Newham Council's Direct Labour Force (DLF) became responsible for the development and maintenance of large housing estates featuring both high- and low-rise accommodation, much of it hugely superior to the late Victorian and Edwardian housing stock that it replaced. By 1970 Newham had the highest concentration of tower blocks in Great Britain (117), but following the 1968 Ronan Point explosion in Canning Town, the council demolished many of these blocks during the 1970s and 1980s (Sainsbury, 1986).

The Newham DLF is a significant movement in the borough's history. Within many working class communities, the notion of a 'job on the local council' offering unparalleled occupational security was one of the common sense understandings of the world of work that emerged from the fragile realities of the 1930s' Depression era. Newham's post-war housing boom exacerbated this perception. In addition, dock-based Transport and General Workers Union (TGWU) affiliated Labour Party councillors were a powerful presence on the education committees of both local councils, influencing the interpretation of major national government initiatives. For instance, under the tripartite system of secondary education introduced by the 1944 Education Act, post-11 education was divided into three types: grammar, technical and secondary modern. Pupils were allocated to each type of school on the basis on their performance in the 11-plus exam that was held in the final year of each child's primary school education. Technical schools were designed to provide a high-standard vocational education for able students, and were enthusiastically embraced by the education committees of West Ham and East Ham. Two technical schools in West Ham and one in East Ham were established, which stands in stark contrast to the UK generally, where at their peak only 2–3 per cent of children attended a technical school (Sumner, 2010).[8]

Well-qualified and high-quality candidates for apprenticeships in local industries, and particularly for the building trades were produced, especially at South West Ham Technical School on the Barking Road, where pupils were required to pass the 11-plus to enter. As the school offered qualifications in metalwork, woodwork, plumbing and technical drawing, the local DLF became a major beneficiary of the cream of local talent who went on to highly prized apprenticeships. Here local education, municipal government, the trade unions, and a local workforce merged with local housing to provide for the needs of the local population. Further, many of the working practices of the DLF mimicked those found in the docks. Working in small semi-autonomous units or 'gangs', DLF employees maintained a considerable semblance of control over the rhythm of their working week, and fiercely negotiated collective bonuses and overtime payments. However, the political landscape was changing.

Even before the Thatcher government's anti-municipal government policies came into being during the late 1970s into the 1980s, members of the DLF sensed change was in the air. As one stalwart of the era explained; 'They (managers) brought in sub-contractors who had been on six-week training courses, and with the drive to "best value" you got the cheapest people using the cheapest materials' (Ron, interview December 2013). When the system dried up many got out: 'Through the 60s and 70s we was building across the borough, and as you was on one site, they was setting up the next one and the one after that . . . yeah security, the work was always going to be there. Then about 1978 that all changed there was no word of where next. I got out in 78 – no future' (Graham, interview July 2013).

The Conservative government that came to power in 1979 cut government funding for councils. The Local Government Planning and Land Act 1980 introduced compulsory competitive tendering (CCT) for direct labour organizations, and a 'block grant' that enabled central government to impose penalties on councils exceeding expenditure targets. The Right to Buy part of the Housing Act 1980 enabled council tenants to buy their homes at a discount of up to 50 per cent of the market value, depending on how long they had been living in the property, and the effect was to drastically reduce the council housing stock: by 1987 over 1,000,000 council houses in Britain had been sold. This served to overheat the housing market, and resulted in working-class council tenants buying their homes at a massive discount before selling at a profit and heading for London's periphery. This exodus, combined with deindustrialization, effectively drained working-class London of much of its human capital, as well as its collective memory. The retreat of the State has continued, but rather than developing a nirvana of home ownership, private landlords and short-term tenants now dominate Newham's housing market.

Power in housing shifted to the landlords with the introduction of Assured Shorthold Tenancies via the Housing Act of 1988, which offered less security of tenure for tenants, and enhanced the power of landlords to evict. Along with the introduction of specialist buy-to-let mortgage products, the Act brought new investors into the property market attracted by rental incomes, rising capital values and a perception that the housing sector entailed a lower risk than equity-based investment. The emergence of this entrepreneurial ethos created a new breed of landlord attracted by rising property values and taxation rules that allowed landlords to deduct the taxable portion of their rental income, and the interest portion of their mortgage repayments as well as maintenance costs on the property. Overall, buy-to-let has had a huge impact in London with one in three new properties being bought by investors,[9] contributing significantly to a sense of neighbourhood instability and uncertainty.

Cumulatively, this constituted a huge blow to the union-dominated public sector. Newham's DLF was decimated from over 1,000 employees, to its present standing of approximately 150. Its locally nurtured workforce, who had often remained living in Newham or on its periphery, now joined the private sector, many becoming self-employed 'white-van men'[10] following the path of redundant dockers and pioneering New Towners into Essex, parts of which became a nostalgic and often resentful alcove where the BBC situation comedy *Only Fools and Horses* played on a loop is a constant, cosy and somewhat reassuring reminder of the way we were (see Fussey et al. 2011).

The docks: boom and bust

The lived experience of Newham's residents has, in common with most of Britain's working class, tended to be ignored. This is particularly true of East London from the 1950s to the late 1960s, an era of high employment, rehousing, innovative schooling, mass trade union membership and confident municipal socialist regimes. The post-war period offered considerable respite from the poverty and unemployment that had forged the East End, and it was during this post-war period, with near full employment for the first time in its history, that the area could savour an unprecedented stability. In particular the docks boomed, and West Ham and East Ham enjoyed a relative prosperity that was unimagined during the 1940s and 1950s. Sol was a cooper working in the Royal Docks whose life cycle typified many of his peers: 'I did a five year apprenticeship and then got called up, Army. Never went abroad. I was a driver. Catterick [North Yorkshire] was the worst place I went. When I got out the docks was buzzing, boats [queuing] up to Tilbury, and I was making barrels for all sorts of firms . . . my old man was an old docker when it was a job for people who couldn't get nothing else. So he made sure I got a trade, and coopering was a good trade. I earned good money, really good money. All them who worked in the docks weren't just dockers, there was trades everywhere, and once the union got hold of things it was a place where everybody could earn.' (interview, January 2012).

This was a confident community, whose ultimate decline commenced with the decade-long demise of the timber and furniture industries between 1961 and 1971, which resulted in the loss of over 26,000 jobs (Hall, 1962: 72). The same decade saw the loss of 40,000 jobs in London's clothing and footwear industries, centred on the East End (Hall, 1962: 44–45). Despite the huge scale of job losses, industrial decline took place surreptitiously, and initially most of the losses were non-unionized and located in relatively small units of production.

Sol's experience of working in the post-Second World War docks was not untypical. Whilst dockers had traditionally been located at the rump of the labour market as casual workers, and although this arrangement continued until as late as 1965, the system became regularized after the creation of the National Dock Labour Scheme in 1947 (Hill, 1976). However, throughout the 1960s container-ization and new handling methods for cargo reduced the demand for manual labour in the docks (ibid.). The massive capital investment in the modernization of deep water docks at Tilbury, some 20 miles east of Newham, where adjacent land was cheap, plentiful and ideal for the storage of containers, clearly signalled the demise of the industrial East End. By 1971, the Port of London's workforce had shrunk to 6,000, and between 1966 and 1976, London's dockland boroughs (Tower Hamlets, Newham, Southwark, Lewisham, and Greenwich) lost 150,000 jobs: mainly in transport, distribution, and food/drink processing, all sectors closely associated with port activity. This represented 20 per cent of all jobs in the area, compared to a decline of only 13 per cent in Greater London and just 2 per cent in Great Britain. Newham alone lost 40,000 jobs (Hobbs, 1988: ch. 6, Ross, 2010).

Chobham Farm

'A cowboy operation in an unresolved wasteland' (Sinclair, 2012: 19).

But the loss of jobs and industry did not happen without a fight. In the 1970s the histories of the north and south of the borough were brought together as industrial labour gave way to a post-industrial future which in itself was to prove transitory. The south of the borough provided the parliamentary constituency of Keir Hardie, the Labour Party's first MP. (Morgan, 1975), and the area was a bulwark of British Trade Union history (Hyman, 1971), via the epic Dockers' Tanner strike of 1889 (Champion, 1890), with a long history of struggle revolving around the obscenity of casualization. Dockers were always going to be a target for a 'modernizing' government and predatory market forces (Hill, 1976).

The combination of bigger ships' holds, increased use of fork lift trucks, container-ization and palletization all contributed to the decline of dock work. Employers were faced with a decrease in their labour requirements, and attempted to make 'fundamental changes in the day to day practices that had suited them admirably for the previous 100 years' (Hobbs, op. cit.: 127). In particular, containers could be handled in a tenth of the time of traditional non- packaged cargoes, and shift-ing to containers enabled a move to workplaces not covered by the National Dock Labour Scheme. These inland ports and depots paid fewer people significantly less than registered dockers' rates of pay and shop stewards, who were directly elected by rank-and-file workers in the workplace carrying the fight directly to the employers; a policy that stood in direct opposition to a reluctant, somewhat timid hierarchy within the Transport and General Workers' Union (TGWU). By the early 1970s the struggle for the shop stewards' committees was to ensure that labour in the 'scab' (non-unionised) ports and container terminals, established in the wake of containerization, should be carried out by registered dockers working, like them, under the official National Docks Labour Scheme. This included the depot at Chobham Farm in Angel Lane, Stratford, part of the semi-decrepit network of goods yards and rail tracks that have now been sunk beneath Westfield Stratford City, and the Queen Elizabeth Olympic Park.

The TGWU had been busy in recruiting new members and had signed up many workers at the new container terminals.[11] In summer 1972, dock workers were secondary picketing the Chobham Farm depot (Peart-Jackson, 1973: 116–117), and came into direct conflict with fellow union members, resulting in Chobham Farm workers complaining to the newly contrived National Industrial Relations Court (NIRC) who subsequently ordered the arrest of three of the shop stewards' committee leaders for failing to attend a hearing. Nationwide strikes across the dock sector, supported by car workers at Longbridge, Birmingham followed, which resulted in the Government backing down before any arrests could be made. Midland Cold Storage (MCS), part of the multi-national Vestey Group, applied to the NIRC for an injunction to stop further picketing: the dockers defied the injunction. The Vestey Group, headed by Lord Vestey, a longstanding adversary of dock workers (Hobbs, 1988: 128–130), owned cattle ranches and abattoirs in Argentina, the transport company that carried the chilled beef to the docks, and the company employing the dockers who loaded the beef into Vestey-owned Blue Star ships. When the beef arrived in London or Liverpool it was unloaded by a Vestey-owned stevedoring company, and moved by a Vestey-owned haulage company to the company's cold stores. 'From there it would be distributed to the nationwide chain of Dewhurst butchers shops . . . he owned them too' (Ross, 2010: 95–96). MCS hired private detectives to identify the strike leaders, and five Transport and General Workers Union shop stewards were named and subsequently arrested for contempt of court as a result of refusing to appear before the NIRC. Four were arrested and imprisoned on 21 July, while the fifth man, Vic Turner, generally regarded as the most prominent figure in the dispute, was arrested and imprisoned as he led a demonstration outside Pentonville prison, where his colleagues were incarcerated (see Hill, 1976: 103–108)

The picket at Pentonville started as soon as the first arrested dockers arrived to begin their sentence, and along with most of the nation's 44,000 dockers, print workers in Fleet Street and the main London food markets stopped work. London lorry drivers and warehouse workers came out in sympathy, as did Aberdeen, Fleetwood and Grimsby fish-workers and trawler crew, along with Welsh and Scottish miners. While the Yorkshire District National Union of Mineworkers announced action for later in the week, three Yorkshire pits came out immediately, as did a wide range of workers across the country including those at Midland Cold Storage. Eventually, in order to establish some authority over the shop stewards' committees, the TUC had to respond, and the General Council called for a one-day General Strike to take place on 31 July. In the meantime 20,000 London bus workers came out, as did the ground staff at London Airport. All the major factories in Sheffield were on strike, along with 10,000 lorry drivers on Merseyside, Lambeth refuse workers, Rolls-Royce workers, ship builders, power station workers and many others across the country (Lindop, 1998: 65–100). The Official Solicitor 'appeared like a fairy godmother' (Barber, 1977: 2) on behalf of the Government to look at the case, and applied to the Court of Appeal. The law was now reinterpreted to state that the Courts held the unions, rather than individual pickets, responsible for their actions, and the men were set free on 26 July.

While the role of the NIRC was discredited, the Industrial Relations Act was dealt a 'mortal blow' (Barber, op. cit., Dorey, 1995: 73), and was repealed by the 1974–1979 Labour government. Following the miners' Saltley Gates victory in February, this was the second time in 1972 that working-class action had manifested as a genuine threat to the Government (Dorfman, 1979: 59–65). However, internal union politics prevented the shop stewards' committee from continuing this gathering momentum, and the TGWU blocked the picketing of the much larger London International Freight Terminal,[12] where 1,500 jobs existed outside of the NDLS. Dock workers voted to end the strike, severance pay was doubled to £4,000, and the key issue of registration of all dockers was effectively surrendered as part of the Jack Jones–Lord Aldington Report, and the demise both of the London Docks and the culture that it fostered was accelerated (Ross, 2010: 148–171).

Subsequently, it became apparent that the post-1979 Thatcher regime had learnt valuable lessons from Chobham Farm and the Pentonville Five, and developed anti-union tactics that targeted funds rather than individual activists. Nonetheless, the events of 1972 focused the nation's attention upon the backwaters of Stratford as never before, triggering a level of working-class militancy the scale of which had not been seen since the 1926 General Strike.[13] Although this momentous episode in labour history has been consigned to obscurity by politicians, entrepreneurs and urbanists, when the archeologists of the future drill down through the cultural plague pit of Westfield, the Queen Elizabeth Park and the Chobham Manor housing estate, one can only hope that there remains something valuable, perhaps even virulent, from the vestiges of Chobham Farm.

While the Olympics are sometimes seen as the harbinger of neo-liberal urban policies, Newham had already experienced the powerful impacts of neo-liberalism, through the loss of industry and privatization of housing stock from the 1980s onwards. The established social order of Newham had fractured. Dock workers and their families took their severance pay and moved to Essex, and the traditional 'ducking and diving' of generations of East Enders was transformed into a fiercer set of strategies based upon the new 'gloves off' entrepreneurship of market society (Hobbs, 2013). Both the fragmentation of the population and disintegration of extended family networks were extensive, as the post-industrial market economy laid waste to traditional communities that were 'emptied out' of marketable labour and traditional forms of governance (Pakulski & Waters 1996: 110; Strangleman, 2007).[14]

Markets: co-existence and commerce

Industrial era West Ham and East Ham were blessed with three vibrant street markets where locals could resist the onward march of supermarkets. Although Angel Lane Market at Stratford was demolished to make way for a shopping mall that opened in 1974, Plaistow and Canning Town proved more resilient. In Canning Town the origins of Rathbone Market date back to 1253, when a charter signed by King Henry III promised that a Wednesday market in West Ham would exist 'forever'. By the 1880s, a group of street traders were well ensconced on the Victoria Dock Road, and were only persuaded to move by the council when the road was being dug up to put in tramlines. The traders eventually moved to Rathbone Street in 1963, when the old market made way for the construction of the A13 arterial road and moved to a smaller site on the Barking Road which at its peak had 160 stalls. However, with the area being redeveloped as part of the regeneration of Canning Town that will build 650 new homes as well as retail out- lets and community facilities, the new Rathbone Market will become a cluster of stalls that feels to many locals like a mere gesture on the behalf of the developers.

For well over a century, one of Newham's few remaining genuine hubs of community has been Queens Road Market in Plaistow. Consisting predominantly of Jewish traders from 1904 to the late 1960s, food, clothes, toys and much more were sold by renowned stallholders such as Israels (toys), Sonny the Cloth (dress- making materials), and a man with several fingers missing who sold live eels. The old market was demolished and the current covered version, built in 1970 as part of a high-rise development, quickly adapted to the increasingly cosmopolitan population (see Lyon & Back, 2012).

> With over 85 per cent of the shoppers coming from African, African- Caribbean and Asian communities . . . With its souk-like ambience, access to fresh, culturally appropriate produce and goods at amazing prices ensures that news of the market spreads far beyond the East End. This human reef has some rarer national groups if one is prepared to explore; who would have thought that Burundians, Ecuadorians, Latvians and the Togolese would be regular denizens of Queen's Market . . . (which) continues to evolve and absorb the social mores of countless nations. Add to this the piquant Cockney humour and you have the sort of cocktail of peacefully coexisting humanity that social engineers can only dream of.[15]

Although the north side of Green Street no longer has the departmental store, which was prominent in the 1960s, it now boasts a thriving collection of Indian- owned gold and sari shops. The south end of Green Street, once dominated by small Jewish businesses, now features a plethora of ethnically diverse constantly churning small businesses. At the Barking Road end of Green Street stands the 35,000 capacity Boleyn Ground, home since 1904 to West Ham United. Every two weeks during the football season local shoppers are outnumbered by predominantly white, Essex-based supporters who return to converge on a locale that for many constitutes an ancestral home. With the clubs impending relocation in summer 2016 to the refurbished Olympic Stadium in the QEOP, the pubs, cafes and pie and mash shops around the ground are already closing their doors, no longer able to survive on a once fortnightly mainly winter trade, and will disappear entirely.

Sport and recreation

As with any working-class area of the industrial era, sport was an important aspect of life in both West Ham and East Ham. Apart from the ubiquitous presence of West Ham United's stadium in Green Street, the borough also boasted the 120,000 capacity West Ham Stadium in Custom House which was used primarily for greyhound racing,[16] speedway[17] and stock car racing. Opened in 1928, the stadium closed in 1972 when it was sold to developers.

At a more micro-level, during its post-war industrial zenith and its immediate aftermath, cultural capital was acquired through interlocking family-based networks relating to sport, work and entrepreneurial pursuits – in particular the licensed trade. These networks were not accidental or disparate phenomena, but were enabled by full employment bolstered by a municipal government inextricably tied to its electorate. This was played out not only in the aforementioned arenas of education and housing policy, but in sports and youth clubs that were part-funded by local government, but staffed largely by unpaid local citizens whose authority and status was ensured by their links to these informal networks. An example is that of Forest Gate Boys' Club, formed in the 1950s by a locally born volunteer and sports fanatic, Len Hoffman, whose day-time job was working for West Ham Education Committee as an attendance officer. Based in a hut in Sebert Road, Forest Gate, the club, which produced national table tennis champions and a number of professional footballers, was open three nights a week plus Saturday mornings and Sunday afternoons. Although the club closed in 1970, Hoffman continued coaching football and table tennis at various venues in East London. At the time of writing he is aged 91 and in his 67th consecutive year in sports coaching.

In 1964 East Ham alone had over 60 youth clubs. Some of the clubs across the two boroughs offered facilities and expertise that, regardless of the oft claimed Olympic Legacy, can only be dreamt of by contemporary youth in Newham. For instance, founded in 1922, West Ham Boxing Club at the back of the Black Lion pub in Plaistow produced hundreds of champions and notable fighters including Billy Walker, Jimmy Tibbs, Mark Kaylor, Nigel Benn, Kevin Mitchell, and Olympic gold medallist Terry Spinks. The club constitutes the last surviving element of industrial era youth provision in the borough. When the lease on their premises at the back of the Black Lion pub expired in 2013 and the club moved into the Curwen Centre in London Road, Plaistow, this marked a new relationship between London Borough of Newham Council and the University of East London which will ensure that Year 7 pupils at the borough's secondary schools can participate in a wide range of sports. Boxing in the borough is further enhanced by the Bowers brothers' world famous Peacock Gym in Canning Town, and by Joey Chapman, an alumnus of both Forest Gate Boys' Club and the Black Lion, who now runs Newham Boxing Club from otherwise redundant municipal premises in Church Street Stratford.

Philanthropic institutes and settlements were prominent all over East London but particularly in West Ham. With its origins in the Mansfield House University settlement, Fairbairn House Boys' Club, founded in 1891, had a membership of 900 by 1968. The club included a library, theatre, workshops, gymnasium, and canteen. The club could also boast a sports ground at Burgess Road East Ham, with a running track, football pitches, tennis courts and an open air swimming pool (Powell, 1973c: 141–144).[18] Newham's schools and sports clubs were also well served by council-owned football and cricket pitches. Much of this is now a memory, but places the bumptious narrative surrounding the sporting legacy of the 2012 Olympics into a context largely forgotten.

On Broadway: nightlife in Newham

Along with St John's Church and the Victorian-built Town Hall,which in 1898 hosted the first socialist municipal administration in Britain, Stratford Broadway, particularly in the 1960s and early 1970s was a booming thoroughfare that hosted a number of important local institutions. These included the headquarters of the much read *Stratford Express* newspaper, and its publisher Wilson and Whitworth, which sat alongside tailors, furniture shops, banks and insurance offices as well as two department stores – the somewhat genteel Boardmans, and another run by the London Co-operative Society. Behind Stratford Broadway was Angel Lane street market and the Theatre Royal, an Edwardian theatre that became famous in the 1960s as home to Joan Littlewood's *Theatre Workshop* (Coren, 1984). However, the most significant feature of Stratford Broadway was its nightlife. The *Edward the Seventh* was a well-ordered pub favoured by local football teams, and *The Swan* was an early 'Music Pub' that never came close to competing with the *Two Puddings*,[19] a pub run with ruthless efficiency by two local entrepreneurs with backgrounds in dock work and amateur boxing (Johnson, 2012). The *Two Puddings*, along with Terry Murphy's *Bridge House* in Canning Town, became popular and profitable music venues with reputations across London and the South East. Terry Murphy, a professional boxer who fought for British titles, and his extended family were well connected in the worlds of local football, boxing and public houses (Murphy, 2007). These two families, along with others such as the Curbishleys, used local networks with their origins in the negotiated world of dock work to become key players in the pubs, sport and show business.[20]

A number of nightclubs were also important features of the area. The *Lotus Ballroom* at Forest Gate was run by the Johnson brothers. Opposite the *Lotus* and housed in an old skating rink was a truly remarkable venue, the *Upper Cut*. This club's opening night in December 1966 featured The Who, and over the next 12 months hosted the cream of British and American touring bands including Jimi Hendrix, Stevie Wonder, and the much revered Stax Tour of 1967 with Otis Redding, Sam and Dave, and Booker T and the MGs. The club was owned by glamorous local heavyweight boxer Billy Walker and his brother George who had been 'Boss of Britain's Underworld', Billy Hill's minder (Hill, 1955), and who went on to become the founder of Brent Walker, and the archetypical tough resourceful entrepreneur of the Thatcher era.[21] This was no cultural or economic void, or indeed gash.

Immigration

However, nor was it an ethnically homogenous zone of privileged white proletarianism. By 1911, about 1.5 per cent of West Ham's and 1.9 per cent of East Ham's populations were of (non-British) European origin (Widdowson & Block, no date), and amongst the middle-class families who resided in North West Ham, and just adjacent to the site of what would become the *Upper Cut,* was a Jewish community of German and East European origin who had migrated four miles eastwards from the original Whitechapel ghetto of the early 1900s. Newham had at various times five synagogues. The biggest in Earlham Grove, Forest Gate opened in 1897 and closed in 2004 (Bloch, 1997). The synagogue in Carlyle Road, Manor Park between the Romford Road and Wanstead Flats that opened in 1900 and closed in 1986 now houses the Sri Lankan Shri Guru Ravidass JI Gudwara Sahib temple, and the Ravidasia Community Centre. The Canning Town synagogue closed in 1966 and was taken over by the Al-Habib mosque and Islamic centre. Mormons now occupy the site of the Upton Park synagogue that closed in 1972 after 61 years. The synagogue in Katherine Road also closed that year, after 49 years.[22]

South Asians had been coming to Newham docks as seamen since the early nineteenth century, and by the mid-nineteenth century had an established presence, mainly in West Ham, initially staying in hostels such as the Lascar Mission, a branch of St Luke's church in Canning Town. In the 1911 census there were 143 Asians recorded in East Ham, and 17 in West Ham (Widdowson & Block, no date). Gradually, small communities of black and South Asian people evolved in the south of the borough, and after the First World War these communities were enhanced by recently demobbed troops and sailors, particularly from India and the Caribbean, many of whom married local women. In 1926 the Coloured Men's Institute was opened in Tidal Basin by Kamal Chunchie on behalf of the Methodist Church, and quickly established itself as a key resource for black and Asian men and their families (Rozina, 1999). By the 1921 census there were 1,000 Indians in Canning Town alone, and by the 1930s the black community in the area was the largest in London (Bell, 2002).

Post-Second World War, the British government ran campaigns to attract labour from the Commonwealth, and during the 1960s and 1970s a significant Pakistani Muslim population grew in Newham. Initially working in river-based processing plants and at the Ford Motor factory in Dagenham, they were joined in 1971 by several hundred East African Asians, predominantly Sikhs, who also settled in Newham after fleeing the regime in Uganda. black and South Asian individuals and families arriving in Newham seldom qualified for council accommodation. With most of the borough's post-war council housing situated in South West Ham, and with an increase in far right National Front Party activity, Canning Town established itself as a distinctly white area whose population, in part, were resistant to non-white newcomers.

By the time the docks had closed Newham could boast long established Asian and black British Caribbean communities, who, despite being subjected to widespread racism in a borough controlled by white-dominated trade unionism generally unable to comprehend the notion of multiculturalism let alone international proletarianism (see Schoen, 1977), were embedded in a localized version of an industrial project that had already absorbed successive generations of immigrants. By the end of the 1960s one section of the larger, more substantial housing stock in the north of the borough had become run down and subdivided into flats and bedsits, providing accommodation for a West Indian community who rapidly established a vibrant colony culture of pubs and clubs, and became firmly embedded into a local economy that was still enjoying full employment.

black and Asian families were left to rent from private landlords (Widdowson & Block, no date) who established a market in the north east of the borough around Forest Gate, Manor Park, Little Ilford, Upton Park and East Ham; areas where housing was larger and more amenable to multiple occupancy (LBN 1982). Soon, upwardly mobile Bangladeshis from Tower Hamlets bought into the housing market (Modood & Berthoud, 1997) in the north east of the borough as they followed the indigenous white eastward's flight that would culminate in suburban Essex (North et al. 2004), while Caribbeans and Africans tended to settle in Stratford and, to a lesser extent, Plaistow (LBN, 1982). Newham remained a destination for Muslim migrants after the Commonwealth Immigrants Acts of the 1960s restricted migration, and family reunion, marriage migration, asylum seekers and refugees all confirmed the north east of Newham as the centre of the borough's Muslim community (LBN 1993, 2005).[23] However, more recent Muslim migrants are spread across the borough in areas that were previously exclusively white domains, such as Canning Town and Stratford.

Late industrial era Newham was a vibrant place of work, family, sport, and leisure, and at its confident post-war peak, bolstered by near full employment, the borough enjoyed a remarkable period of prosperity that was evident in every aspect of social life. But when the docks closed, followed by the emptying out of the working population, the area went into decline. The population became poorer, less homogenous and prone to a factionalism that was the antithesis of the admittedly ragged communitarianism that had marked the borough's all too brief socio-economic peak.

Newham today

After years of debate concerning the actual size of the borough's population (Hayman, 2011; von Ahn, 2006; House of Commons London Regional Committee, 2010), Newham today is home to a population of over 300,000 people.[24] Newham has had the highest birth rate in the country for several years. In 2009 Newham had the highest number of births (6,003), the highest general fertility rate (105.8) and the highest total fertility rate (2.96) in London (LBN & NHS Newham, 2011: 14, citing ONS data). An 8 per cent increase in the number of dwellings in Newham between 2001 and 2009 also suggests that population falls are highly unlikely (LBN & NHS Newham, 2011: 83). Inter-censual estimates of Newham's population tend to ignore post-2004 migration from Eastern Europe in favour of an emphasis on migration from South Asia (Hayman, 2011). Consequently, as public services are part funded by central government on the basis of local authority population calculations via the Local Government Settlement, concerns were frequently expressed that Newham, due to under-estimates of the population size, has been severely under-funded – possibly by £5.8 million in 2010/11.[25]

At the time of the 2001 Census, Newham was the UK's most ethnically diverse local authority with almost 61 per cent of residents being from non-white ethnic groups. The cluster of electoral wards on the boundary between Newham and Redbridge – Little Ilford, Manor Park, Loxford and Forest Gate – are the most diverse in the country (Piggott, 2004). There are more than 30 different ethnic communities in the borough, where more than 300 languages are spoken (Newham Language Shop, 2005). Some 35.6 per cent of Newham's residents were born out-side of the European Union, 13.1 per cent of whom described themselves as black African, 12.1 per cent Indian and 8.8 per cent Bangladeshi.[26] In 2006, 71 per cent of Newham's school pupils had a first language that was 'known or believed' to be other than English (second only to neighbouring Tower Hamlets, with 75 per cent),[27] while a 2008 survey found that school pupils in Newham spoke 144 different languages.[28] A recent analysis of police custody data in Newham reinforces this point, with prisoners from 132 nationalities recorded over a five-year period.[29] Against this background, Newham's mayor Sir Robin Wales has claimed that Newham is 'the most diverse community for its size in the world'.[30]

As mentioned above, in the 1970s and 1980s the National Front targeted Newham, and racist violence was commonplace. In the face of organized racism black and South Asian communities in Newham became politically organized, and established the Newham Defence Committee and the Newham Youth Movement, which eventually led to the foundation of the Newham Monitoring Project in 1980 (LBN, 2002). Also in 1980, the murder of a young Muslim male prompted the founding of the Newham Muslim Citizens' Association, which evolved into Newham Muslim Alliance (Stratford Community History, 1996). Right-wing groups continued to be active in Newham during the 1990s, but since 2000 their strength and influence has dissipated to the point of insignificance.

Eastern Europe and institutional ignorance

The decade since the 2001 census has seen major changes to migration flows, particularly with large-scale migration from Eastern Europe. It is, for example, claimed that as many as 30,000 Lithuanians may have moved to Newham since the A8 Eastern European nations joined the EU in 2004.[31] However, we found that generally amongst both practitioners and policy makers their understanding of the notion of multiculturalism in Newham was restricted to the shadows of Empire. More specifically, this knowledge was limited to those of Caribbean, African or South Asian heritage, regardless of how long they or their families had resided in the UK. However, in the light of media attention in the run up to the Olympics, Eastern European immigration was increasingly presented as posing a serious criminal threat to Newham and the 2012 Olympics.[32] As ever, police data relating individual and isolated cases was cited as typifying pathological tendencies amongst a group defined not by their class or economic situation, but by their ethnicity (Hobbs, 2013).

Despite this, however, within Newham police there emerged a rather more sympathetic view that challenged this stereotype. This was due almost entirely to the empathy that was developed between a Detective Inspector and members of the Lithuanian community (Cushion 2010). Based upon careful work carried out of his own volition, the picture he presented of Newham's Lithuanian population was of a poorly educated, God-fearing, hard-working population with a penchant for alcohol abuse. One in ten of all recorded crime in LBN in 2009/10 was credited to 'Lithuanians'.[33]

Lithuanians constitute a relatively isolated community. Their version of colony culture resembles that of the Irish in particular who, also driven by poverty into cramped and insanitary living conditions, engaged in low paid manual work and became associated with alcohol-induced disorder. Indeed, alcohol and drug abuse have become a characteristic of this loose knit community of migrant workers, as they seek to attain some relief from exploitative tenuous labour and poor housing. As the DI explained: 'They usually live in over-crowded places – either sharing rooms and communal areas or squatting a premise. They then drink too much and arguments break out and they thump one another when very drunk'. In late January 2011 a 37-year-old Lithuanian male was found dead in the house he shared with six other Lithuanian men. A problem drinker, he had died as a consequence of a blow to the head. The suspect, also an alcoholic and acquaintance of the deceased, turned himself in to police within 48 hours.[34]

Like generations of immigrants and sojourners before them, Lithuanian newcomers proved to be vulnerable to landlords, with up to 20 crammed into small Edwardian terraced houses built for a family of four or five, while others reside in equally cramped conditions in illegally sub-let social housing, in illegal extensions built onto back gardens, in shipping containers, and in the store rooms of shops and business.

Overcrowding and churn

Even in 2004, however, before this new migration pattern had become established, three of Newham's electoral wards were estimated to be the most overcrowded in England.[35] Today, evidence suggests that the picture may be very much worse, with the emergence of illegally built temporary accommodation in the rear gardens of domestic houses,[36] while LBN officers report that local schools are seeing increasing numbers of pupils with room numbers included in their addresses: one sub-divided property being home to 32 children. Newham's population is notably youthful: at 31.8 years (2011 estimate) the average age of borough residents is the lowest in London,[37] with almost 40 per cent being under the age of 25 compared with the London average of 32 per cent (2005 estimate).[38]

Today around 20 per cent of residents enter or leave Newham each year,[39] while additional intra-borough movements mean that as many as 30 per cent of council tax accounts change ownership annually.[40] This data indicates substantial population churn: a potentially major obstacle to building community cohesion.[41] Of particular note, in a borough where 35 per cent of housing is privately rented,[42] is the fact that the majority of churn occurs in the private rented sector where 44 per cent of private rental tenants live in their property for less than a year (LBN & NHS Newham, 2011: 83). In contrast to the more settled Hackney, Islington and Brixton, all London boroughs with large stocks of attractive period housing, Newham remains unique, its population arriving from the global south and east to eventually earn enough to as quickly as possible move out of the borough, eastwards into Essex (see LBN, 2007, and LBN & NHS Newham, 2011).[43]

Senior public service workers have conceded that faced with such fragmentation and churn they struggle to implement genuine community consultation. That said, a number of senior LBN officers indicated that discourse concerning the fluidity or fragmentation of communities in Newham is unacceptable to the councils's political leadership, who insist on a narrative that emphasizes Newham as a homogenous community. Such ideal homogeneity has structural problems. Newham is the sixth most deprived local authority in England, and is third in London behind fellow 'Olympic boroughs' (and immediate neighbours) Hackney and Tower Hamlets.[44] In 2008, the unemployment rate was 10.3 per cent compared to the London average of 6.9 per cent,[45] while in 2010, 22 per cent of Newham's working-age residents were in receipt of benefits from the Department for Work and Pensions, compared to the London average of 15 per cent.[46] Similarly, in 2009, 37 per cent of Newham's pupils were eligible for free school meals, against the London average of 26 per cent.[47] Deprivation in Newham is widespread rather than existing in specific pockets,[48] which has important implications for the delivery of all public services as they cannot be easily geographically prioritized.

Not surprisingly, in a 2008 survey of Londoners, Newham residents reported the lowest levels of satisfaction with their local area, the highest levels of anti-social behaviour, and the second lowest levels of community cohesion.[49] In 2009, Newham recorded the lowest borough average 'ward well-being' score in London, and Newham's housing stock is also a cause for concern. In 2009 almost two-fifths of Newham's dwellings were considered unsuitable for their residents.[50] Meanwhile, demand for housing has been increasing, with one third of households registered on London Borough of Newham Council's housing register in 2010, up from around 10 per cent in 2000.[51] Looking further ahead, it is projected that between 50,000 and 80,000 new homes will be built in Newham by 2030, expanding the resident population by up to 100,000 (LBN & NHS Newham. 2011: 7, 84).

Meanwhile, pre-Olympics, the borough's old industrial infrastructure has proven ripe for commercial exploitation. London City Airport was opened in 1987 on the site of the King George V Dock, and the ExCel exhibition centre opened in 2000 at the Royal Victoria Docks. In 2011, these developments were joined by Europe's largest urban shopping centre, the Australian-owned Westfield, conveniently situated adjacent to the Olympic Park in Stratford.

Conclusion: ashes

Newham, then, can be understood as a highly complex and challenging place to live and work, and a somewhat bizarre choice to stage the Olympics. But it is no 'gash'. It has a history featuring work, industry, immigration and poverty, interspersed by a brief period of full employment and relative prosperity. Mobility rather than stoic, and at times intransigent, communality now typifies the borough. Crucially, in terms of understanding contemporary Newham, we must first attempt to comprehend the real lived impact of complex processes upon the borough's citizens; processes and experiences that are often hidden when terms such as 'post-industrialism', 'globalization' and 'neo-liberalism' are used in sterile, somewhat zombified ways. As we can see above, the draining of actual capital out of the area by the closing of the docks and their associated industries was accompanied by direct assaults upon municipal socialism and union-based labour. Combined with the new housing market that was created as a result of 'right to buy' and 'buy to let', the area was emptied of its most marketable labour, creating a void that has been filled by a low paid, unstable, churning population of non-unionized labour disproportionately reliant upon poor-quality privately rented accommodation.

The flotsam and jetsam of the borough's recent industrial past have been quickly swept away following the award of the Games to London in 2005. Old factories, warehouses and a swathe of good-quality social and private housing were cleared and 450 people rehoused. This was not slum clearance. They were just in the way. West Ham United's Boleyn ground, a place of tradition, memory, nostalgia and very occasionally entertainment, will be bulldozed to make way for a 700-home East End 'village' when West Ham relocate to the Olympic Stadium. Sir Robin Wales, Mayor of Newham, explained: 'We have always maintained that West Ham United's relocation to Stratford had the potential to deliver an Olympic legacy beyond Queen Elizabeth Olympic Park as a key part of the comprehensive regeneration of Green Street and Upton Park. The prospect of much needed homes, jobs and community spaces for this area is an exciting one.'[52] At least seven pubs and a number of cafes will close around Upton Park as a result of the shift.

Industrial-era employment alongside its associated political organization, its institutions and cultures had proved to be efficient, if at times fractious vehicles of proletarian assimilation for generations of new arrivals to Newham. However, post-industrial immigration to the borough cannot rely upon the docks or river-related processing and production, and the influence of trade unions no longer enjoys predominance within local government, most crucially with regard to education and housing. These were the props upon which not only the population of Newham, but much of the post-war consensus relied, and its demise has ensured that the very notion of community when applied to diverse, fractious, fragmented urban working-class populations has little contemporary relevance. New arrivals are no longer roughly absorbed into the local political economy and its interlocking enabling structures (Vertovec, 2006).

Of the millions who visited the Olympic Park in the course of the 2012 Games, few had visited this part of London before, and even fewer had any knowledge about the people who lived within Newham's boundaries. For the duration of the Games the Olympic Park was little more than a sterile peninsula in the north west corner of Newham, into which the public was funnelled directly from adjacent transport hubs. While the local authority branded Newham a place to 'Live, Work and Stay', the reality for many of its residents, drawn from every corner of the world, has been that Newham is more a transit lounge than destination. If place-related identities, relations and histories are formed and asserted via uniformity (Korpela, 1989), its absence suggests that Newham's remarkable character can only be inferred from its component parts (Latour, 1988: 85.).

While examples of everyday ragged, contested, and essentially informal conviviality and communality can be observed routinely in playgrounds and at school gates, on street corners, in shops and markets (Gilroy 2004: 161), in the waiting rooms of probation, housing, and social work offices and of course in faith (Madge et al., 2014), there is little conformity or potential for organization or activism amongst these small fragmented informal networks, for: 'There is history but no shared narrative of difficulty, and so no shared fate' (Sennett, 1998: 147).

Notes

1 The factory relocated to Thetford in the early 1960s, and the Jeyes Estate was built on the site by the Greater London Council.
2 See http://hansard.millbanksystems.com/commons/1910/mar/23/dreadnought-bilding-thames-contract.
3 For a detailed analysis of industrial West Ham see www.british-history.ac.uk/report. aspx?compid=42755.
4 Tate and Lyle were sold to American Sugar Refining in 2010. The firm still has a presence in Newham, and its 850+ workforce makes it the third largest employer in the borough after the council and the police.
5 The factory closed in 1983.
6 See http://www.mirror.co.uk/news/uk-news/blitz-bomb-killed-600-in-school-248302.
7 For an evocative view of housing conditions in West Ham and the incredible effort to rehouse its population after the war, see these two films made in the late 1940s: http://www.newhamphotos.com/p1027275707/h6BBFA268#h6bbfa268, http://www. newhamphotos.com/p1027275707/h6BBFA268#h6f8b4305.
8 In addition, St Bonaventure's Roman Catholic boys school in Forest Gate had grammar, technical and secondary modern provision.
9 Property yield is the annual return, calculated by expressing a year's rental income as a percentage of how much the property cost. The highest average yield available in London was to be found in Newham, 'Top buy-to-let hot spots in Britain', *Daily Telegraph* 11/12/2014.

10 'White-van man' is a somewhat derogatory term coined by the media in the mid 1990s to describe working-class self-employed tradesmen. The term became associated with independently minded working-class conservatism. 'Wooing White-van Man'. the *Economist*, 2/5/2015.

11 For an example of the messy reality of union politics at Chobham Farm see Sinclair's account of his time there as a casual worker (Sinclair, 2012: 15–29, 39–40). One of our research team worked on the site for several months in 1969, and at that time, as Sinclair notes: 'We were doing dockwork four miles inland from the Thames. Once a week, no choice about it, we paid our dues to the Transport and General Workers Union. A mark on the pink card.' (op.cit.: 17). However, whether workers were signed up to the TGWU or not, pay, conditions and health and safety did not measure up to those found just three miles to the south behind the dock wall.

12 Now the site of the Queen Elizabeth Olympic Park.

13 As a result of his opposition to the strikers, Reg Prentice, Labour MP for Newham North East, was deselected and joined the Conservative Party. Bill Chapman, the shop steward who took responsibility for organising the strike HQ in Plaistow, went on to become Mayor of Newham, while Vic Turner continued as a union activist assisting in the Upper Clyde Shipyards and the 1972 miners' disputes. He lost his job when the Royal Group finally closed and worked for Newham Council as a Trade Refuse Officer. He was elected to the council in 1984, serving as Mayor 1997–1998. Chobham Farm, or Chobham Manor as it now is, is proving to be an effectively bucolic brand for a segment of the post-Olympic housing 'legacy'.

14 While the Transport and General Workers Union had impacted upon every aspect of local life, and in particular housing and education, since a referendum in 2002 Newham became one of just three London boroughs to have an elected Mayor, Sir Robin Wales. Newham is run by 60 elected councillors and in 2006 Labour held 59 of the seats with the nominal opposition coming from one candidate elected on a Christian People's Alliance ticket.

15 See http://www.friendsofqueensmarket.org.uk/index2.html.

16 West Ham Stadium had the biggest and fastest track in the country where at its peak over 30,000 people would watch dogs racing over a 600 yard circuit.

17 At one point London boasted eight speedway teams, and at its peak West Ham attracted crowds of over 80,000 to watch its highly successful multi-national teams (Bamford & Jarvis, 2001. Belton, 2003).

18 In addition, particularly in the light of the huge publicity given to the opening in February 2014 of the Olympic Aquatic Centre (http://www.standard.co.uk/lifestyle/health/london-aquatics-centre-swim-in-the-wake-of-2012s-olympic-legends—for-just-350-9151382.html), it should be noted that before the 2012 Olympics, Newham had boasted three municipal swimming pools in East Ham, Romford Road and Balaam Street, in addition to a huge outdoor swimming pool, the Beckton Lido, which opened in 1937 and closed 50 years later.

19 Stratford also boasted some fine Victorian pubs clustered around Maryland Point, including the smallest pub in the East End, *The Hope,* now renamed *The Chevy Chase.*

20 Matt Johnson, the son of *Two Puddings'* proprietor Eddie, was a member of the band 'The The'. Terry Murphy's son Glenn became a successful TV and film actor. The five Curbishley brothers were sons of a docker. Alf Curbishley ran the *Lord Stanley* pub, Bill Curbishley managed the Who and Led Zeppelin as well as being a film producer. Alan Curbishley played football for West Ham, and later managed the club. Paul Curbishley played football in the USA and remains involved with the professional game in the UK.

21 See 'Obituary: George Walker', *The Telegraph*, 25 March 2011.

22 See Colin Marchant, *Faith Flows in Newham Project,* http://www.urbantheology.org/journals/journal-1-4/faith-flows-in-newham.

23 A 2005 report stated that Newham has the second largest number of asylum seekers in London, with 240 asylum-seeking families in dispersal accommodation and an additional 2,600 households who are supported by the National Asylum Support Service (LBN, 2005).

24 http://www.newham.gov.uk/Pages/News/Newhamspopulationhasrisen.aspx.

25 House of Commons London Regional Committee (2010: 15, para. 40). Author correspondence with LBN officers confirmed that the £5.8m figure was for the year 2010/11 (e-mail 28 July 2011).

26 See http://www.statistics.gov.uk/census2001/profiles/00BB-A.asp.

27 ICC (2007: 39).

28 See http://www.aston-mansfield.org.uk/wp-content/uploads/2012/09/newham-key-statistics.pdf, citing Newham Information Service and the 2008 Schools Census. This marked a significant increase on the 105 languages recorded in 2002.

29 MPS Newham (2011), which also indicates that the proportion of police prisoners not holding a UK passport rose steadily during this period.

30 In evidence to the House of Commons London Regional Committee (2010: Ev. 15–16).

31 The A8 nations that joined the EU in 2004 were the Czech Republic, Estonia, Hungary, Latvia, Lithuania, Poland, Slovakia and Slovenia. Between 2006 and 2010, Lithuanians comprised the second largest group of prisoners detained in police custody behind UK passport holders, their numbers having risen from 102 detained in 2006 to 221 in 2010. Of 12,900 custody detainees in 2010: 62 per cent (8,047) were UK passport holders; 7 per cent (881) were Lithuanian; three per cent were from each of Romania (393), India (328) and Poland (326); 2 per cent were from each of Pakistan (299), Nigeria (248) and Bangladesh (207); and, one per cent were from each of Portugal (190) and Somalia (158) (MPS Newham, 2011).

32 See for example: 'The "Money Mules" of East London', *BBC News*, 4 February 2011); and, 'Police Smash Gang Trafficking Poles to UK for Benefits Scam', *London Evening Standard*, 2 November 2011.

33 We were told by several reliable (non-police) sources that online Lithuanian passports were being sold for the equivalent of £700, enabling the holder to legally work in the UK. This suggested that some Lithuanians coming to the attention of the police were actually of other, non-EU nationalities.

34 40 per cent of the Drug and Alcohol Service for London (DASL) on Romford Road, Newham, are Lithuanian-born migrants. In the years 2009–2011, 200 Lithuanians have called on DASL for assistance.

35 Newham was identified as the most overcrowded local authority in England. Green Street is estimated to have 25 per cent overcrowding, while East Ham North was estimated to have 23 per cent overcrowding; (DCLG, 2004).

36 See, for example, LBN 2011, which reports that Newham Council has established a 'task force to tackle the growing menace of ramshackle illegal out-buildings in gardens often housing people living in squalor'.

37 http://data.london.gov.uk/datafiles/demographics/average-age-borough.xls   linked from http://data.london.gov.uk/datastore/package/average-age-borough.

38 LBN (2011: 24).

39 'In 2007/08 19.5% of residents either left or entered the borough, a figure significantly higher than the London average of 13.6%' (LBN & NHS Newham, 2011: 7).

40 According to the Newham Household Survey 2009, 21 per cent of households had moved within 12 months and a further 9 per cent had moved within 2 years (quoted in LBN & NHS Newham, 2011: 83).

41 Of particular note, concerns have been raised that, '... although households in the five [Olympic] boroughs will gain [from the presence of the Olympic Games], these families may then move out of the boroughs, to be replaced by more deprived incomers-leaving the deprivation profile of the boroughs more or less unchanged' (Scanlon *et al.*, 2010: 8).

42 Data from Newham Household Survey 2009, between the census in 2001 and the Household Survey in 2009, indicates that the proportion of owner-occupied properties fell from 44 per cent to 32 per cent (LBN & NHS Newham, 2011: 83).
43 For example, in 2006–2007 new National Insurance Number registrations were equivalent to 6.6 per cent of Newham's population, second only to the City of London (ICC, 2007: 30).
44 Based on the 'rank of average score' as measured by the 2007 English Indices of Multiple Deprivation. (see Noble *et al.*, 2008: 86).
45 2008 data from ONS provided by Newham (www.newham.info) under the 'unemployment' theme: http://www.newham.info/IAS/profiles/profile?profileId=126&geoType Id=6&geoIds=00BB (accessed 13 July 2011).
46 2010 data from DWP provided by Newham Info under the 'deprivation' theme: http:// www.newham.info/IAS/profiles/profile?profileId=40&geoTypeId=6&geoIds=00BB (accessed 13 July 2011).
47 2009 data from the Department for Children, Schools and Families provided by Newham Info under the 'education' theme: http://www.newham.info/IAS/profiles/pro file?profileId=42&geoTypeId=6&geoIds=00BB (accessed 13 July 2011). Importantly, this figure masks significant variation between different ethnic groups, with only 5 per cent of 'other Asian Tagalog Filipino' pupils eligible for free school meals at Key Stage 2 in 2008, compared with 91 per cent of 'black African Somali' pupils at the same point (von Ahn, 2010: 12, table 3).
48 According to the 2007 English Indices of Multiple Deprivation Newham ranks second behind Hackney for 'rank of extent', which measures the 'proportion of a district's population living in the most deprived [areas] in England' (Noble et al., 2008: 81, 86).
49 Ipsos MORI (2008). It should be acknowledged that: (a) that Newham Council's own Household Panel Survey data indicate a more positive picture in absolute levels, for example in relation to community cohesion (they do not include comparative analysis); and (b) that Newham Council believe that the face-to-face methodology used in their Household Panel survey is more robust than the self-completion postal survey used in the Understanding London Life survey (source: e-mail correspondence with Newham Council's's Head of Public Policy and Research [Kieran Read] 06 April 2011).
50 The Newham Housing Survey 2009 identified that 38,800 households were living in unsuitable housing, with overcrowding being the main reason (LBN & NHS Newham, 2011: 85). At that time there were 101,000 dwellings in Newham (LBN & NHS Newham, 2011: 83).
51 DCLG Housing Strategy Statistical Appendix data provided by Newham Info under the 'housing' theme: http://www.newham.info/IAS/profiles/profile?profileId=44&geo TypeId=6&geoIds=00BB (accessed 13 July 2011).
52 The Garden of Remembrance where the ashes of many West Ham United fans are scattered will be 'retained, protected and incorporated into the new development.'

References

Armstrong, G., Hobbs, D. & Lindsay, I. (2011) 'Calling the Shots: The Pre-2012 London Olympic contest', *Urban Studies, 15*: 3176–3184.
Ashworth, W. (1964) 'Types of Social Economic Development in Suburban Essex', in Glass, R. (ed.) *London Aspects of Change.* London: Macgibbon & Kee.
Bamford, R & Jarvis J. (2001) *Homes of British Speedway.* London: Stadia.
Barber, R. (1977) *Trade Unions and the Tories.* London: Bow Group.
Barrett, D. & Calvi, N. (2012) *Sugargirls.* London: Collins.
Bell, G. (2002) *The Other Eastenders: Kamal Chunchie and West Ham's Early Black Community.* London: Stratford: Eastside Community Heritage.

Belton, B. (2003) *Hammerin' Round.* London: History Press.

Bermant, C. (1975) *London's East End: Point of Arrival.* London: Eyre Methuen.

Besant, W. (1901) *East London.* New York: The Century, Co.

Bloch, H. (1997) *Earlham Grove Shul: One Hundred Years of West Ham Synagogue and Community.* London: The Congregation.

Champion, H.H. (1890) *The Great Dock Strike in London, August, 1889.* London.

Coren, M. (1984) *Theatre Royal: 100 Years of Stratford East.* Quartet Books.

Crampton, M. (2012) *The Trebor Story.* London: Muddler Books.

Cushion, J (2010) 'Engaging Eastern European Communities to Tackle Problems in the Night Time Economy', *BME National Workshop*, Peterborough, 6 July 2010.

Damer, S. (1976) 'Wine Alley: The Sociology of a Dreadful Enclosure' in P. Wiles (ed.) *The Sociology of Crime and Delinquency in Britain.* London: Martin Robinson.

DCLG (Department for Communities and Local Government) (2004) *The English Indices of Deprivation.* London: HMSO.

Dickens, C. (1857). 'Londoners Over the Border', *Household Words*, *16*(390): 241–244.

Dorey, P. (1995) *The Conservative Party and the Trade Unions.* London: Routledge.

Dorfman, G. (1979) *Government versus Trade Unionism in British Politics since* 1968. Basingstoke: Macmillan.

Foley, M. (2011) *Disasters on the Thames.* Stroud: The History Press.

Fussey, P., Coaffee, J., Armstrong, G. & Hobbs, D. (2011) *Securing and Sustaining the Olympic City: Reconfiguring London for 2012 and Beyond.* Aldershot, UK: Ashgate.

Gilroy, P (2004) *After Empire: Melancholia of Convivial Culture.* London: Routledge.

Hall, P.G. (1962) *The Industries of London since 1861.* Hutchinson: London.

Hayman, A. (2011) 'Newham Issues DCLG Legal Threat', *Local Government Chronicle,* 21 April.

Hill, B. (1955) *Boss of Britain's Underworld.* London: Naldrett Press.

Hill, G. and Bloch, H. (2003) *The Silvertown Explosion: London 1917.* Stroud: Tempus Publishing.

Hill, S. (1976) *The Dockers.* Heinemann: London.

Hobbs, D. (1988) *Doing the Business.* Oxford: Oxford University Press.

Hobbs, D. (2006) 'East Ending: Dissociation, De-industrialisation and David Downes', in Newburn, T. and Rock, P. (eds) *The Politics of Crime Control.* Oxford: Oxford University Press.

Hobbs, D. (2013) *Lush Life: Constructing Organised Crime in the UK*, Oxford: Oxford University Press.

House of Commons London Regional Committee (2010) *London's Population and the 2011 Census: First Report of Session 2009–10.* HC349. London: House of Commons. http://www.publications.parliament.uk/pa/cm200910/cmselect/cmlonreg/ 349/349.pdf.

Hyman, R (1971) *Workers' Union, 1898–1929.* Oxford: Oxford University Press.

ICC (Institute of Community Cohesion) (2007) *Estimating the Scale and Impacts of Migration at the Local Level.* Report prepared for the Local Government Association. London: LGA.

Idle, E.D. (1943) *War over West Ham.* London: Faber and Faber.

Ipsos Mori (2008) *Understanding London Life.* London: Ipsos Mori.

Johnson, E. (2012) *Tales From the Two Puddings: Stratford, East London's Olympic City in the 1960s.* London: Fifty First State Press.

Korpela, K. M. (1989) 'Place-identity as a Product of Environment Self-regulation', *Journal of Environmental Psychology*, *9*: 241–256.

Korr, C. (1986) *West Ham United: The Making of a Football Club*. Chicago: University of Illinois Press.

Larkin, E. (2009) 'Stratford Locomotive Works', in *An Illustrated History of British Locomotive Workshops*. Royston: Heathfield Railway Publications.

Latour, B. (1988) *The Pasteurization of France*. Cambridge, MA: Harvard University Press.

Lindop, F. (1998) 'The Dockers and the 1971 Industrial Relations Act, Part Two: The Arrest and Release of the "Pentonville Five"', *Historical Studies in Industrial Relations*, 6: 65–100.

Lock, J. (2013) *The Princess Alice Disaster*. Robert Hale Ltd.

London, J. (1903) *The People Of The Abyss*. London: Macmillan.

London Borough of Newham (LBN) (1982) 'Newham Ethnic Communities Background Report: The Ethnic Composition of Newham's Population', *London Borough of Newham: Department of Planning and Architecture*. Available on inquiry from the Archives and Local Studies room in Stratford Library.

London Borough of Newham (LBN) (1993) 'Newham Borough Trends Part 1: Newham Overview', 2nd Edition, November 1993. Available on inquiry from the Archives and Local Studies room in Stratford Library.

London Borough of Newham (LBN) (2002) *The Newham Story: A Short History of Newham*. London: London Borough of Newham.

London Borough of Newham (LBN) (2005) *Focus on Newham: Local People and Local Conditions*. London: London Borough of Newham.

London Borough of Newham (LBN) (2007) *Focus on Newham: Local People and Local Conditions*. London: London Borough of Newham.

London Borough of Newham (LBN) (2011) 'Curbs on "Shanty" Dwellings', *The Newham Mag, Issue 227*, 19 August–2 September: 5.

London Borough of Newham & NHS Newham (LBN) (2011) *Joint Strategic Needs Assessment 2010: The London Borough of Newham*. London: London Borough of Newham.

Lyon, D. & Back, L. (2012) 'Fishmongers in a Global Economy: Craft and Social Relations on a London Market', *Sociological Research Online, 17*(2): 23.

Madge, N., Hemming, P. & Stenson, K. (2014) *Youth on Religion: The Development, Negotiation and Impact of Faith and Non-faith Identity*. London: Routledge.

Modood, T. & Berthoud, R. (1997) *Ethnic Minorities in Britain: Diversity and Disadvantage*. London: Policy Studies Institute.

Morgan, K. (1975) *Keir Hardie, Radical and Socialist*. London: Weidenfeld and Nicolson.

Metropolitan Police Service (MPS) Newham (2011) *KF and KO Custody Summary 2006–10 –Nationality*. Unpublished internal report.

Murphy, E. (2007) *The Bridge House, Canning Town: Memoirs of a Legendary Rock and Roll Hangout*. London: Pennant Books.

Newham Language Shop (2005) 'Newham Council Community Language Survey'. Available from http://www.languageshop.org.uk.

Newton, D. (2008) *Trademarked. A History of Well-Known Brands – from Aertex to Wright's Coal Tar*. Stroud: Sutton Publishing.

Noble, M., McLennan, D., Wilkinson, K., Whitworth, A., Barnes, H. & Dibben, C. (2008) *The English Indices of Deprivation 2007*. London: Department for Communities and Local Government.

North, D., Ramsden, M., Birch, J. & Sanderson, I. (2004) 'Barriers to Employment in Newham', London Development Agency, Access to Jobs and CEEDR, Middlesex University.

Pakulski, J. & Waters, M. (1996) *The Death of Class*. London: Sage.

Peart-Jackson, M. (1973) *Labour Relations on the Docks*. London: Saxon House.

Piggott, G. (2004) 'Ethnic and Religious Groups in London', British Society for Population Studies Annual Conference on Ethnicity, Refugees and Group Conflict, 13–15 September.

Powell, W.R. (ed) (1973a) 'Becontree Hundred: East Ham', *A History of the County of Essex*, 6: 1-8.

Powell, W.R. (ed) (1973b) 'East Ham – Economic History and the Marshes', *A History of the County of Essex, 6*: 14–18.

Powell, W.R. (ed) (1973c) 'West Ham: Philanthropic Institutions', *A History of the County of Essex*, 6: 141-144.

Ross, C. (2010) *Death of the Docks*. London: Authorhouse.

Rozina, V. (1999) 'Kamal A. Chunchie of the Coloured Men's Institute: The Man and the Legend', *Immigrants and Minorities, 18*(1): 29–48.

Sainsbury, F. (1986) *1886– 1986 A Volume to Commemorate the Centenary Of The Incorporation of West Ham as a Municipal Borough in 1886*. London: London Borough of Newham.

Scanlon, K., Travers, A. & Whitehead, C. (2010) 'Population Churn and its Impact on Socio-economic Convergence in the Five London 2012 Host Boroughs'. London: Department for Communities and Local Government.

Schoen, D. E. (1977) *Enoch Powell and the Powellites*. Macmillan, London.

Sennett, R. (1998) *The Corrosion of Character*. New York: Norton.

Sinclair, I. (2012) *Ghost Milk*, London: Penguin.

Strangleman, T. (2007) 'The Nostalgia for Permanence at Work? The End of Work and its Commentators', *Sociological Review 55*(1): 81-103.

Stratford Community History (1996) *Newham Women: Lives, Memories, Opinions*. Stratford City Challenge: Community History.

Sumner, C. (2010) '1945–1965: The Long Road to Circular 10/65', *Reflecting Education*, 6(1): 90–102.

Thompson (1974). *The Woodgrange Estate: A Brief History'*. London: London Borough of Newham.

Townsend, C.A. (2003) 'Chemicals from Coal: A History of Beckton Products Works'. London: Greater London Industrial Archaeological Society.

Trench, R. & Hillman, E. (1984) *London Under London: A Subterranean Guide*. London: John Murray.

Vertovec, S (2006) *The Emergence of Super-Diversity in Britain*, Working Papers 06–25. Oxford University: COMPAS.

von Ahn, M. (2006) *Newham's Population and the Office of National Statistics Mid-Year Estimates*. Unpublished paper, October.

White, J. (2007) *London in the Nineteenth Century: A Human Awful Wonder of God*. London: Vintage.

Widdowson, J. & H. Block (no date) 'People Who Moved to Newham'. London Borough of Newham: Newham Libraries Service educational package. Available from the Archives and Local Studies room in Stratford Library.

3 Youth as an Olympic threat

> All that was solid about the post-war welfare consensus – from lifelong employment to welfare safety net – has been actively unravelled and seemed to have melted into air.
>
> (MacMahon, 2007: 24)

The post-industrial political economy of Newham has created a fragmented terrain lacking the cognitive and political props of the industrial era. Policing in the borough during the industrial era was based upon local knowledge that was often acquired and utilized in an informal manner, and with an intrinsic character that had more to do with the dominant cultural characteristics of the local community than with the rigid institutional rules of the police organization. This was largely enabled by the homogeneity of Newham's predominantly white proletarian population that shared a common sense of order with a police force experiencing, certainly in comparison with today, few institutional restraints upon its everyday practices (Hobbs, 1988).

As Mayhew noted: 'It is a moral impossibility that the class of labourers who are only occasionally employed should be either generally industrious and temperate – both industry and temperance being habits produced by constancy of employment and uniformity of income' (1849: 83, in Hobbs, 2001). With casual work only being phased out during the late 1960s when the docks were in their death throws, theft and the networks that they engendered were key characteristics of local culture, rather than an exceptional manifestation of transgressive intent. These networks were not regarded by the general population as a threat, but part of a locality grounded in the realities of casual work and the attractions of entrepreneurial endeavour. As Newham is on the river 'and the river meant plunder' (Bermant, 1975: 122), it was only a few families in this locality who did not partake of the loot gleaned from ships and warehouses. Whether it was pocketfuls or lorry loads was a matter of proportionality and risk awareness rather than morality (Hobbs 1988, 2013).

Like East London generally, Newham had always been a space associated with transgression, although its criminal collaborations lacked the gothic glamour of the Kray twins, whose base was a few miles down the road in Bethnal Green (Hobbs, 2013). The area that is present-day Newham nurtured notorious individuals including Alf Lucy, Jacky Reynolds and his 'Upton Park gypsies' who collaborated with the self-styled boss of Britain's underworld Billy Hill, and the Tibbs and Nicholls families whose bloody feud was based upon family honour rather than anything approximating an underworld vendetta. To the south of the borough, Canning Town was a breeding ground for several generations of armed robbers (Hobbs, 2013), as well as numerous collaborations of part-time and professional thieves who plundered the docks and its periphery.

Generally, youthful combat has always been an ideal preparation for a career in crime (Fraser, 1998: 1–4; Leeson, 1934: 147; and McDonald, 2001: 9), and in every generation a minority of youth have commodified their violence by exploiting reputations enhanced by community protection (Suttles 1968), and violent adventurism in adjacent territories (Whyte, 1943: 10). It is here within nascent extortion networks that criminal careers are nurtured (Yablonsky 1962: 147–148; Hobbs, 1988: 8; Hallsworth & Silverstone, 2009: 362). Certainly during the industrial era, Newham produced its fair share of violent youth collaborations, and 'some of those boys went on and on' (Hobbs, 2013: 113) to form careers in armed robbery and gangsterism (Smith, 2005). However, those progressing into serious acquisitive adult crime were rarities, and youth collaborations were generally regarded as an unthreatening and temporary phenomenon.

Subcultures: youth and the industrial social order

With one notable exception,[1] youth gangs in the UK are a 'newly noticed kind of human behaviour' (Hacking, 1999: 136). According to the influential definition of Klein (2005), 'A street gang is any durable, street oriented youth group whose own identity includes involvement in illegal activity', suggesting a degree of imprecision (Hancock, 2006: 180) that renders much gang research 'an argument over the correct description of a ghost' (Katz & Jackson-Jacobs, 2004). Indeed, the absence of any relatively precise definition has made it difficult to find a youthful form of collaboration that cannot be designated as 'gang related'. In this chapter we will discuss how Newham's post-industrial turn addressed in Chapter 2 has impacted on local youth, and how the notion of the gang provided for the police and local council a potent threat to the 2012 Olympics.

Traditionally, within British academic discourse, gangs and subcultures constituted contrasting views of working-class youthful collaborations distinguished by the socio-economic differentials that typified and divided British and American cultures. These differentials were created within the context of production-based cultures, and industrial era Newham, particularly during its post-Second World War peak and up to its post-industrial neo-liberal adaptation, saw a comparative sense of order prevail. The strain theories of Cohen (1955) and Cloward & Ohlin (1960) that located gang membership as a reaction to failure within a fiercely aspirational culture were rejected by British scholars in favour of subcultures as the primary, albeit temporary form of British youth collaboration. Subcultures dominated British Youth scholarship for 40 years (Campbell & Muncer, 1989)[2] before the nuances of subcultural analysis were largely abandoned and the previously inconceivable, and essentially alien concept of the 'gang' began to seep in to the British consciousness.

For UK youths of the industrial era, subcultural membership constituted a brief interlude, before they took their places in a mono-class society with distinct, visible and attainable horizons (Cohen, 1972). The structural inequalities they encountered were similar to those experienced by the previous generation, which led youths to adopt traditional practices based upon traditional values which were integral to cultural transmission (Parker, 1974; Gill 1977). Styles of resistance (Hall & Jefferson, 1976) were temporary (Hobbs, 1988), and lacked the malice and negativism of the American gang (Downes, 1966: 204–206) as youths retained a stake in the industrial project. Unskilled, low-paid proletarian futures (Downes, 1966: 237; Davies, 2008) were embraced along with traditional leisure pursuits shaped by the ecology of the working-class street and the extended family where 'Loose collectivities or crowds within which there was occasionally some more structured grouping, based on territorial loyalty' (Cohen, 1973: 128) prevailed. The regimes of work that dominated post-Second World War working class life in Newham had moulded 'arena(s) of empowerment' (Sennett, 1998: 43) that lent some coherence and dignity to everyday life. The near full employment discussed in the previous chapter created a rough-edged stability within tightly-knit communities that enabled subcultural membership to bloom as a temporary bridge between childhood, which ended on leaving school at the age of 16, and the world of work.

It is important, however, not to become dewy eyed with 'Smokestack Nostalgia' (Strangleman 2013) in regard to that era's youth. black youth were largely excluded from the world of work into which white members of subcultures tended to segue (see Fieldhouse, 1999). Neighbourhood and familial links to inherited 'masculinist working traditions' (Gunter, 2010: 142) embodied in white-dominated manual occupations such as dock-related employment, the printing industry, market-portering and some aspects of the building trade were seldom available to black youth of the industrial era, reducing their stake in the 'ordered and respectable working class life' (Rustin, 1996: 4) that awaited local white youth at the end of a benign period of subcultural experimentation. The halcyon era of post-war industrialism was short-lived (Hall, 1962; Hill, 1976; Hobbs, 1988: Ch 6.; Ross, 2010), and the self-contained communality and subsequent 'structure of feeling' (Williams, 1977: 128–135) of working-class life has gone, and in its place are socially fragmented areas 'of structural unemployment, economic precariousness, a systematic cutting of welfare provisions and the growing instability of family life and interpersonal relations' (Young, 2007: 59).

This was to have consequences.

The gang and post-industrial social order

The industries upon which communities such as that described by Downes were founded are now distant memories, and new arrivals to Newham cannot aspire to membership of working-class institutions that have largely disappeared. Alienated from work that could have previously included them securely in community life (Currie, 1985: 278), youths no longer enjoy the type of benign relationship with their parent culture that had been pivotal to British subcultural studies, and which had provided a model for assimilation. Filling that social abyss is the gang, now established as a social problem whose threat to social order is constantly reinforced by an infrastructure of youth governance that has evolved in direct proportion to its conflation (Hallsworth, 2013; Horne & Hall, 1995; and Hobbs, 2013). In the post-industrial city vulnerable and disposable 'contingent workers' (Persaud and Lusane, 2000: 26), deprived of both the negotiating power and unifying potential of trade unions, now reside alongside multifarious youth and parent cultures, co-existing in de-industrialized cosmopolitan territories, where nihilism is able to thrive (Hobbs, 2013). In common with so many aspects of social policy from the Thatcher era onwards, the UK looked to the USA for solutions.

In 2001 American gang researchers established *The Eurogang Network*, with the intention of linking researchers in Europe who, according to Klein (2001), were in denial of the growing gang problem. In 2007, the Home Office set up a specialist subgroup, the *Tackling Gangs Action Programme*, overseen by a *Task Force on Gangs and Guns* and chaired by the Home Secretary to develop policies designed to deal with the problem of gangs. However, Hallsworth and Young locate a 2008 report as the formal acknowledgement of the British gang problem (Home Office 2008),[3] where: '. . . the gang was for the first time explicitly linked to the problem of urban violence and rising weapon use in the UK . . .' (Hallsworth and Young, 2008: 176).

Gangs were being addressed via vague and unhelpful definitions (Klein, 1995; Klein, 2005), and the term is often used as 'veiled expressions of bourgeois disapproval' (Ball & Curry, 1995:227), towards a diverse range of transgressive youthful behaviours. However, whatever sobriquet it attracts, youth action is played out mainly in public space, and enables a minority of young people to impact significantly upon their local communities (Pitts, 2008). At the same time it is apparent from the recent work of British scholars that post-industrial British youth have been heavily influenced by consumer capitalism (Hallsworth, 2005, Hallsworth and Young, 2008; Aldridge and Medina, 2008; Pitts, 2008), which in turn has 'promoted a culture of intense personal competition, and spur(red) its citizens to a level of material consumption many could not lawfully sustain' (Currie, 1985: 278). Subsequently youth collaborations have come to the forefront of much urban entrepreneurship (Hagedorn, 1998; Davis 1990: ch. 5; Sanchez-Janowski 1991), and in the case of the drugs' trade in particular (Williams, 1989, 1992; Mieczkowski, 1990; Hamid, 1990), individualism and pecuniary advantage are promoted over traditional communal priorities (Bourgois, 1995). Consequently, and, in contradiction to the façade of resistance promoted by gangs, strategies that are closely related to those of the post-industrial mainstream are valorized (Sullivan, 1989: 163, Brotherton & Barrios, 2004).

The downgrading of Newham's industrial base has created a fractious urban hinterland where youth collaborations are 'not the product of youth culture, but of working class culture turned upside down' (Schneider, 1999: 50). Youthful deviance, including 'street collections that approximate gangs' (Hallsworth & Young, 2008: 177), must be located within the context of the political economy of post-industrial working-class cultures, and in particular the adoption of market prerogatives where there is 'no common sentiment, no common interest' (Zorbaugh, 1929: 180). This is the condition of the London Borough of Newham, and this is the context both for the emergence of innovative youthful collaborations, and the construction of 'gangs' as an Olympic threat.

The emergence of the Newham gang problem

In the mid-2000s, the behaviour of a cohort of young males aged between their early teens and early 20s was causing considerable consternation in Newham police and council circles. The majority of these youths were black and visible minority ethnic (VME), and their behaviour was encapsulated by the term Serious Youth Violence (SYV).[4] Newham police in early 2011 launched a specialist unit, the Serious Youth Violence Team to address a series of stabbings and a rise in the use of guns amongst local youth, some of whom were rumoured to be affiliated to named territorial-based gangs. These territories were often associated with postcodes, and territorial rivalries were sometimes linked with efforts to 'control' Newham postcodes. Such was the concern over this violence that within four months the SYV Team had expanded to one DI, one DS, seven DCs and two PCs, and was soon renamed as the Gangs and Firearms Unit (GFU). The DI brought in to head the unit came with a reputation forged in the Flying Squad and the Serious Crime Directorate, and at his interview for the GFU post he was left in no doubt about what the job entailed: 'It was all Commanders and A-Cs (Assistant Commissioners) telling me about the Portuguese Mafia (PGM), the Young Blood City (YBC) and Maryland Gang . . . nick 'em, smash 'em, clean it up . . . then start on the others . . .'. However, as he explained during his first week in office, and echoing the views of some of the more sceptical British academics, 'We use the term "gangs", but they're not really gangs. They're groups of boys and youth who live in the area, hang around together and get involved in serious crime . . . Eighteen months ago this borough didn't have a gang problem and indeed you were not allowed to use the word "gang". Now we can talk about it'.

Figures for the Newham MPS district released in April 2011 showed an 8.2 per cent rise in youth violence on the previous year. At its peak the GFU held investigations into 35–40 crimes, and its proactive remit involved covert operations, notably around disrupting drug and gun supply lines.[5] The GFU could also lead investigations to ascertain what might constitute a 'gang-related' incident and to react to events that might provoke imminent reprisals. As the DI explained: 'Within two hours of a stabbing we've had Commanders phoning asking for Intel about home visits and management of offending.'

Based on arrest data, the GFU established a database of gang members, 95 per cent of whom were black, and who allegedly wore coloured bandanas to denote their territorial allegiance. However, despite this simplistic modelling, for the DI the problem was complex and subtly nuanced, and what passed as data emanating from London's police Centre drove the activities of the GFU: 'In the London-wide top 25 Most Dangerous gang nominal (member) Newham has four in there. Newham is a Tier 1 borough. This means it has a serious gang issue. There are 20 Newham names in the matrix. You cannot enforce your way out of this problem . . . I had to move from enforcement to engagement . . . Now all gang members know my name. Two years ago we didn't have a gang issue. Now nearly one in five are "ours". No other borough has as many in the top 25.'[6]

However, while it was apparent that some young men in Newham were explicitly affiliated to groups based upon territorial imperatives, and utilized violence that was sometimes drug related, identifying members, affiliates and associates was as much a problem for local youths as it was for the police. A few days after the DI commenced work, an 18-year-old boy was walking through Newham's Custom House district on his way to meet a friend. The pair intended to go to a music venue, and as he walked three vehicles containing 12 youths that the police identified as being Green Gang members on a mission to avenge a slight on one of their members by their Custom House equivalents, alighted their cars. When the youth was asked where he was from he replied, 'Custom House', thinking that this was the right answer. It was not and he received seven stab wounds, including two to the face. The boy lived; three of his attackers were arrested and faced charges of Grievous Bodily Harm.

Very quickly, and often regardless of the rigour of any intelligence database, the word 'gang' became an emotive working metaphor for the police in Newham. However, as the DI realized early in his appointment, other agencies were more resistant to the term: 'Look at our "Gangs in Schools" meeting[7]. . . only five out of 20 headteachers in the borough attended. They don't want to know – or admit – there's a guns and gangs issue. It reflects bad on their school if they say they've got serious youth violence and gangs'. Yet the problem was complex, a fact often acknowledged by those whose daily task was to confront a chaotic youth culture that defied simplistic definitions. For instance, we witnessed one situation where staff in a Plaistow school had to decide whether or not a 12-year-old boy was a gang member after he came to school with a green handkerchief poking out of his back pocket. One teacher insisted that this was a bandana that signified gang affiliation, and as a consequence the school's designated police liaison officer should be informed, and the child banished from the classroom. The defiant but slightly tearful boy eventually surrendered the piece of cloth to the school's world-weary headteacher, who had sat next to the boy and gently pleaded with him to 'do the right thing'. One of Newham's high-profile murder victims whose death was attributed to gang activity had been a pupil at the school.

Even within Newham police, there was some confusion, and some young men who received wounds from peers were not the remit of the GFU. To illustrate the complexity of the issue one Inspector recounted a recent incident: 'A few months ago a big fight between rival Afghanis left one youth with a wound from a meat cleaver and his brain spilling out. He's still critical. We've now apparently got something called The Panther Gang in Newham because the council have re-housed 30 men from Afghanistan who had previously lived in Yorkshire.

They've moved to Canning Town and we've got violence between them and Afghanis living in Ilford. We think it's over drug markets not gangs'.

Clearly the drugs/gangs nexus proved problematic for an organization seeking clarity around gang membership. Another incident was equally ambiguous: 'Chicken shop . . . Barking Road last Friday. Ten Asian youths enter and grab all the knives in the premise. We get there and one gets nicked for possession of an offensive weapon. We think it's part of a drug turf-war between two Asian criminal families . . . and related to a kid who was stabbed weeks earlier. But this is not what we call 'gang violence.'

The vagueness surrounding gangs and gang violence, and the lack of definitional clarity is a feature of 'gang-talk' generally (Hallsworth and Young, 2008), but the pragmatic concerns of the DI had to cut through any ambiguity. His unit's remit as he saw it was both protecting members of the various Newham 'gangs' from each other, as well as protecting innocent members of the public. Further, the very notion of the 'gang' was often irrelevant to the simplistic brutality of many of the scenarios that his unit were tasked to deal with, where even the gold standard result of a custodial sentence was merely another episode in a chaotic continuation of serious youth violence. One incident which the DI recounted illustrated this: 'One 25-year-old nasty piece of work, when in prison heard of his 15-year-old brother getting slapped by someone in the school yard. When he comes out he goes down to the school to find the aggressor, waits outside and when he sees him, puts a hammer across a 16-year-old's head. The latter's school mates jump in and the 25-year-old ends up with multiple stab wounds. He's rushed to the Royal London (hospital). I'll tell you now, if it wasn't for the brilliance of the medics there, we'd have the highest murder rate in London – they save us so many bodies'.

The gang was clearly an inappropriate tool to deal with the wide range of violent crime committed by a minority of Newham's youth, and association with a named group could not be verified by consulting a reliable official database. For some young men lie, exaggerate, fantasize, and also assume gang membership as a protective cloak.

Nine lives: evidence and protection

Amongst this cacophony of voices, and regardless of the clarity or otherwise to be found in the rising crescendo of official and semi-official pre-Olympic 'gang talk', some young men were making an unambiguous claim on gang membership and all of the stylistic and territorial accoutrements that went with it, including violence.

19-year-old JC nearly lost his life in February 2011 when he was attacked by a dozen-strong group of youths wielding knives and machetes as he departed a railway station near his home. Prostrate and semi-conscious, JC was stabbed in the head as one of his assailants instructed others to 'finish him off'. A neighbour of JC's saw the attack and bravely rushed into the melee causing the attackers to run off, and at a subsequent identity parade JC picked out his assailants, allegedly members of the Custom House gang, who were charged with Grievous Bodily Harm.[8] The attackers, who wore white bandanas on their lower faces, were punishing JC for his friendship with the Green Gang, but the attack and subsequent arrests were not the end of the matter, and there were two further stabbings involving the Green/Custom House gangs. The stakes were high for the police, and a successful prosecution was vital to stem the escalation of violence. In the build-up to the court case petrol was poured through the letter-box of JC's home, which he shared with his mother and sister.

On being visited at home mid-morning by the DI and his colleague, JC entered the living room wearing pyjamas and a carefree expression. This was in stark contrast to his mother, a worried woman in her late 30s with concentric dark rings around her eyes. Although proclaiming his non-involvement in the Green Gang, JC had convictions for theft, robbery, assault, drug possession and possessing an offensive weapon. He had never worked, and his post-school education consisted of a short course at an FE College that was little more than an attempt to get him to understand the basics of constructing a CV. However, his mother was in the final year of a criminology degree at university, and she had proven helpful and supportive towards the police. She was convinced that JC was not a 'gang member'.

The police wanted JC to testify, and had to protect him from intimidation and then – hopefully after the conviction of his assailants – protect him from any further attacks. To assist this process the Home Office-funded Safe and Secure Scheme had been pioneered in Newham by the Serious Crime Directorate, with help from the YOTS, and had sought to help victims of gang attacks by moving individuals out of Newham to a new location, and provided a 12-month mediation package to facilitate employment or skills training. JC's 12-year-old sister also lived in the house, and his mother insisted on keeping the family together.

The DI explained to JC: 'I know you're not in the Green Gang but others think you are and others in it are known at times to sit on this sofa. Your attackers consider you a Green Gang member and nearly killed you. I also know that last time an officer visited here sitting here was a lad – Craig – in a green T-shirt and green baseball cap who celebrates being in the Green Gang . . . Now, some people put two and two together . . .'. The silence that followed was broken by his mother who explained: 'He just knows them all; he grew up around here. I tell him all the time "Don't walk with them", but circumstances mean that he gets associated. It's my fault; I bought the green T-shirt he was wearing when he was attacked. He'll never wear green again. His dad lives in Custom House. He knows that lot; he's told them "You attacked my son and blah, blah . . .". One told him it was because he was wearing a green T-shirt'.

A letter produced by Newham Council was read out by the DI. This agreement between the council and family related to information sharing; all agencies involved were listed. At the end of the explanation both JC and his mother were asked if they were happy with what they had heard, and they signed the letter. He was now in the Safe and Secure Scheme but was not to reveal this to anyone. In return for the protection the scheme offered he had to co-operate with the police and the case for the prosecution. Failure to comply with these criteria would lead to the scheme being withdrawn. The DS who accompanied the DI, and who had remained largely silent, finished the visit with a homily addressed to both JC and his mother. 'Remember they've tried to burn you out of your place. Think smart – you've wasted about four of your nine lives'.

The multi-agency gang

In 2009/10, Newham MPS dramatically increased the use of stop and search with the explicit intention of deterring knife carrying by young men. A particular feature of this tactic was the routine authorization of controversial 'Section 60' (s60) powers, which allowed police officers to stop and search anyone in a defined geographical area without having to justify their action on the basis of specific suspicion. By 2010/11, Newham accounted for around one third of all s60 stops and searches in London.[9] In addition, the GFU and various Newham Council agencies were regularly meeting to discuss co-ordinated action against the newly discovered gang problem, and in replication of the anti-organized crime strategy of the era, the aim was 'disruption'.

In February 2012 the Met Commissioner Bernard Hogan-Howe made his first visit to the borough since his appointment two months previously. He was there to launch the Met-wide Trident Gang Crime Command which was designed to deal with the '150 gangs in London . . . 62 cause the most trouble . . . these cause a fifth of all serious violence, a fifth of robberies, half of all shootings and 15 per cent of rapes'. Part of this launch was a series of dawn raids following a fight in the food hall of the Westfield Shopping Mall before Christmas (see Chapter 4). As a result of the raids 21 young men were arrested and 11 charged. The head of Westfield security accompanied officers on the raid, for Westfield had funded the overtime that made the raid possible (see Chapter 4). In addition, council personnel were to accompany police in order to deliver letters informing the occupants that if youth-offending behaviour continued to attract the attention of police the family risked losing the roof over their heads. These letters contained the following:

Gang crime in London needs to stop. We must protect our community from violence.

We have changed the way that we work so that many more of our officers are now dedicated to tackling gangs. This means we can deal more quickly and force-fully with any gang crime or gang member than ever before.

We are working even more closely with our partners like Local Authorities, Youth Offending Teams, Prisons, and Courts. Although we don't want you to end up in the criminal justice system we will use harder enforcement if we have to.

WE BELIEVE THAT YOU ARE IN A GANG SO YOU WILL BE PART OF A NEW TARGETED APPROACH UNTIL WE ARE SATISFIED THAT THIS HAS STOPPED FOR GOOD.

We want to help you. We understand that leaving a gang can be difficult but there are people in your borough that can help you do this. You can call the number

---

on this letter to get this help started – you won't necessarily have to deal with the police. Don't miss this chance to change your life.

It's up to you but if you continue to be involved with gangs, we will use the full power of the law to deal with you. We will use any means necessary such as:

- Stop & search in the street whenever there are grounds to justify it.
- Using Gang Injunctions – these will ban you from being in certain places or having any contact with certain people.
- Eviction from your home.
- Prosecuting you for ANY offence you commit.
- Asking your Local Authority to investigate your family situation and take action if they feel that you or any other young person is at risk.
- Taking your car from you if it has been used in a crime, or if you don't have it insured or taxed.
- Seizing ANYTHING you have which you have bought using money from a crime.

This is the time for you to take control of your life, call the number and get the help that you need.

Doors were kicked in, and a series of police raids gleaned money and guns, all of which firmed up the thin line between 'gangs' and 'organized crime', two social constructions of American origin that were quickly finding their way into the local police lexicon (Hobbs, 2013). Parents and elderly relatives were left stunned and weeping as the homes of working families and dysfunctional households alike were left in disarray as police officers and council officials conducted dawn raids. Young men were arrested, disabled dependents were taken to places of safety, and children delivered into the care of social services. The parents of youths suspected of violence or drug dealing were faced with the agony of deciding whether to pass on information in exchange for an emergency housing transfer out of East London. Others had panic alarms installed by police and council, or joined the Safe and Secure scheme to escape the environment that had ultimately brought the police into their homes.[10]

Much of Newham's youth violence echoed the brutality of previous generations of the borough's young men,[11] featuring youths drawn from the same social housing, who like their counterparts of the industrial era developed a culture around respect, territory and the use of weapons. However, during this previous era, 'the injured found their own way to hospital, the tabloids stayed away, and nobody attributed (violence) to gangs . . . or used it as a racially loaded metaphor for "Broken Britain"' (Hobbs, 2013: 240). In 2010, the pupils of Rokeby Secondary School were moved three miles south to Canning Town, so that boys from the Stratford area had now to pass daily into territory that was hitherto 'forbidden' to them. What just a few decades earlier would have been regarded as fights between rival schools now became part of Newham's gang problem. Further, Rokeby and its catchment area were adjacent to both the Olympic stadium and the Westfield Shopping Mall which was, a year before opening, subject to Twitter and Facebook posturing by 'gangs' making a claim on ownership. Newham police believed the mall had great potential for gang-related violence, and claimed that gangs from as far afield as Hackney and Southwark were 'looking at it' (see Chapter 4). As we shall see in Chapter 4, the mall was inextricably linked with the Olympics.

Although at this stage (late 2011) the Games were seldom mentioned with regard to SYV, the Olympics were now looming rather than forthcoming, and the policing atmosphere was heating up, as exemplified by four police operations that commenced in early 2012 which combined to constitute an unprecedented drive against local youth.

Operation Laraki (funded by Operation 5 Rings, an Olympic police funding source) pursued a cleansing policy of the Stratford Town Centre area and perimeter of the Olympic Park, performed mostly by uniformed police drawn from the TSGs. This initiative was combined with *Operation Menhir*, an anti-knife carrying initiative which involved plain-clothed locally based police directing uniformed officers to individuals who were subjected to 'stop and search' on the bridge linking Stratford to the Westfield Mall. In addition came *Operation Massachusetts*, which from April 2012 proclaimed itself as a problem-solving initiative to address youth violence in Stratford. It identified and targeted 50 gang members involved in 'organized criminality' and saw both the youths and their parents receiving letters from the council threatening their housing tenancy should the youths continue their delinquency. The final project was entitled *Operation New Hampshire* which involved council officials working with Newham GFU to remove over 60 gang-related videos from social media sites. These videos were alleged to contain material that constituted hate crime, incitement to violence and to have implications for the safeguarding of minors.

Enforcement, intervention and diversion

In March of 2011 the Mayor of Newham funded 30 extra police officers for the borough, specifying that they were to be deployed primarily to address serious youth violence, and requiring the police to report back to him on the nature and scale of the problem. To this end a meeting was called in early May 2011 at the council's Dockside HQ. The meeting lasted 40 minutes. Present were representatives from Newham Community Safety and the Newham Youth Offending Team, as well as the GFU Inspector. The Mayor wanted value for money, and was about to hear that the problem of SYV/gangs was not insurmountable. As the following account of the meeting illustrates, he also needed to know that interventions of various types worked; jobs, resources and reputations were at stake.

According to many members of LBN and Newham MPS, the Mayor had 'a thing about gang colours' (a reference to the association of specifically coloured clothing with gang affiliation in Newham),and a map of the borough charting gang associations was produced. The DI explained to the meeting that the word 'gang' brought a definitional problem and should not be equated with images from the USA, suggesting that the structure of these formations was less about strict hierarchies and more about 'organized chaos'. The following 'landmark' incidents were then presented:

- *Murder* (January 2009): of Green Gang member who attended a house party in Plaistow and was stabbed to death by Custom House youths who were convicted of the murder at the Old Bailey.
- *Murder* (July 2009): of a Tower Hamlets resident, and member of the 'Bloodsheddam Gang' who attended a party in Newham and was stabbed to death during an altercation with the Beckton Boys.
- *Murder* (January 2010): of a Custom House member stabbed eight times after attending a house party in Canning Town.
- *Murder* (October 2010): of a youth shot dead by a rival gang. The origin of the dispute was a brick thrown into the home of a girlfriend of a youth who promptly called on his gang associates to avenge the insult.

The meeting then heard that from November 2010 there had been a series of Grievous Bodily Harm assaults and large-scale street fights. To end his talk the DI made a plea for more resources based upon the principles of enforcement, intervention and diversion, and the last image in his Powerpoint presentation was of a self-loading pistol. The GFU Inspector explained: 'This is something directly linked to Newham . . . We got a tip-off that this gun and others were about to be sold and distributed to gangs in Newham. We got a judge to sign a warrant at half-three in the morning and when we got there we found five sawn-off shotguns, one self-loading rifle, two semi-automatic handguns, one revolver, two silencers, 86 cartridges and 120 rounds of ammo . . .'.

The gun cache was actually that of an incarcerated professional criminal that had been found in Essex, and while there was no connection to Newham gangs, it was offered as proof of the success of anti-gang policing, and as a vital part of his plea for further investment in solving Newham's gang problem. As the GFU Inspector later explained to us: 'We can say he was part of a gang . . . we don't have to say where! And we're after resources and more men so that might help!'. Here we can see the explicit and highly pragmatic use of the term 'gang' as a generator, not of crime and violence, but of police resources.

However, the Mayor was not impressed: 'So, how do we stop it? Six months in [from the formation of the SYV Unit] is that it?'. Another silence followed, broken by the GFU Inspector who replied: 'It has to be a long-term strategy . . . recognising the problem . . . changing the kids' affinities . . . There's nothing for them to do'.

On hearing this, the Mayor with theatrical rage exclaimed: 'Bullshit . . . Fuck that . . . This has to stop . . . There's loads to do here. They've got all they need. I'm not having that shit . . .'. Adding another 'bullshit' for good measure, the Mayor then opined that he wanted such people 'out of Newham'. He continued by citing a Newham youth project in Canning Town, of which no one in the room seemed to be aware. He then added: 'Disrupt everything . . . continue to do so . . . as long as it takes'. He turned to the YOTS representative asking: 'What are you doing about stopping them getting into gangs?'. The representative explained that she had 200 young people on her books, before moving on to the issue of gang members in relation to council tenancies. The Chief Executive's representative added that each case had to be considered individually: '. . . one case saw the tenancy held by an 86-year-old grandparent whom the gang member lived with'.

The now calm Mayor asked: 'Education . . . where is it?'. The YOTS representative explained that schools liaise with YOTS, albeit the relationship had not always been co-operative. The Chief Executive's representative added to this, explaining how the headteacher of one secondary school a few months earlier had been assaulted as a result of apparent gang-related disorder (or what used to be called a fight between school pupils), but had declined to make a statement to assist the prosecution of the offender. The Mayor again exploded: 'Fuck this . . . for two and a half years now all schools in Newham have had police dedicated to them . . . The system's a bloody disgrace: the pupils are out of school at lunchtime and get out of school at two-thirty every afternoon . . . Why are schools not part of this [the SYV Partnership]? Don't they get OFSTED inspections?'.

After a few carefully worded interjections from Newham's CID Superintendent the meeting began to draw to a close, but not before the Mayor demanded of the GFU Inspector: 'How many are involved in all this? . . . Don't inflate it'. The answer was 300. A Mayoral command followed: 'Draw up a plan. Tell us how to go about it – if we get the officers. Destroy them. Keep going till it's no longer worth their while . . . This is the fault of the bloody Mayor of London . . . I'd have voted for the Labour Mayor if a Labour Mayor had stood . . .'.[12] Turning to the Chief Executive's representative, the Mayor commanded: 'If any of the housing associations won't play ball I want them in my office. They'll do exactly what we do . . . they're subsidized by the rest of us . . .'. Addressing the Borough Police Commander the Mayor's message was: 'Invite the schools in. Draw a list up of how many gang members are in each school and we'll contact all Heads to publicize the problem'.

The discussion then turned to public knowledge. The Chief Executive's representative asked: 'What are the levels of resident awareness of such groups? And what information had local media publicized on these issues?'. The Mayor intervened: a media story on gangs throughout the borough could be damaging and he and the Borough Commander had to prevent that being broadcast. At this point the GFU Inspector reminded those present that a recent successful raid by the GFU and LBN personnel on the Custom House Gang was refused publicity by 'council people'. The Mayor, angry once again, responded: 'Who pulled it? We want publicity for all our successes. But we want it sensitive, careful and not sensational'. The Mayor's logic then became confusing: 'We won't put up with this . . . I'm willing to name and shame but we don't want to raise the profile of the gangs . . . I don't want to hear any "legal" shit around this. It's a problem – "organized" or not'.

A senior council official in charge of publicity then used a word hitherto unheard that afternoon. The word was 'Olympics'. As she stated: 'I can just see in a year's time thousands of unaccredited journalists all looking for a story about Newham . . . they've got one here'.

The TAG team: entering the ring

In his late 40s, ST, a Jamaican-born former offender explained to a somewhat bewildered audience of three MPS detectives that of the 20 black youths he came across in Westfield while shopping two days previously, he would have liked to 'bust' two of them. Appearing as the potential nemesis of deviant Newham youth, ST headed an organization called Teaching Against Gangs (TAG). He had impressed a senior officer in the MPS at a conference, and was invited to address the GFU following the previous week's Westfield opening.

ST declared that all his team had a God-inspired mission to convert those who were taking to gangsterism and 'Road Life'. TAG worked elsewhere in London, and several councils funded their work that was based upon street-level confrontation and negotiation with the perpetrators of violence. To facilitate their departure from the 'Road Life' TAG had connections with a variety of businesses to provide for alternative careers. ST explained that the crucial dimension in his work was credibility; and the TAG team had this in abundance. Established in 2008 TAG claimed they could address the destructive influence of gangs via building quality relationships with gang-affected individuals through intensive mentoring. TAG's ex-gang personnel meant they were not intimidated by notions of area codes, or the presence of guns or knives. In recognition of the often complex nature of gang related needs TAG worked with families and key organizations, be they local authorities, the youth offending services, schools, police, probation service, faith groups and community and voluntary organizations. The TAG programme also sought to develop leadership skills, breaking the gang mentality, addressing past hurts and emotional pain, assisting family dysfunction, and where relevant reconciling absent fathers with children, as well as challenging sexist attitudes to women and sexual behaviour. A dedicated 24-hour phone line was available for all who sought to talk over such issues.

ST claimed that gangs from Hackney and Peckham had been showing great interest in Westfield, and that confrontation with local youths was inevitable. Aware of a spate of insults and counter-insults on social networking sites, ST considered that the Newham boys were playing with fire in insulting their opposite numbers from Waltham Forest and Hackney. In particular, they were out of their depth, as the latter were more violent entities. After 60 minutes the meeting came to an end and the GFU Inspector and ST agreed to communicate further to consider some form of arrangement. The one-page pitching document from TAG arrived within 24 hours asking for £45,000 for gang intervention work in Newham. TAG offered to provide a localized mapping of Newham's gang problems. This would include the visiting and counselling of both perpetrators and those most at risk from living the 'Road Life'. On top of this TAG would give contexts around conflicts, explain gang allegiances and flag up safeguarding concerns. TAG undertook visiting and counselling work with individuals given to them as 'referrals' by social services, the youth offending team, schools, probation service, and police: all of this featured an information-sharing proto- col for both risk planning and programme management. TAG began its work in Newham in early 2012, just as a number of disturbances involving youths in the Westfield Mall in late 2011 (see Chapter 4) contributed to a growing orthodoxy concerning gangs, and one group in particular were emerging as emblematic of this emergent Olympic threat

The Portuguese Mafia

In 2011 the state of affairs beyond Stratford had become a source of concern. Over the past two weeks there had been 17 incidents of gold jewellery being snatched from the necks of Asian women. Amidst the depressing statistics, a final moan of the DIs concerned Scotland Yard's obsession with something called the 'Portuguese Mafia' (PGM). 'They want to do "research and Intel profiling" on the Portuguese Mafia. I don't need it thanks very much . . . they would rob in the park and they did a whole spate on two bus routes that got crimed-up in both Newham and Tower Hamlets. We got custodial sentences for four of their top men and another three are awaiting trial. This busted them. They are today an ASB (Anti- Social Behaviour) problem . . . I said the PGM are not our main problem . . . he said he was offering help because he'd heard they were and Newham needed cleaning up because the Olympics were coming.'

The PGM were a group of 30–40 youths aged between 15 and early 20s who met most days in the Spring and Summer from midday onwards in Stratford Park and West Ham Lane. In winter they had gathered in the warmth of the Stratford Centre Mall. The core of what the police called the PGM were 'black' and had arrived in London via Lisbon. Some were Lisbon born, while others were from the former Portuguese colonies of Mozambique, Angola and Guinea-Bissau. According to a wall chart in Stratford police station, the PGM consisted of 31 individuals including two white British youths, two of Middle Eastern origin, one Anglo-West Indian and one Anglo-Polish. The nomen- clature of 'Portuguese Mafia' originated in the summer of 2010 following a series of Section 60 Stop and Searches. When asked who they were the group responded with the words 'Portuguese Mafia', and although it was initially conceded that the name was only a 'tongue-in-cheek' term, it quickly took on a life of its own.

The PGM nomenclature was discussed at Newham MPS senior management level in early June 2011. One senior officer considered the term 'mafia' over- romanticized their sense of criminality and only assisted in their enjoyment of notoriety. For this reason the mugshot display in Stratford police station saw the word 'mafia' overlaid with that of 'robbers' thanks to an upper case printout and some sellotape. Some did commit robberies, and they could be intimidating to shoppers and park strollers. When challenged by the mall's pri- vate security personnel they could be defiant and abusive. Later, when Stratford was classified as a dispersal zone,[13] police were empowered to arrest anyone who was gathering in large numbers and refusing a request to move away, causing the group to retreat to Stratford and West Ham Parks to while away the hours, chatting and smoking dope. Also found in two Portuguese-owned cafes in Newham, the PGM were considered by the police to be the most 'confrontational' of all youth groups in Newham, and their defiance in the face of the police occasionally resulted in arrests.[14]

Many of the young men associated with the PGM had arrived in Newham destitute and claiming refugee status, and ten of them had been housed in the E15 Foyer,[15] where they received some English language tuition and job counselling. This left them with too many hours to kill, and too little money. They had no links to Newham, and with no work, family, education or training, their lives were confined largely to West Ham Lane and Stratford Park. This street, only a few hundred metres from glossy Westfield, also hosted Stratford police station and two dozen small businesses, a third of which sold fast food.

Portuguese speaking friends located in other London boroughs would travel to Stratford to meet with them, and they were joined by local youths who shared their appreciation for cannabis. At times the group in the park could be 20-strong, and although some of them robbed locals of their phones and other valuables, the majority of these young men were not robbers. But the so-called PGM had no youth workers or institution that could represent them. Their English was poor. They were public, visible and intimidating. No police officer made it their task to get to know them and the only Intel available was distinctly negative. Thus, in local police consciousness, they were black, foreign, and surly.

The PGM did not have a 'turf' to defend, and so did not get involved in territorial disputes with other groups of youths. However, violence was a feature of the PGM and a number of stabbings and a shooting were attributed to them but were they a 'gang'? In response to this question the GFU Inspector scrolled down on his computer the MIB (Met Intelligence Bureau) profiles on Newham gangs and found not a single mention of the PGM: 'They're a group of mates who meet every day . . . We can't decide if they're a gang or not'. The answer to the question had three dimensions: they were not on the radar of the GFU because they did not exist in the gang MIB intelligence; on another level their existence did not fit the identikit gang profile of those who had grown up in the borough and contested the control of territory; and thirdly, they were primarily dismissed as a 'bunch of robbers', and thus policed by the dedicated Robbery Squad. As one of the GFU Sergeants explained 'They [Robbery Squad] have ownership of them . . . so they're "robbers" not "gangsters"!'.

The PGM had emerged as an ambiguous deviant group whose transgressions defied easy categorization. There was an undeniable problem of youth violence in Newham, and violence along with street robbery did not bode well for the reputation of the Olympic Borough, or for the careers of anyone associated with the smooth running of the Games. However, as the event drew ever closer, categorizations of deviant young men became explicitly linked to administratively convenient labels. And youth violence continued.

'The gang thing'

A 16-year-old boy was stabbed to death in a feud involving Newham youths. The killers were from E15, while the dead boy was from E13. Three young men in their late teens received life sentences for the killing, and when sentencing was handed down the Old Bailey erupted into violence, and a fight involving 100 youths from the respective postcodes ensued when friends of both the deceased and the convicted found themselves sharing the same underground train.

The dead boy's sister spoke tearfully of her brother's funeral, and her feelings towards her estranged mother: 'She played up the gang thing. She placed a green balaclava on the grave. She asked on Facebook for green flowers to be part of the wreath. There was a documentary two weeks ago about knives and she was on it . . . But she's an addict and mentally ill. We have nothing to do with her.' The 40-year-old mother of the deceased, a multiple addict, was estranged from the family, having been rehoused ten miles away by the council. In her grief at the time of the murder she invited friends of her son to arrive at the funeral in gang colours, and the parade of 'gangsters' was videoed and posted on social media. The previous evening the family home had three windows broken by missiles thrown by youths riding mountain bikes. The 13-year-old niece of the deceased youth described to police the clothing of one youth who threw the missiles, and the colour of the bicycle. She mentioned how upon departing he held his hands together and imitated a firearm being discharged. Later the same day, a car with blacked-out windows had cruised slowly past the house. Having completed a high-speed spin the driver then lowered his window and stared as he passed the watching family. The victim's sister had spent many nights in a friend's home concerned for the safety of her 12-year-old daughter. The family did not want to be moved. They liked the neighbourhood.

Built two decades previously, the council-owned home was a basic two-up-two-down and well looked after. However, the windows remained cracked and the letter box in the front door hung on its hinges after the home had been attacked a few weeks earlier. A new letter box had been added to the door, capable of dousing anything flammable. A reinforced front door and ground floor windows were to be installed. A CCTV camera provided by the council would cover the approach to the home. The uncle promised police he would note car registration plates that drive by slowly. The police in return promised that the alarm button which had been installed would 'bring the cavalry when pressed'.

When the Court of Appeal turned down an attempt by those convicted to have their sentences quashed, there were consequences for the extended family of the deceased. His niece was verbally abused by youths claiming to be 'Custom House', his grandfather had bricks thrown at his windows, and his uncle was attacked in the street by three youths. The uncle had refused to make a statement to police, but explained that 'anyone aged 16–20 seems to be after me'. When the dead youth's younger brother, now aged 17, visited his doctor's surgery, he did so in a minicab because the E15 boys congregated on a corner near the surgery and he feared for his safety. An aunt of the deceased described how a 40-strong group of youths including one carrying a samurai sword and another letting off a shotgun had attacked the family home.

The English riots of August 2011: the Newham experience

In August 2011 England suffered widespread major disorder, and Newham experienced two days of rioting and looting which cast a spotlight upon the borough's youth. As a result of these riots, and despite any lack of causal evidence, gangs were suddenly regarded not only as a major social problem, but also as a serious threat to the 2012 Olympics. Further, the police response to the violence proved inadvertently to be an ideal dress rehearsal for public-order scenarios that could emerge during the Games. The English riots of August 2011 have been covered in detail and from differing perspectives by other scholars,[16] but our concern here is the manner in which they were played out in Newham. The two days of rioting in the borough were to have serious consequences for how the Newham police and the British government approached the 2012 Olympic Games.

By mid-afternoon on Monday 7th August the Stratford Centre was closed on police orders, and other shops in the vicinity were advised by police to close. Later in the day, all four Newham police stations were closed and their front doors shuttered. A notable police presence was evident outside Stratford railway station and private security guards stood in greater numbers than usual in the stairway that led to the Westfield Mall. In High Street North in East Ham, dozens of businesses were broken into and looted. By 22:00 hours on Monday, Forest Gate police station was disgorging police units that travelled in convoys with sirens and blue lights to the latest incident.

With the Chief Superintendent away and the Superintendent new to the neighbourhood, senior policing command was somewhat shorn of specialist local knowledge. Six Junker bomb-proof and bullet-proof neo-military specialist riot vehicles arrived in the borough. The cumbersome vehicles had been dispatched to Newham at the behest of the police Centre. When they arrived in Newham nobody knew what to do with them and, apart from a brief sortie to East Ham's beleaguered High Street North by one of the vehicles, they were parked outside Forest Gate police station until it was pointed out that the presence of military-style vehicles on the streets was not a great public relations message to relay to the general public. They were subsequently parked in the car-park of the East London Rugby Club in West Ham. The President of the club was an ex Newham Chief Superintendent, who had recently been appointed as the (civilian) Head of Enforcement for Newham Council.

By the early hours of Tuesday 8th August police from Thames Valley, Northamptonshire and Cambridgeshire had arrived in Newham. At 01:35 reports came through of repeated attempts being made to enter Stratford Centre by a large group of youths, and all over Newham reports of large groups converging on stores were now being reported to the police. A youth was arrested at the rear entrance of Plaistow police station whilst carrying a Molotov cocktail, and the Junker neo-military vehicles were deployed in and around High Street North.[17]

In Beckton a group of men were unsuccessful in breaking into an ATM. The biggest casualty was Argos (High Street North) which lost goods to the value of £28,000. Hundreds of computer games were stolen from a computer store and a small supermarket lost £6,500 in cash. A NatWest Bank had an undisclosed sum of cash stolen, and money was also stolen from gambling machines at an amusement arcade.

Some violent disorder was counteracted by the threat of even greater violence. Green Street remained untouched – the largely Indian proprietors of the shops organized to protect their property, and when one 24-hour store came under attack the looters were discouraged by a vigilante group of the storeowner's friends who fired a shotgun. At a Turkish-run mini-market looters were repelled by shots being fired at them by the owner's friends. By Tuesday evening additional police from Humberside, West Yorkshire and Derbyshire had arrived in Newham, and three Newham police vehicles had been badly damaged in attacks by youths on the streets of Canning Town. Social media suggested that the Olympic site was to be attacked.

By August 16th Newham police had identified 180 scenes of crime, most relating to looting and criminal damage, as well as three cases of GBH. Newham police had 72 named suspects, of these 31 had been arrested. The youngest suspect was a black youth aged 11, the oldest was a white 70 year old who had stolen an ironing board.

In the MPS it was generally considered that Newham had not been as affected by the disorder as other London boroughs, and had not suffered an 'iconic event', a category used by the MPS for crimes of murder and arson.[18] However, the UK Prime Minister claimed that the riots were gang-related[19], and the conversation in Newham followed suit, particularly amongst senior members of Newham Council. Despite the pre-riot intensity of the policing of youth in Newham there had been no intelligence forthcoming of the imminence of the disturbances, and few of those arrested had any previous convictions or gang affiliations. Yet the riots succeeded in embedding gangs in the police and wider consciousness as a serious risk to the Olympics. In the subsequent post-mortems on the riots, a senior council member, emboldened by the Mayor's funding of extra police and the consequent increase in Newham Council's influence over policing in the borough, lambasted the force for not clamping down on gangs and denied the effectiveness of 'soft' diversionary tactics. 'I've seen 50–60 cause mayhem over the last couple of days . . . we don't need touchy-feely . . . we don't want *The Guardian* approach to all this . . . The only thing that ever works is being tough with people. Take the ringleader out – most people are followers. They're involved in heavy crime. We don't want free swims and night classes'.

In the wake of the riots, concerted multi-agency action against gangs was intensified. Efforts to provide a more nuanced analysis on behalf of any number of concerned agencies, including some sections of Newham police, were swept away as youth violence was conflated with organized crime and gangs (Hobbs, 2013). Crucially 'gang talk' (Hallsworth and Young, 2008) became louder within a sophisticated organization that prided itself on being 'intelligence driven', and as a consequence senior MPS officers responsible for key aspects of Olympic-related tasking began talking of Newham's gangs as a major threat to the Olympics.

In addition, although the riots were not 'Olympic related' the police had identified Westfield as a potential target, and to the detriment of the rest of the borough, had deployed resources accordingly. This may account for why Newham was the only borough reinforced by specialist anti-riot vehicles. Had the Olympic borough suffered the same levels of disorder as other parts of London, for instance Tottenham or Croydon, the commercial viability of the Games, and the cumulative reputations of a number organizations, agencies and individuals would have been seriously damaged.

There were lessons to be learned from the August 2011 riots. The police looked at their equipment, in particular radios and vehicles, both of which had been found wanting. Muster points for officers were reconsidered. In addition, the riots enabled the establishment of important personal relationships between Newham police officers and officers from the provinces in terms of providing mutual aid, as many of these provincial officers returned to Newham the following year for the Olympics. Newham was no longer a strange unfamiliar place. Overall the riots acted, inadvertently, as a convenient test event for securing the Games.

Gangs, youth and the Olympics: a kind of legacy

In February 2011, the Newham MPS Senior Management Team had all agreed to remain in their respective positions for the duration of the Olympics. A year later, all bar one, a Chief Inspector, had left, or were leaving the borough. It was a good time to be absent from Newham police ranks, as the racism of MPS officers re-emerged from the 'underground' (Foster, Newburn & Souhami, 2005).

In January 2012, a story broke across national media, revealing racist comments made by a Newham police officer to a 21-year-old black youth during the 2011 riots. The arrested youth had surreptitiously recorded on his mobile phone the officer calling him, amongst other things, a 'nigger' and a 'black cunt'. In what was to be a major internal MPS enquiry, the accused officer and three others in the same police vehicle, all Newham based, were suspended from duty. Days later a 15-year-old youth, also arrested at the time of the riots, made complaints about his treatment in a Newham police station. Police CCTV cameras revealed that whilst on the floor in the custody suite the youth had been subject to kicks and a knee in the back from a uniformed officer.

While the Olympics were still several months away, the national (and soon to be international) reputation of Newham's police force was on the line, in terms of securing public order, controlling violent crime, and contributing positively to intercultural relations. Meanwhile a 17-year-old black youth living in a care home and well known to the police was involved in a feud with an individual in South London. Staff from the care home had contacted the police on suspicion that he had concealed a shotgun and was likely to use it. Two members of the Newham GFU had called on the youth, obviously hoping to deter him from his mission and also to obtain the weapon. The youth's contempt for his visitors was manifest in his total silence in their presence, broken only by the repeated playing on his i-phone of the now viral YouTube clip of the racist comments made by the Newham police officer the previous August. A kind of legacy had been assured.

Conclusion

Newham was in a permanent state of flux, its youth were no longer able to enjoy the relative luxury of subcultural membership before joining mainstream working-class society. Since at least the early 1990s, Newham's phenomenal population churn has included groups of young African, European and Asian men escaping war and economic trauma, drawn to the borough by cheap housing. They have joined young men whose families have been established in the borough for generations, and when a small number are associated with street robbery, public disorder or street dealing, they are attributed with emotive and hard to shake monikers such as the Portuguese Mafia.

Fitting perfectly with the net-widening imprecision of its contemporary use, the term 'gang' suggests a level of competence and organization somewhat removed from the rootless, chaotic street life of Newham's youth collaborations. For Newham's young, fluid, and constantly churning population, territories established in the industrial era that were built upon a strong cross-generational sense of neighbourhood patriotism no longer have the same relevance, resulting in an increasing reliance upon artificial or symbolic territorial boundaries (Katz, 1988: 146).

While some young men have adopted the collaborative identity offered by the gang, it has been clear to us that those 'kinds of group-based violence today being identified as gang-related, constitute a longstanding, perennial, deeply embedded feature of street life in British society' (Hobbs, 2013: 61). Yet for the police the term offered an imprecise, constantly morphing category in which to place a whole range of youth crime. Further, in recognizing the vague idea of 'gangs', both the police and local government have located a pragmatic means of categorizing problematic youth activity, while giving the impression of institutional understanding, and by implication, valorizing the institutional capacity to respond.

The growth of the gang problem in Newham corresponded to the growth of the Olympic infrastructure and, whether in an amorphous rioting mob or in a violent criminal gang, local youths were now defined as constituting a threat to London's Games that was to dominate the policing of Newham throughout 2012. Political and commercial futures along with organizational reputations were in jeopardy, and in an environment where so much risk associated with terrorism was vague and cloaked with secrecy, gangs were ideal and highly visible hooks upon which to hang fears and devote resources: a 'suitable enemy' (Christie: 1986) *par excellence*.

Notes

1   Patrick's (1973) work on gangs in Glasgow is the exception. An account of territorially based fighting gangs that conforms in many ways to Thrasher's structured gang, with its leadership and defined roles. The loose membership and image of the

group as a collectivity based on spontaneous violence, is indicative of Yablonsky's 'Violent Gang'. An inter-locking network of inequality had produced an enduring gang subculture hinging on dissociation from middle-class norms, in an environment of socio-economic hardship that had narrowed the possibilities for action (see Fraser, 2015).

2 Downes (1966) found an absence of aspirational culture amongst East London youth and identified dissociation, the process by which all aspects of middle-class life, and in particular the primary engine of aspirational culture, education, was rejected (see Willis, 1977; Corrigan, 1976, 1979).

3 For a comprehensive overview of the evolution of the British gang as a major policy concern see Chapter One of Hallsworth (2013).

4 Plaistow Police Station was home to the Serious Youth Crime Team (SYCT) established in 2009 to investigate one particularly gruesome crime involving three Asian males and an Asian female, which was classified as a Conspiracy to Murder. This morphed into the SYU team then later became the Gangs and Firearms Unit (GFU).

5 In early August 2011 a young man from Custom House was stopped in a random search and found with a pump action shotgun, 50 wraps of heroin and a bullet-proof vest that originated from the Hertfordshire Constabulary.

6 By 2012 Newham police had identified up to ten youth gangs. However, new mutations were constantly being 'discovered', and the evidence base for inclusion in the Newham Gang Matrix was somewhat sketchy.

7 The meeting was called by the Newham MPS in late 2011, and held in a corporate suite at West Ham FC. The all-day event had speakers from the police, the local Youth Offending Team (YOTS), and two Third Sector organisations *Teaching Against Gangs* (TAG) and *Fight for Peace* explained their role in diversion and enforcement around SYV/gangs. Invitations to the event were sent out to all primary, junior and secondary school headteachers in Newham, but only five attended.

8 The main assailant was well known to police, and had previous convictions for violence. He was given bail, and part of his bail conditions involved wearing an electronic tag as he was being monitored by a private company who failed to inform the police that he continually breached his bail conditions. The Youth Offending Team (YOTS) added to the confusion. The accused failed to attend YOTS meetings on time seven times in a row. The first breach should have seen him arrested and returned to custody.

9 In 2010, Newham conducted almost 18,000 s60 stops and searches, out of an MPS total of a little over 53,000.

10 Technology was utilized in the pursuit of evidence. In mid-2011 the GFU received eight body vests funded by Newham Council. These contained micro body-cameras costing £540 each.

11 See Aldridge and Medina (2008) and Gunter (2010) for studies that unpack contemporary youth cultures which in very different ways have much in common with the sub-cultural era.

12 Section 92 of the 1996 Police Act refers to 'The council of a county, district, county borough (London borough, parish or community) may make grants to any police authority established under section 3 whose police area falls wholly or partly within the council's area'. The Mayor's 2011 initiative of a Section 92 plan for 30 new police officers had stalled due to in-fighting over costs. The debate was taking place at Home Office and London Mayoral level. The blame being apportioned here was towards London's Mayor Boris Johnson.

13 Sections 30–36 of the Anti-Social Behaviour Act 2003 (ASBA) gave police forces in England and Wales the powers to: disperse groups of two or more people from areas where there is persistent anti-social behaviour, and to take home any young person under 16 who is out on the streets in a dispersal zone between 9pm and 6am and not

accompanied by a parent or responsible adult. http://www.cps.gov.uk/legal/d_to_g/dispersal_orders/.

14 A couple of years earlier one member was deported, and returned to Newham a few months later under a different name, where he resumed his part-time occupation as a robber.

15 Based upon a French model, foyers were set up in the early 1990s to provide secure accommodation and an opportunity to engage with education and employment for young people who were unable to live at home. However, as we will discuss in our concluding chapter, in recent years funding cuts across all spheres of government have made the future of these remarkable institutions problematic. As we discuss in Chapter 4, from the perspective of Newham police the E15 Foyer was a 'crime generator'.

16 See for example Newburn, (2015), Newburn et al. (2015), Treadwell et al. (2012), and Winlow et al. (2015).

17 CCTV footage showed a newsagent in the High Street lock up his shop and join the looting of a shop a few doors away. Footage also showed one looter wearing the uniform of the store he was looting. The immediate silencing of the internal alarm system of a well-known sportswear retailer was attributed to staff who knew the whereabouts of the de-activating switch, and who subsequently became part of the looting fraternity.

18 During this same week a weapon discharged in the Wood Green area of North London was found to have originated from a Newham address. The father of a girl living in Forest Gate whose boyfriend was from Wood Green heard enough from his daughter to make him contact police. He gave an address in Wood Green where police found a handgun and ammunition under the floorboards of a 14-year-old boy's bedroom.

19 The urban riots in the UK during August 2011 were partly attributed by the Prime Minister David Cameron to 'opportunist thugs in gangs' (*Guardian*, 11 August 2011). See also the response by Hallsworth: 'Academic seeks new understanding of rioters' (the *Guardian*, 20 November 2011).

References

Aldridge, J, & Medina, J. (2008). *Youth Gangs in an English City*. Manchester: University of Manchester Press.

Ball, R. & Curry, D. (1995) 'The Logic of Definition in Criminology: Purposes and Methods for Defining "Gangs"', *Criminology*, 33(2): 225–245.

Bermant, C. (1975) *London's East End: Point of Arrival*. London: Eyre Methuen.

Bourgois, P. (1995) *In Search of Respect*. Cambridge: Cambridge University Press.

Brotherton, D. & Barrios, L. (2004) *The Almighty Latin King and Queen Nation: Street Politics and the Transformation of a New York Gang*. New York: Columbia University Press.

Campbell, A. & Muncer, S. (1989) 'Them and Us: A Comparison of the Cultural Context of American Gangs and British Subcultures', *Deviant Behaviour 10*: 271–288.

Christie, N. (1986) 'Suitable Enemy', in H. Bianchi & R. von Swaaningen (eds) *Abolitionism: Toward a Non-repressive Approach to Crime*. Amsterdam: Free University.

Cloward, R. and Ohlin, L. (1960) *Delinquency and Opportunity: A Theory of Delinquent Gangs*. New York: Free Press.

Cohen, A. K. (1955) *Delinquent Boys: The Culture of the Gang*. New York: Free Press.

Cohen, P. (1972) 'Subcultural Conflict and Working Class Community', *Working Papers in Cultural Studies* No. 2. Birmingham: Centre for Contemporary Studies, University of Birmingham.

Cohen, S. (1973) *Folk Devils and Moral Panics*. London: Paladin.

Corrigan, P. (1976) 'Doing Nothing', in S. Hall & T. Jefferson (eds) *Resistance Through Rituals*. London: Hutchinson.

Corrigan, P. (1979) *Schooling the Smash Street Kids*. London: Macmillan.

Currie, E (1985) *Confronting Crime: An American Challenge*. New York: Pantheon.

Davies, A. (2008), *The Gangs of Manchester*. Liverpool Milo Books.

Davis, M. (1990) *City of Quartz*. London: Verso.

Downes, D. (1966) *The Delinquent Solution: A Study in Subcultural Theory*. London: Routledge and Kegan Paul.

Fieldhouse, E. (1999) 'Ethnic Minority Unemployment and Spatial Mismatch: The Case of London' *Urban Studies*, *36*(9): 1569–1596.

Foster, J., Newburn, T. & Souhami, A. (2005) *Assessing the Impact of the Stephen Lawrence Inquiry*, Home Office research study, 294. London: Home Office.

Fraser, A. (2015) *Urban Legends: Gang Identity in the Post-Industrial City*. Oxford: Clarendon Studies in Criminology.

Fraser, F. (1998) *Mad Frank and Friends*. London: Little Brown.

Gill, O. (1977) *Luke Street: Housing Policy, Conflict and the Creation of the Delinquent Area*. London: Macmillan.

Gunter, A. (2010) *Growing Up Bad? Road Culture, Badness and Black Youth Transitions in an East London Neighbourhood*. London: Tufnell Press.

Hacking, I. (1999) *The Social Construction of What?* Cambridge, MA: Harvard University Press.

Hagedorn, J.M. (1998) 'Gang Violence in the Post-Industrial Era', in M. Tonry -&- M. Moore (eds) *Youth Violence*. Chicago, IL: University of Chicago.

Hall, P.G. (1962) *The Industries of London since 1861*. Hutchinson: London.

Hall, S. & Jefferson, T. (1976) *Resistance Through Rituals: Youth Sub-Cultures in Post-War Britain*. London: Routledge.

Hallsworth, S. (2005) *Street Crime*. Cullompton: Willan.

Hallsworth, S. (2013) *The Gang and Beyond: Interpreting Violent Street Worlds*. London: Palgrave.

Hallsworth, S. & Young, T. (2008) 'Gang Talk and Gang Talkers: A Critique', *Crime Media Culture*, *4*(2): 175–195.

Hallsworth, S. & Silverstone, D. (2009) 'That's Life Innit': A British Perspective on Guns, Crime and Social Order', *Criminology & Criminal Justice 9*(3): 359–377.

Hamid, A. (1990) 'The Political Economy of Crack Related Violence', *Contemporary Drug Problems 17*: 31–78.

Hancock, L. (2006) 'Urban Regeneration, Young People, Crime and Criminalisation', in B. Goldson & J. Muncie (eds) *Youth Crime and Justice*. London, Sage.

Hill, S. (1976) *The Dockers*. Heinemann: London.

Hobbs, D. (1988) *Doing the Business*. Oxford: Oxford University Press.

Hobbs, D. (2001) 'Deviance and Ethnography', Atkinson, Delamont, Coffey, Lofland & Lofland, *The Sage Handbook of Ethnography*. London: Sage.

Hobbs, D. (2013) *Lush Life: Constructing Organised Crime in the UK*. Oxford: Oxford University Press.

Home Office (2008) *Saving Lives. Reducing Harm. Protecting the Public: An action plan for tackling violence*. London: Home Office.

Horne, R. & Hall, S. (1995) 'Anelpis: A Preliminary Expedition into a World Without Hope or Potential', *Parallex*, *1*: 81–92.

Katz, J. (1988) *Seductions of Crime*. New York: Basic Books.

Katz, J. & Jackson-Jacobs, C. (2004) 'The Criminologists Gang', in C. Sumner (ed.) *The Blackwell Companion to Criminology*. Oxford: Blackwell.

Klein, M. (1995) *The American Street Gang: Its Nature, Prevalence, and Control*. New York/Oxford: Oxford University Press.

Klein, M. W. (2001) *The Eurogang Paradox: Street Gangs and Youth Groups in the US and Europe*. Dordrecht and Boston: Kluwer Academic Publishers.

Klein, M (2005) 'The Value of Comparisons in Street Gang Research', *Journal of Contemporary Criminal Justice,* May 2005, vol. 21, no. 2: 135–152.

Leeson, B. (1934) *Lost London.* London: Stanley Paul and Co.

MacMahon, W. (2007) *Bowlby's Contribution for an ASBO Age*. London: Crime and Society Foundation.

McDonald, B. (2001) *Elephant Boys*. Edinburgh: Mainstream.

Mieczkowski, T. (1990) 'Crack Distribution in Detroit', *Contemporary Drug Problems, 17:* 9–30.

Newburn, T. (2015) 'The 2011 English Riots in Recent Historical Perspective', *British Journal of Criminology,* 55(1): 39–64.

Newburn, T., Cooper, K., Deacon, R. & Diski, B. (2015) 'Shopping for Free? Looting, Consumerism and the 2011 England Riots', *British Journal of Criminology.* 55(5): 987–1004.

Parker, H. (1974) *View from the Boys: A Sociology of Down Town Adolescents.* Newton Abbott: David and Charles.

Patrick, J. (1973) *A Glasgow Gang Observed.* London: Methuen.

Persaud, R & Lusane, C (2000) 'The New Economy, Globalisation and the Impact on African Americans', *Race and Class, 42*(1): 21–34.

Pitts, J. (2008) *Reluctant Gangsters: The Changing Face of Youth Crime*. Cullompton Willan.

Ross, C. (2010) *Death of the Docks*. London: Authorhouse.

Rustin, M. (1996) 'Introduction', in T. Butler & M. Rustin (eds) *Rising in the East.* London: Lawrence & Wishart.

Sanchez-Jankowski, M. (1991) *Islands in the Street: Gangs in American Urban Society.* Berkeley: University of California Press.

Schneider, E. (1999) *Vampires, Dragons, and Egyptian Kings: Youth Gangs in Postwar New York*. Princeton, NJ: Princeton University Press.

Sennett, R. (1998) *The Corrosion of Character*. New York: Norton.

Smith, T. (2005) *The Art of Armed Robbery*. London: Blake.

Strangleman, T. (2013). '"Smokestack Nostalgia," "Ruin Porn" or Working-Class Obituary: The Role and Meaning of Deindustrial Representation', *International Labor and Working-Class History, 84*: 23–37.

Sullivan, M. (1989). *Getting Paid*. Ithaca NY: Cornell University Press.

Suttles, G. (1968) *The Social Order of the Slum*. Chicago: University of Chicago Press.

Whyte, W. (1943) *Street Corner Society: The Social Organisation of a Chicago Slum.* Chicago: University of Chicago Press.

Treadwell, J.; Briggs, D., Winlow, S. & Hall, S. (2013) 'Shopocalypse Now: Consumer Culture and the English Riots of 2011', *British Journal of Criminology, 53*(1): 1–17.

Willis, P. (1977) *Learning to Labour: How Working Class Kids Get Working Class Jobs.* London: Saxon House.

Williams, R. (1977) *Marxism and Literature.* Oxford: Oxford University Press.

Williams, T. (1989) *The Cocaine Kids*. Reading, MA: Addison-Wesley.

Williams, T (1992) *Crack House*. Reading, MA: Addison-Wesley.

Winlow, S., Hall, S., Briggs, D, & Treadwell, J. (2015) *Riots and Political Protest*. London: Routledge.

Yablonsky, L. (1962) *The Violent Gang.* New York: Macmillan.

Young, J. (2007) *The Vertigo of Late Modernity*. London: Sage.

Zorbaugh, H. (1929) *The Gold Coast and the Slum*. Chicago: University of Chicago Press.

4   Contested domains

Shopping and enforcement

The 2012 Olympics involved a merging of various policing systems designed to respond to a range of threats. Some of these threats, specifically terrorism, were of an almost apocalyptic nature, and stemmed from global tensions and trans-national movements.[1] Other threats, such as youth gangs, although ostensibly a mundane local policing problem, were placed by the 2012 Games into a global context. This chapter will address the emergence of both terrorism and local youth gangs in the context of the Westfield shopping centre, a new space with its own policing requirements, and with a significance in terms of the political economy of the Olympics that far outweighed its overt function as a mere shopping mall. We shall also address the manner in which Westfield, and Games Time Newham more generally, became the focus of multifaceted policing strategies that are unique, and would subsequently emerge as significant foundations of the 2012 Olympic legacy.

The mall of malevolence

The Westfield Stratford City mall was opened in September 2011, having cost almost £1.5 billion in its development, and featuring over 250 retail units spread across approximately 175,000 square metres. The mall's management claimed to have generated some 27,000 construction jobs during its development, and 10,500 established positions, 2,000 of which had gone to 'local long-term unemployed'.[2] Crucially, the mall was ideally situated for the Olympics and its millions of prospective visitors as the main entrance point for the Olympic Park, adjacent to the bus terminus, and located between Stratford overground train and under-ground stations. At the entrance steps to Westfield, and across the road from the old Stratford shopping mall, was Meridian Square: a sizeable public space allowing Olympic visitors and onlookers to gather and mingle before entering the mall and the park.

In police planning for the Olympics, an estimated 67 per cent of all Olympic spectators were expected to pass through Westfield en-route to the Olympic Stadium. However, these figures did not account for people who would merely be shopping during the Games. Working on projections compiled by the MPS, Olympic peak days would see 150,000 shoppers supplemented by 161,000 spectators, giving a figure of 311,000 entering the main Westfield Boulevard. The lowest-risk days would see 100,000 shoppers and 50,000 Olympic spectators in the mall.

The mall was iconic, the biggest of its kind in the UK. It was also integral to the notion of Olympic Legacy; it was to be the place which attracted post-Olympic visitors to the newly invented commercial zone of 'Stratford City'. The nearby Olympic Village would be sold and the 3,600 residential units taken over by residents who would not only shop, but also enjoy their leisure time in the mall with its shops, restaurants, cinema complex and all-night casino: all without any need to exit Westfield and enter into 'old Stratford'.

To plan for the securing of the mall, the Westfield Security Tasking Group first met in early February 2011: some nine months prior to Westfield's scheduled opening, and at a time when the site was entering the 'fit-out' stage involving the electrical, plumbing, carpentry and general shop-fitting work. In attendance at the Tasking Group meeting, convened in one of the stacked portacabins that constituted part of the Westfield Leasing Suite, were nine men and three women. Only two people, the Head of Westfield Security (WS) and the Head of Westfield Olympic Security (HOS), were not serving police officers.[3] Flamboyant and talkative, the HOS led regular tours of the Westfield site for prospective tenants across his vast domain.

Today, security was the focus of the 45-minute tour. The HOS expressed his concerns that the mall was an ideal target for a potential terrorist attack either before or during the Olympics, and with chilling echoes of the transport route taken by two of the four 7/7 bombers, he considered the potential attackers' approach: 'You've got the train from Leeds, got off at Luton, made your way to St. Pancras then got the shuttle to Stratford and here you are in Westfield'.

The tour revealed the scale of the mall. Some 5,000 vehicles could park within its bowels. The retail units covered three levels. The anchor tenants, Marks and Spencer and John Lewis, had negotiated deals for the best sites and this very week had been given the keys to begin their respective fit-outs. On top of all this were five storeys of office space which, for the duration of the Games, were to host a variety of functions for the National Olympic Committees of the USA, Australia, Great Britain and Israel. The latter's presence, the tour party learned, was a direct consequence of the pro-Israeli stance taken by Westfield's owners Frank Lowy and his family. The HOS acknowledged that the Israeli Mossad were included in ongoing security negotiations.

While the mall's potential for retail profits was described as 'massive', the prospect of terrorism was deemed 'possible'. The HOS took several opportunities to gather the group around him and deliver facts, figures and homilies regarding possible Olympic security scenarios. At the first stop it was explained to the group that a nearby footbridge was to transport all passengers from Stratford underground and overground stations over the six railway lines and into the mall; from here an 800-metre walk would bring them to the Olympic Park entrance. The walkway presented a dilemma in that the Westfield owners wanted it to be festooned with benches, outdoor cafes and foliage in order to mimic an archetypal 'high street'. However, the HOS realized that these installations would hinder the 'total surveillance' capacity sought by the mall's 850 CCTV cameras, and was having to negotiate the matter with the mall's senior management.

At the second stop the HOS revealed his primary concern. The walkway branched left, and revealed the Olympic stadium some 300 metres in the distance. Access to the stadium was to be ticket only, via a security barrier that was at the perimeter of the Olympic Park, where tickets would be checked and spectators searched. At its busiest the stadium would host 80,000 spectators, and there would inevitably be considerable congestion at the park entrance as ticket holders alighted from trains arriving at Stratford International station, located some 100 metres away down a very steep 100-step stairway. In the opinion of the HOS, this confluence represented the spot where a terrorist, with a backpack loaded with explosives, could cause maximum devastation on the greatest number of people.

Reflecting on this sobering prospect, the group made its way to the third stop, where the HOS spoke about 'crime in Olympic time'. This referred to his fear that, a week or so into the Games, some of the 10,500 athletes who had already been knocked out of their events in the opening heats would be drawn to the mall and commit crime.

Crime potential and the Westfield Mall

The tour participants then attended a meeting chaired by a Chief Inspector from the Counter-Terrorist Command who held the highest rank in the room. At this point the HOS revealed that he had 'clearance', presumably to the highest levels of security intelligence, and that no fewer than four other men employed in managerial positions at Westfield had the same status. Members of the committee gave accounts of their work and planning. A counter-terrorism (CT) Sergeant showed the meeting the 'flyers' to be distributed around the site next week announcing an Olympic Site Security Unit (OSSU) consisting of 20 officers This police unit would provide, for the most part, highly visible patrols as well as carry out searches on site staff, and operate 'expo dogs' with the ability to smell explosives. The same officer also revealed that the unit would soon be taking possession of a number of small vessels capable of cruising the waterways around the Olympic Park.

The HOS explained that in addition to OSSU the dedicated mall policing team would consist of one Sergeant and six Police Constables paid for by Westfield, and accommodated in a dedicated police office in the mall basement. On behalf of Westfield the HOS had asked for eight MPS officers; Newham MPS meanwhile were considering providing two of their officers free of charge in return for Westfield funding a police radio network, and a police office at a cost to the mall of £268,000. An officer responsible for 'crime design' explained to the meeting that a dye was to be placed on building materials entering the site so that if anything was removed illegally the dye could reveal the origins of the theft.

The Newham-based Detective Inspector in charge of 'volume crime' in Stratford, the only police representative from the borough, spoke about her remit to record 'Olympic-related crime'. She had attended previous meetings of this forum and was aware of the problems of previous months, namely theft of high-value copper cable. Today, however, she restricted herself to itemizing what had been reported over the past few weeks. These were:

1   Theft of a power-tool worth circa £1,500. This provoked deliberation on the perceived East European attitude to borrowing building tools from fellow building workers.
2   Theft of Westfield site ID cards and the discovery of two false ID cards. These potentially very serious breaches of the Westfield security system did not merit alarm as the issue was interpreted as relating more to East European workers seeking to make a few pounds than to the preparation of a terrorist atrocity.
3   The potential for crime opportunities for local car thieves provided by the vehicles of the fit-out crews.

The focus of the meeting then shifted from the mundane to the spectacular. A counter-terrorism Inspector spoke of his two main fears, namely, the availability of weapons in London, and the possibility of a 'Mumbai-style' Al-Qaeda attack. That was the extent of the information given. The Olympic Comand Zone (OCZ) rep told of two new police officers joining the unit to work 'behind the scenes' on 'insider threat'. Another officer from the Westfield team spoke of consideration being given by Westfield management to Behavioural Analysis Screening (BAS) – i.e. predictive profiling of people for criminal potential.

Identify and minimise

The next meeting of the Joint Westfield Security Tasking Group took place some six weeks later. Fifteen persons were present in an 80-minute meeting chaired by a CT Chief Inspector. The Borough DI spoke of the reported theft of copper cable and the Olympic Site Security Unit (OSSU) Sergeant claimed that his leafleting campaign in the Olympic Park site was 'well received', and had resulted in 'a small amount of info' from the mall's workforce. Twenty five men going under the name of the 'Blacklist Support Group', had protested against an Olympic site blacklist created by the building industry. The Sergeant told those gathered that 'this could be a future issue'. This illegal blacklisting never appeared in any analysis of 'Olympic-related crime', and given that this was on the site of some historically important labour disputes (as discussed in Chapter 2), it serves as a useful reminder that down in the 'gash' some things do not change.[4]

The HOS commended the newly begun OSSU for their recent searches conducted between 06.00–09.00 hours. All 1,500 workers entering the site were subject to stop and search, using hand-held scanners, x-ray machines and sniffer dogs, and with personnel drawn from the OCZ, Safer Transport, UKBA and the

Department of Work and Pensions. This resulted in 38 arrests, one worker in possession of cannabis was sacked, and 30 others failed drug tests and were also were sacked. Two were arrested when they were found to be wanted on warrants, two were found to be in possession of 'points and blades', and one man was taken away by UKBA for immigration offences. The meeting was then informed that a threat assessment drawing on input from MI5 and other agencies and compiled by SO15 (Counter Terrorism Command) highlighting 'CT, domestic extremism and austerity/animal rights' had been received by the HOS that morning. It is significant to recall here that the HOS is a civilian employed by a shopping mall, and this ready access to 'Intel' effectively gifted highly sensitive material to the commercial sector.

The remit of the OCZ to police the one-mile circumference outside of the Olympic Park was presented. Alongside three other OCZ police personnel, the advisor had written a tactical plan, and explained that the OCZ's focus was on insider threat and suspicious activity. The OCZ would work jointly with SO15 and Newham-based CT)officers: 'We need to know all Westfield permanent staff and identify and minimize the opportunities for hostile recon(naissance)'. This was to be achieved through various CT initiatives aimed at training security personnel, shop staff, and others (such as waste removal personnel) in order to identify threats. A final contributor, a crime prevention design advisor, added that he had test-sampled glazing to minimize the damage to human bodies from glass-shard showers caused by explosives, and was consulting with Westfield management regarding the installation of laminated glass.

In the weeks preceding its opening there was a huge amount of media interest in the UK's largest shopping mall. The number of shops and car parking spaces were highlighted. The transport interchanges were promoted. However, privately, MPS counter-terrorism officers considered that an attack on the mall was a realistic proposition. For any disaffected group the mall represented *par excellence* the opulence and decadence of Western consumerist culture, it was inextricably linked to the 2012 Games, and was owned by a one-time Israeli 'freedom fighter', a billionaire who had given huge sums of money to the state of Israel. The Israeli Olympic Committee were using space in the mall for their parties and meet-and-greets, along with the USA and Great Britain.

However, while a terrorist attack was a possibility or a realistic proposition, the previous year had seen increasing social media chatter amongst groups of young Londoners making claim and counterclaim regarding who would 'own' the mall. This was a contest that Newham's police believed would inevitably be settled through violence.

Who's feeling dangerous? The opening of the mall (September 2011)

The Westfield marketing team had predicted that 250,000 people would visit on the first day, and at the Tuesday morning opening of the mall litter-droppers, cigarette butt-discarders and chewing-gum spitters were apprehended by an eight-strong uniformed enforcement team employed by Newham Council, and issued with fixed penalty fines of £60. Elsewhere an array of flower, fruit, and coffee stalls, and the owners of a three wheel 'Tuk-Tuk' vehicle, which transported a coffee making machine and half a dozen collapsible chairs for customers, were all required to leave Meridian Square. The 'Tuk-Tuk' owners were circulating a petition which claimed that the council were seeking to place permanent structures in the square 'to act as a counter-terrorist measure'.[5]

Despite the vastly expensive upgrades of the previous few years, the transport system failed miserably during the first week of Westfield. The wider context for the opening day was not auspicious. Westfield had been planned during the mid 2000s' boom period before the global economic downturn that commenced in 2007. By the time of Westfield's opening day the UK Retail Price Index had risen to 4.5 per cent, unemployment had reached 2.5 million, with the biggest rise for any area in the UK occurring in the London Borough of Newham. Meanwhile, the iconic department store John Lewis had reported a 47 per cent reduction in annual profits and the Confederation of British Industry reported that sales on the British high street had fallen at their fastest rate in 16 months.

At the mall's opening ceremony,[6] headlined by a one-time member of the Pussycat Dolls pop group, Westfield CEO Frank Lowy dismissed the 'doomsayers', claiming that '20,000,000 people a year would visit the mall', and that 2,000 jobs had been created. The Mayor of London, Boris Johnson, with characteristic hyperbole, spoke of the mall creating 18,000 jobs and offering the greatest addition to the area since the Middle Ages. He spoke of the 'cultural backwater' that was Stratford, and how a shopping mall and the Olympics would be the pioneers of change. He told of shoppers travelling from Paris to visit 'le Westfield' where a Hermes scarf was 20 per cent cheaper, where Levis jeans were £70 compared to the Parisian £84 and where a Big Mac meal cost £4.74 rather than £5.47. Accompanying Johnson on the platform were the Mayor of Newham Sir Robin Wales, and significantly, Hugh Robertson, the UK Minister for Sport. The opening ribbon was cut by Johnson at 11.30 hours and the mall was declared open to the accompaniment of Lady Gaga's 'Poker Face'. Then, entering on a down escalator, came the singer Nicole Scherzinger with a six-strong dance team. Her opening sentence asked those present: 'who's feeling dangerous?'.[7] The actual number of people visiting Westfield on the opening day varied in estimates between 160,000 and 190,000; Westfield's management later claimed that one million people had visited the mall in the first seven days. However, some of the Westfield management were expressing consternation over the behaviour of some mall visitors, such as in the amount of chewing gum discarded on the complex's flooring, or the number of babies in pushchairs impeding the free movement of shoppers. Apparently the general decorum of Stratford's shoppers did not compare well with the mall's counterpart, located in more upmarket West London.

Leave it to us: partnership issues

The actual levels of crime evidenced in Westfield during the first week were a contentious issue. On the opening day there were five crimes reported. The first, within 90 minutes of the mall opening, was a sexual assault: a young woman had her breasts grabbed by a male. But this does not tell the full story. One opening day crime, a theft, was not recorded because it was committed by the mall's security guards who stole a youth's Blackberry while searching him. The youth made a complaint to police which went to the highest echelons of the mall management, and the company that employed the guards faced the prospect of losing its £1 million security contract. The issue was smoothed over, and the company got richer on the second day by virtue of the mall's management requesting a further 30 personnel to deal with the volume of visitors. On day two there were just three crimes.

Some visitors were not welcome, and on the first day an altercation had seen a youth, part of a group of 20, vault the counter of a hardware store and steal a knife which he waved at another group of youths. By the time security and police had answered the call from shop staff, the youths had disappeared. Security staff were warned by the mall's Security Manager to take special interest in large groups of youths to the point of 'man marking' them. Local youths quickly adapted and began entering the mall in groups of two and three and reconvening once inside. While in the first week Westfield could not claim to have hosted a single gang-related crime, 24 hours after the opening day, a drug-trade inspired altercation believed to be between alleged members of the Maryland Gang and the PGM resulted in a stabbing just metres from the mall entrance, followed two hours later by a revenge stabbing on the forecourt of the E15 Focus building.

For Westfield's managers a passive commercial utopia was vital, and they sought control around both enforcement in the mall and any consequent crime-related publicity. This strategy had angered the OCZ Superintendent who predicted at the Westfield opening ceremony that private security personnel would be unable to deal with potential crime and disorder in the mall. At the same time, he stated that the MPS Westfield team of eight uniformed officers assigned to 24-hour policing of the mall would be inadequate. Four days after the mall opened Newham police had to enter Westfield to assist in an arrest.

The daily management of security in the mall was, as yet, not clearly demarcated. There was a dedicated Security Manager responsible for the private security personnel contract, while an Olympic Security Manager (HOS) gave strategic advice on behalf of LOCOG. Newham police allocated an Inspector, a Sergeant, and six Police Constables to the mall. The Security Manager was quick to praise his place of work and always had statistics and positive stories to hand: 'One million visitors in the first week. *Forever 21* [Westfield store] took £1 million on its first day. There's a lot of nosing around, not shopping, but they'll be choosing where to shop when they come back at Christmas. There are masses coming in just to eat'.[8]

Indeed the volume of visitors had meant security and police had to close some entrances and redirect pedestrians at pinch-points.[9] The mall had also attracted a number of local youths, assumed by both the police and mall security to be connected with serious youth violence (SYV), and as a consequence the deployment of Newham officers in the mall's first two months had been intensive in an attempt to secure the reputation of Westfield in the face of the risk of violence or 'gang activity'. The decision to give the Olympic Park area and Westfield its own postcode meant that if the notion of 'postcode wars' had any credibility, the clearly-defined territory of 'E20' constituted a potentially contested space for local youths. This was certainly the view taken by the Westfield Security Manager, who explained: 'We've got a policy of breaking up any gathering of youths larger than four in number. We're also going to throw them out if they're not shopping. We'll remind them that the purpose of this place is to buy things'. The other threat was from terrorism. To this end a variety of plain clothes officers from specialist units had been working the mall, tasked with identifying 'hostile reconnaissance'.

Responsibility for implementing and paying for security in Westfield was contested by police and other agencies, leading at times to breakdowns in communication over security planning. LOCOG had responsibility for the 'Last Mile' at London 2012: that is, the one-mile radius surrounding the approach areas to all Olympic venues, which in the case of London 2012 also encompassed the Westfield Mall. The local police perspective was that all Olympic security inside this area was LOCOG's remit, which included searching spectators, and deciding who would be allowed entrance to Olympic venues. However, while the mall was in the Last Mile, it was impossible to differentiate between shoppers and spectators who were obliged to walk through Westfield on the way to the Olympic Park. Accordingly, LOCOG demanded that Westfield should pay for security out of the increased profits from the Games. While negotiations had been undertaken to address issues of ownership, not all of the relevant agencies were talking to each other. For instance, a test event on the Olympic site conducted by G4S[10] had included a simulated explosion, which resulted in calls to the police from the public, resulting in a Newham MPS emergency response that included specialist explosives officers. According to the OCZ Superintendent, Newham police had not been informed of the G4S exercise, and the security company had been acting independently.

The (Olympic) Mall: total policing

In the run-up to the Games, Westfield was making money, the tills were ringing, and the 2011 Boxing Day sales saw an estimated 210,000 visitors in the mall. Yet the fear of local youths as an Olympic threat, as discussed in Chapter 3, appeared to be becoming a reality when the next day four youths from Hackney clashed in the lower-ground-floor food mall with a group of 26 local boys who Newham MPS officers later claimed were members of the Maryland/Young Blood City (YBC) gang. One of the locals told the Hackney boys that the mall was the YBC's and that they were guilty of 'trespass', and a fight ensued during which one of the Maryland group was stabbed. According to both the police and the management of the mall, a 'gang fight' had occurred.

Further violence involving local youths occurred days later with a running fight in the mall. Two youths received knife wounds before the combatants were apprehended by mall security and uniformed police. None of the youths were known by police as gang members. Within 24 hours seven youths had been arrested and another ten identified via the mall's CCTV system. The incident was perceived as being drug-related, but was never resolved. While the Head of Newham CID acknowledged that these two incidents were not necessarily about 'gangs', it was 'serious youth violence', and 'It's a flagship mall. You cannot assault people when others are out shopping with their kids . . . Those charged and found guilty will get sentences out of proportion to the actual incident. They'll get the whole picture from us as well . . . We'll look at their housing, rent, schools and vehicles . . . Total Policing'.[11]

Patrols around Stratford were intensified, and as we discuss in Chapter 3, gangs were increasingly being referred to within police circles as an Olympic threat. At a multi-agency meeting in Stratford it was disclosed that robbery rates in Stratford were up by 7 per cent on the previous year, which had caused consternation 'in town' (i.e. at Scotland Yard). A gang truce was discussed and quickly rejected, and the Westfield Security Manager presented some figures of his own. In the five months since opening, Westfield had attracted 13 million visitors. This averaged 90,000 per day in December with one day attracting 135,000. The Newham police crime analyst discussed 'young offender targets', and bemoaned a lack of inter-agency co-operation. At this point the Head of Westfield Security explained that he was seeking access to MPS data, and information regarding the records of suspected offenders regarding benefits and housing. This remarkable admission regarding the control and surveillance ambitions of a shopping mall employee went unchallenged. The same individual elaborated on the Westfield situation: 'Up to and during Christmas we swamped the place with police and private security. There was very little crime of note until two weeks ago. The bridge [on the approach from Stratford into Westfield Mall] was the place where we disrupted potential trouble-makers with security personnel, wands [weapon detectors] and sniffer-dogs [for drug possession]. It worked for a while . . . then they began entering in ones and twos via the tube system. Then they gathered 25-strong inside . . . We operate a 'deter and disrupt' tactic and identified key members. The future is smart water-spray guns for staff. Our nominals (gang members) are known to be carrying weapons . . . If knives are pulled we'll spray them on their way out and identify them later. We've got a facial recognition system being pioneered with Australian experts'.

The room responded to this 'Intel' and tactical response with apparent indifference. The Chair then added some context which played down the immediacy of the issues, prioritizing the long-term over the imminent Olympics: 'We have a generation who will be a problem for this area. This place is not to become a magnet for them. We need zero tolerance . . . The Olympics are coming but in late September they're gone. Then what? This is about a ten-year security issue for Stratford. The Olympics are not our priority'.

The two incidents of disorder in the mall were elaborated upon. The second incident revealed 'Warrior Square, a new gang previously unknown to us'. Interestingly, in the light of our scepticism regarding the construction of the gang problem in Newham (Chapter 3), the chief suspect for the January stabbing that had been designated by the police as gang related, was a youth not known to police and with no history of violence. Another issue that the GFU Inspector stressed was that contrary to the narrative being built around Westfield and the Olympics, the mall was not a contested site for Newham gangs. Youth from Beckton and Custom House would not enter Westfield. It was out of bounds to them because it was in Stratford and was considered the turf of local youth.

Meanwhile, Westfield's management were becoming increasingly proactive, and exerting a considerable influence over local policing. They paid TAG staff to patrol the mall for three weekends to spot gang build-up and to intervene, before donating £12 thousand to the GFU to pay for the overtime required for raids on the homes of the YBC. This remarkable example of the private funding of public policing highlights the commercial sector's ability to take the lead, without resort to the systems of political accountability that still exist within the mandate of British policing.[12]

From January 2012, the cumulative focus of Westfield management, Westfield security, Westfield-based police and Newham police would, according to the OCZ Superintendent be, 'street gangs, squats, raves and some hostile recon(naissance)'. This latter concept prompted the Westfield Sergeant to explain that in the opening weeks of the mall, nine plain clothes officers 'utiliszing behavioural detection tactics', conducted stop and searches on 30 people. They did not find any terrorists, but did find one individual wanted for theft. Furthermore, two men with long histories of burglary were removed from a location just adjacent to the mall managers' offices.

Contested domains

Meanwhile, other aspects of territorial co-operation and contestation were being played out between the public police and private security. Searching vehicles was the remit of G4S (on behalf of Westfield), who would search up to 10 per cent of vehicles using sniffer dogs. However, LOCOG had made it known that their VIPs 'were not to be searched if entering Westfield on the way to the Games'. Furthermore, G4S aroused considerable suspicion amongst the police, and one Superintendent had warned his staff not to reveal any police details requested by non-police personnel, as apparently G4S had been asking for information which he believed was on behalf of Westfield. Matters got more explicit; the Superintendent was vehement in advising that: 'The Last Mile is not our responsibility; nor is getting people in and out of Westfield'. However he admitted that one section called Cherry Park had already been subjected to a Home Office attempt to determine who had responsibility over the area. Territorial rights and responsibilities were becoming ever more complex as new agencies came into the Olympic reckoning; old agencies battled for their corner, and 'ownership' of many interlocking pathways, walkways and roadways remained contested until shortly before Games Time.

Westfield Mall paid the wages of six Police Constables, a Sergeant and an Inspector, and were allowing police a dedicated office in return for a peppercorn rent. Although two police officers working full-time in Westfield were funded by Newham MPS, Westfield would pay 'pre-agreed overtime', but could not instruct on the posting of PCs or decide on shift times. On issues of CT, the uniformed police were instructed by MPS CT to pass on any Westfield request to them: a decision which was compounded by the revelation that Westfield had sought from the police details of the anti-corporate pressure groups Occupy and UK Uncut.

The Police/Westfield ten-year contract which could be renegotiated by either side after three years, was brokered by the OCZ Superintendent, despite the fact that he had never received negotiation training. Indeed, in common with so much of police/private sector relationships and agreements, Westfield tasking relied on a mid-ranking officer's brokering abilities to strike a deal in what that officer perceived as the best interests of the MPS and the local contexts of policing. The Superintendent had also created a document setting out the potential managerial/ policing issues for the 2012 Games. The document sought to address a gap in the planning for the Games by 'the Centre'; that is, the omission of a specific plan to address the impact the Games might have on Newham. To address this lacuna the Superintendent produced a 20-point risk assessment to present at a meeting of the 32 MPS Borough Commanders: 'I've got to get a police force together to police the Olympics . . . We're working on a 62-day Games Time plan. I'm expected to be Superintendent as normal as well as run the six boroughs . . . We have a legal framework to reduce crime and disorder, a crime directive to work with the ambulance service, the fire brigade, local authority and the BTP. All have their own targets like we do . . . we'll have to manage expectations, manage our credibility, but the figures could impact and if targets aren't met funding might not follow.'

There were serious issues regarding how MPS staff would get to work during Olympic time, and where they would be allowed to park borough-wide. Manpower deployment in the light of an estimated 52 per cent of the normal workforce being abstracted to Olympic duties or lost to expected illness all loomed large: 'Then there's the Cultural Olympiad and the local authority programmes; will cops attend to police events because the [Newham] Mayor says he's paid for 30 cops recently and wants them to? There are 1,500 street parties planned for Newham. The local authority will do their best to licence and certify events via the Safety Advisory Group but what is an Olympic policing issue? What becomes of joint patrols with (Newham) Enforcement/YOTs/Trading Standards?'.

Despite the fact that the OCZ Superintendent was the only officer we met throughout our research with a detailed overview of the Olympics as they related, not only to Newham, but to all of the other Olympic boroughs, he was moved to a neighbouring borough in October 2011.[13] In addition to his regular duties he was tasked with discussions with the 2012 Legacy Company and the 2012 Olympic Village Legacy Company, and given responsibility for a borough-led Olympic response. All 32 Met police boroughs had an Olympic-related risk template designed by him. However, during the 62 days of 'Games Time' he would be permanently assigned to the Olympic Park as a Commander, and his primary remit would be Westfield.

When the departing Superintendent met the Borough Commander, it was decided that the business portfolio remit held by him for the previous two years (meant to reassure businesses on Newham concerned about both Westfield and

Olympic developments) would now be given to his successor at Superintendent level. However, the task of policing the post-Games Olympic Park would be kept by the Superintendent supported by an incoming Detective Sergeant. The six Olympic boroughs' task of co-ordinating policing would remain with the Superintendent, but in a 'monitoring and co-ordinating capacity'. The borough-wide Olympic risk was to be the remit of the incoming DS.

Meanwhile, beyond the privatized space of Westfield, other social control agents, unhampered by the complex high-stakes politics, were taking a distinctly proactive stance to prepare the borough for the spotlight that was expected to fall on the borough hosting the 2012 Games.

Enforcement and local difficulty

The TET offensive

> (TET) is similar to 'Zero tolerance', 'Back to Basics' and 'Big Society'; it's anything you want it to mean . . . It started out as 'Pro-Active Licensing' then when the gaffers realized we were doing more than that they re-named it. I call it the Enforcement Team; they want 'Total Enforcement'. I hated that . . . makes us sound like fuckin' Rambo.
>
> (Detective Chief Inspector)

According to the 2008 MPS crime classification Newham experienced more serious violence than any other borough in the MPD. Newham had the fourth highest alcohol-related hospital admissions in London, and over 50 per cent of violent crime in Newham was alcohol related. Furthermore, a MPS public perception survey (Goldstein Awards, 2011) revealed that 52 per cent of Newham's population were fearful of alcohol-related late-night disorder. In addition, the crime figures for robbery, assault, wounding, gun and knife possession and murder in Newham were far above national averages. Although at this stage the Olympics were seldom mentioned in either the MPS or LBN circles, none of the above constituted good PR for the borough hosting the Games. As a consequence, Newham's Licensing Sergeant was replaced by a Detective Inspector, and the Licensing Unit was expanded to accommodate collaborations between the police and LBN, in particular planning, building regulation, health and safety, and community safety. The strategy was to target premises associated with violence. The title given to this collaboration was the Total Enforcement Team (TET),[14] a police-dominated unit that was heavily reliant not only upon LBN co-operation, but also upon council funding. The council bought the police computers, gave them a dedicated office in East Ham Town Hall and purchased a nine-seater mini-van for their operations. They would also fund overtime, and of course pay the wages of any council-employed staff working with the team.

What started out as a solution to drunks hitting each other had morphed into something far more adaptable. The Mayor disliked the proliferation of fast-food outlets and nail salons, which he believed cheapened the ambience of the borough. He disliked the plastic bowls of 'fruit and veg' that many small corner stores displayed on their shop fronts. He also sought to enforce minimum wage legislation. Labour MP's Ed Davey and Stephen Timms had previously raised the issue of non-compliance with minimum wage legislation in Parliament, and Newham's 'Hidden Economy Group' (also known as the Employment Compliance Unit) became involved along with the Health and Safety Executive and other national agencies. The time-honoured East End problem of overcrowding, exacerbated by recent housing policy changes (see Chapter 2), was also prominent, and action was taken against rogue landlords.

TET personnel also clamped down on pseudo-educational establishments such as bogus colleges that exploited newcomers from overseas. TET personnel also raided and closed 35 brothels in 12 months. 'Shisha' bars, where customers share shisha (flavored tobacco) from a communal hookah or nargile which is placed at each table, were considered by TET to be associated with violent disorder and locations for the exchange of stolen goods, and 20 were closed down for trading without a license. Licensed premises associated with violence were targeted, and in the first 18 months of TET's existence 46 were forced to close. Chicken shops were also targeted by police in concert with various council officials including Trading Standards and Food Safety, the UK Border Agency (UKBA), and Her Majesties Revenue and Customs.

Another so called 'crime generator' that attracted the attention of TET was the E15 Foyer building. Home to 210 young people aged between 16 and 24, E15 was opened in 1996 as part of a UK-wide initiative to support vulnerable young people with a home and training for work. Referred from housing departments and a range of agencies, a minority of E15 residents kept irregular hours and were the bane of local estate residents who reported problems ranging from anti-social behaviour, resulting from 'hanging around', to drug dealing and arranged fights that were filmed on i-phones and posted on YouTube. Within police circles the Foyer was also associated with 'gang' activity which raised the stakes considerably, and during 2011 injunctions on nine individuals were obtained, banning them from visiting the Foyer. The fear of attracting residents with gang membership also saw a 'suitability to reside' protocol implemented requiring potential residents being checked against an MPS database for violent offences and gang membership. The problematic nature of these police databases was discussed in Chapter 3.

Police action in relation to the Foyer was rooted partly in traditional police/ youth conflict, based on both myth and reality, and partly in an attempt to protect a vulnerable portion of the local populace from a range of violent and exploitative situations. By 2012, a new security firm manned the reception, while a dedicated police room at ground level and an ID visitor management system was also introduced. In addition, an information sharing protocol was established with the Foyer's management and the police, and the immediate vicinity around the Foyer was designated as a dispersal zone in an attempt to prevent youths congregating. In short, there were extensive and quite unprecedented levels of surveillance.

By the end of 2011, and with the Olympics just ten months away, Newham was no longer a failing borough in police terms. Between October 2010 and October 2011 the figures for incidents of serious violence had fallen by 18 per cent. This was in addition to a 22 per cent drop the previous year. Furthermore, 81 per cent of incidents had been detected, up on the 73 per cent of the previous year. Although the Games were still seldom mentioned in terms of policing the borough, the fact was that Newham was being cleaned up nicely in preparation for the Olympics. The TET attracted plaudits from the ACPO Licensing Lead, the Deputy Commissioner of the MPS, the Home Office, and the Regional Health Authority. In October 2011, and for no apparent reason, TET was rebranded as the 'problem solving' team. It was suspected that many of the duties formerly addressed by TET would now be done by the Section 92 officers of the council alongside the Council's Enforcement Team[15].

The creed of enforcement

For the police, Westfield and multiple state and commercial agents were not the only major players in the build up to the Games. The Mayor of Newham had money, and he was using it in a variety of ways across the borough in order to supplement the policing of the borough. For instance, Section 92 legislation when fully operational would see 66 additional police officers in Newham. Under an agreement reached in May 2011, the Mayor would pay the cost of 35 of these officers; the MPS would 'match fund' the remainder. The Mayor, however, specified that the officers would be specifically devoted to duties that fitted the rubric of 'enforcement', which was his mantra regarding crime, a term that echoed across various LBN forums. Although the term was seldom defined, it became his shorthand for rapid legal responses to a wide range of infractions that he considered to be a blight on the borough.

In 2006, one year after the Olympics had been awarded to London, Nick Bracken (Bracken) was given the position of Newham Chief Superintendent. Then considered a 'failing borough' (in terms of crime clear-up rates), the Olympics were coming and something had to be done. Whilst the word 'Olympics' was not mentioned by his appointment panel, Bracken considered his appointment as having an obvious, if unstated, 'Olympic' purpose. He had to clean up the borough, and between 2006 and 2009 a variety of Newham crime problems, notably robbery and crimes of violence, were drastically reduced.

From 2009, Bracken had a MPS desk job in the West End, and when his 30-year service was up in 2011 he decided to retire and take a job as LBN's Head of Enforcement and Safety, and in doing so, became part of the Mayor's inner circle. His appointment fostered some consternation amongst local police regarding a civilian encroaching on the local policing remit, and these fears seemed to be confirmed when, in May 2012 as part of the rebranding of the council's 'Public Safety' officers as 'Enforcement Officers', the borough witnessed the introduction of new 'cop-lite' uniforms very similar to those of regular police, albeit the white shirts were accompanied by grey trousers and sweaters. The headwear was similar in design to the MPS, differing only in having a grey chess-board band around it, and the 'high- vis' jackets were very similar to those worn by the MPS, including the body surveillance cameras attached to the left breast. At the top of the organization sat Bracken whose uniform, most notably the head-wear, mimicked that of a MPS Commander.

The inspiration for the scheme came from the French Police Municipale, a system of public order that was funded and controlled by both local government authorities and the central state. In Newham it fully embraced the Mayor's emphasis on 'enforcement', being largely concerned with low-level, localized nuisance and anti-social behaviour, actively seeking out more targeted, proactive, and multi-agency working practices which Bracken elaborated upon: 'Let's say there's a location that everybody pisses in and it's a nuisance and health hazard – well, put a gate there and block access to it . . . that's an engineering solution. Then find out who's selling alcohol locally and who's pissing up the wall. Is there illegal selling of booze? Are those pissing street-drinkers? Do we then advise the shopkeeper of his duty according to the terms of his licence? Do we see if the problem-drinker needs intervention from health agencies? Then if all else fails we use enforcement. Nick (arrest) the bloke for pissing and he gets a Fixed Penalty Notice and an £80 fine. The off-licence gets raided and we have a good look at what else they have in the back . . . All in my management structure will be getting the equivalent to a police warrant card to identify who they are and who they work for . . . we'll use specific by-laws if needs be . . . we've got 40 new cops paid for by the Mayor . . . my plan is to pair them up with council employees, that way if we find people doing stuff we don't want them to do . . . they get the force of criminal law on them.'

Bracken had considerable local knowledge and the relationships that he had forged over five decades working in the borough continued, as we shall discuss later, to be influential during 'Games Time'. Since his appointment Newham had begun more prosecutions for a variety of legal transgressions than any other London borough. Publically vociferous in his disdain for the IOC and other Olympic apparatchiks, Bracken sought to get what he dismissively termed 'Stratford's Sports Day' out of the way, so that he could get on with the job in hand, which he perceived as the everyday enforcement of local issues such as rogue landlords, fly tipping: 'you name it: chicken shops, bin bags, rowdy youths. He (the Mayor) wants it done'.

The Mayor was proving increasingly influential on policing issues, and Newham's municipal police who, in anticipation of their enhanced role in this new world of social control by the time the Games commenced, were already negotiating innovative training, and systems of accreditation (cf. Waterford, 2005; Crawford, 2006), and had become very much part of the local polic-ing remit which, in the build up to the Games, was increasingly focusing upon Westfield and its immediate surroundings. The complexity of policing and security arrangements around Westfield and the 'Last Mile' had brought to the fore a startling assemblage of control within which the various branches of the police, as representatives of the State, were often placed in a subservient position to the commercial and Olympic entities who completed the assemblage. However, in the wider borough there was a less ambiguous implementation of policing in direct support of the Mayor who regarded the forthcoming Olympics as an unprecedented opportunity to change Newham forever, acting against people, places and practices that all too often were ignored by the borough police.

But if chicken shops, rogue landlords, public urination and inappropriate displays of fruit were now being robustly confronted in the run up to the Olympics, the police outside of Newham were starting to come to terms with threats to the Games that were of a more serious, if hypothetical kind.

Notes

1 For a detailed reading of the security measures taken at the 2012 Olympics, see Fussey & Coaffee (2012).
2 See http://uk.westfield.com/stratfordcity/community/regeneration/.
3 The HOS had retired from the MPS just the previous year with the rank of Superintendent. This new position earned him a handsome salary to supplement his pension, along with the envy of many of his former colleagues.
4 See 'Olympics Workers Cross-checked Against Unlawful Blacklist', (**the Observer**, 20 January 2013).
5 These structures constituted metal poles and stone obstructions designed to deter a vehicle carrying a bomb.
6 See https://www.youtube.com/watch?v=rDBfvf1fRDw.
7 Boris Johnson might have felt 'dangerous'. A few minutes after the singing act had begun, a large pane of glass in the mall's roof fell and shattered metres just away from the Mayor.
8 The Westfield branch of Gregg's boasted the largest opening day takings in the budget baker's s60-year history (*Evening Standard,* 6 October 2011).
9 However, while the basement food oasis was frequently packed, the floors featuring high-end fashion stores were sometimes literally empty of shoppers.
10 Private security provider and Games sponsor.
11 'Total Policing' became the institutional mantra of the MPS after Sir Bernard Hogan-Howe took over as Commissioner. According to the MPS, total policing involves: 'A total war on crime, total care for victims and total professionalism from our staff' (see http://content.met.police.uk/Site/totalpolicing).
12 However, Westfield did not provide everything that the police requested of them. Westfield refused to install and fund a dedicated police radio system in the mall, and as a consequence a £300,000 system was funded by the Metropolitan Police Authority (the MPA was superseded by the Mayor's Office for Policing and Communities in January 2012).
13 At the same time the borough's most senior Detective departed for Central London. The borough's Chief Superintendent was also moved early in 2012 to a more senior position elsewhere in the MPS.
14 After Bernard Hogan-Howe was appointed Commissioner of the MPS in 2011, Total Policing appeared on the header of all MPS stationery.
15 As explained in Chapter 3, Section 92 of the 1996 Police Act enables a local authority effectively to fund local policing.

References

Crawford, A. (2006) 'Networked Governance and the Post-regulatory State? Steering, Rowing and Anchoring the Provision of Policing and Security', *Theoretical Criminology, 10*(4): 449–479.

Fussey, P. & Coaffee, J. (2012) 'Balancing Local and Global Security Leitmotifs: Counter-Terrorism and the Spectacle of Sporting Mega-Events', *International Review of the Sociology of Sport 472*: 68–85.

Goldstein Awards (2011) 'Newham Borough – Proactive Licensing Team'. Available at: http://www.popcenter.org/library/awards/goldstein/2011/11-24.pdf.

Waterford, A. (2005) *Selling Security. The Private Policing of Public Space*. Cullompton: Willan.

5   Pre-event police planning

'Table Top' exercises

We turn now from a specific focus on Newham-centric issues of policing, to consider how police and security planning in advance of the Olympics was concerned with potential threats and risks which emanated from beyond Newham. Before any sport mega-event takes place, police and other emergency services (such as fire and emergency medical services) focus on establishing high levels of preparedness and responsiveness. Central to the pursuit of maximum security resilience is the simulation exercise, in which different decision-makers and other officials from these services come together to discuss and to test themselves on how they would best respond to diverse imagined scenarios, such as 'worst case' catastrophes like a large-scale terrorist bomb, as well as major fires, breakdowns in transport infrastructure, outbreaks of public violence in and around stadiums, and numerous other such incidents (cf. Boyle & Haggerty, 2012).

Given the seven year run-up to London 2012, police and other emergency services had a relatively long period to undertake simulation exercises. Notably, several 'Table Top' exercises were staged by central police management at Scotland Yard, beginning around seven months before the Olympic opening ceremony. According to the UK government guidelines, in general terms 'Table Top exercises are based on simulation', 'involve a realistic scenario and time line', and are run in ways that 'simulate the divisions between responders who need to communicate and be co-ordinated'. In addition, these responders 'are expected to know the plan', and should 'test how the plan works as the scenario unfolds'. These exercises require good preparation, are low cost (with the exception of staff time), and are ideal for identifying procedural flaws.[1]

In this chapter, we discuss five of these Table Top exercises which we attended in the build-up to London 2012. The simulations refer to the mundane, the commercial and the catastrophic, and exposed conflicts regarding both ownership of the problem and the consequent command structures in relation to multiple police agencies, commercial and Olympic hierarchies and the British military. In addition, there is the conundrum posed by the notion of Olympic-related crime. While all of the hypothetical scenarios discussed at these Table Tops ultimately had implications for the host borough, Newham police had little input at this stage, and the borough's population were barely mentioned, bar in respect to their possible threat to Olympic visitors.

Simulation: Table Top talking

Table Top 1: project to delivery

The first Table Top exercise was staged at the Police National Training Centre in Coventry, around 250 days prior to the Olympics. Central questions that were discussed and debated were: what crimes and other incidents are anticipated by these services in their scenario planning? How do these services view their roles and distribute responsibilities? The aim of the event was to clarify roles and responsibilities with respect to incidents that might occur before and during the Olympics, and to consider what constituted 'Olympic-related crime', and how they should look upon their general roles and duties during the Games.

Over 100 participants were in attendance, primarily police personnel from the six London 'Olympic Boroughs' and specialist units within the MPS. The Newham police were de facto the 'local' Olympics police force, hosting the multi-venue Olympic Park, as well as the Athlete Village and the ExCel Centre. There were nine tables in the room, around one tagged 'Newham Territorial Police' sat 14 police and civilians, of which only four were Newham based. In the top right corner of the room sat senior officers from Olympic 'Gold', 'Silver' and 'Bronze' levels of command.

Crucial to proceedings was the construction or simulation of possible incidents that might be encountered before and during the Olympics. The first day of the two-day event featured a large screen broadcast of images taken from the internet that were a combination of the informative, the symbolic and the apocalyptic. The informative revealed the smiling photographs of members of the MPS Olympic Command. The symbolic were images of, variously: Windsor Castle, University College Hospital, the Olympic Park, the Olympic Stadium, the Olympic Cycle Track, the Olympic yachting venue, London train stations and the entrance to the East London Limehouse link dual carriageway. The apocalyptic showed: a post-riot police van being towed away covered in graffiti; an image of the Queen striding towards a baying mob protected by riot police who were striking protesters with batons; a 'hoodie' male in his late 20s in post-theft pose carrying one of the five Olympic rings; a group of ten armed police in riot-issue protective clothing; Trafalgar Square ablaze as two youths sat atop a statue; and Tower Bridge visible as the Thames flooded the surrounding streets. There was no commentary accompanying these images, which the organizers had downloaded directly from a variety of internet sites.

The event was chaired by a MPS Superintendent who explained that the meeting was about moving from 'project' to 'delivery'. Key issues included: clarifying command posts and roles; who would be responsible for what, where and when; how reserve units and specialists would be brought in; and, what would be the protocols for taking responsibility. In his words the purpose of the event was to: 'Find out what are the confusions and work it through . . . find out who's doing what. It's generic stuff, you can't plan for everything'. The Chair also reassured participants that, before and during the Olympics, 'Nothing will happen that doesn't already or might not happen at any other time of year'. In effect, and despite some of the disturbing images on the introductory video, this exceptional event was to be viewed as generating unexceptional policing challenges.

On day one, the event participants were presented with a document which was to 'set the scene' by providing the 'simulated background' in which the Olympics might occur. The initial scenario was positive, imagining the British Olympic team performing well, inspiring public celebrations and street parties, despite wet weather. However, the document turned to envision more complex issues and greater challenges, which included the following:

- First came issues around transport. For example, the background scenario considered 'a growing public outcry' occurring over Olympic-related traffic disruption, alongside protests by London black cab drivers against their exclusion from the Olympic Route Network.[2] Elsewhere, the document considered the impact of high rainfall, leading to flash flooding. Instead of being the 'policeman's friend', rain in this scenario might undermine the effectiveness of air and rail terminals' procedures, while also reducing tourist numbers. Meanwhile, the simulation continued; engineering works along with Olympic road restrictions were disrupting traffic flows.
- Second, the problematic wider consequences of economic austerity were envisioned. For example, the emergence of large and difficult to predict protest movements in inner cities. Also, potential industrial unrest involving waste-management workers in London was outlined, alongside its negative effects on the positive image that the UK was trying to project globally from the Games.
- Third, the contextual impact of national and international conflicts: for example, where planned, British military withdrawal from Afghanistan may be delayed; where 'extremist groups' may stir up tensions over the staging of the Olympics during Ramadan (thereby disadvantaging Muslim athletes); or, the possibility (considered highly unlikely) of any kind of attack by dissident Irish Republican groups.
- Fourth, unanticipated individual or collective acts of disorder. For example, the possibility was explored for a peaceful anti-Olympics protest to attract 'flash mob' crowds. Routine acts of drunkenness and disorder were also anticipated, leading to the need to deploy specialist police units trained for public order incidents, and resulting in turn in 'many arrests'. These potential incidents and challenges provided the 'simulated background' for this security event.

On day two, the next stage for the participants to consider involved 'simulated breaking incidents' which might subsequently occur before and during the Olympics. These incidents were described on sheets of A4 paper passed by their creators (a Sergeant and an Inspector) to specific tables at regular intervals throughout the day. The participants were required to discuss the incident before deciding how they would act or deploy resources. The simulated breaking incidents included the following:

- First, there was a report from the Counter-Terrorism Command of a 'suspect package' being found at an Olympic Training Arena. The package carried a Birmingham address, and consisted of a bag containing a cylindrical object which was both leaking and foul smelling.
- Second, the participants were informed that economic and industrial problems were continuing to beset the UK. A leading trade union announced that strike action was being considered by waste-management and recycling workers. The national economy meanwhile teetered on the brink of further recession. Public sector workers remained opposed to the financial cutbacks imposed by the government a year earlier, and unemployment had spiralled. Both the government and opposition parties were concerned about possible impacts on the Olympics, and sought to persuade all groups that a successful, harmonious and uninterrupted event would be in everyone's interests.
- Third, the impact of Games-related crime was considered. Breaking scenarios pointed to how routine crimes were being exacerbated by professional criminals, so that the police needed to liaise with both public and private partners to restore public confidence. Games and parallel event locations were reporting increased levels of crime, particularly pickpocketing and shop theft by organized groups, predominantly Eastern Europeans. Similar tactics were evident on the London Underground as pickpockets robbed vulnerable tourists. Increased numbers of British Transport Police (BTP) officers were to be deployed at key points. Since the Olympic Opening Ceremony, the Westfield Shopping Centre, adjacent to Olympic Park, had seen a 20 per cent increase in shoplifting; London's major streets had also reported rising levels of shop theft. The areas within the 'Last Mile' of Olympic venues were especially targeted by pickpockets. Incidents of people turning up at the Olympic Park entrance points in possession of counterfeit Olympic tickets had caused some unrest.

Attention was directed at potential crime among Olympic competitors, and the simulated breaking scenarios included an East European Olympic squad being involved in an altercation over athlete drug use, during which a physiotherapist had been threatened. A serious sexual assault was reported within the Olympic Village and a female athlete with head injuries was receiving care; one male suspect had been arrested. The participants recommended that the investigation should be led by police at Olympic Bronze level, media releases should be reviewed, and a community impact assessment drawn up.

Meanwhile, further simulated reports centred on a murder near the route of the men's Olympic cycle race. The participants acted to ensure that, following an expedited search of the crime scene by local police, the route would be reopened approximately one hour before the event was due to begin.

Youth gang tensions were also included in the breaking scenarios, for example through a report from North London of a life-threatening shooting. The participants planned for, variously: one group of officers to investigate; protection measures to be put in place for the hospitalized victim; and various police units to be allocated roles. The impact of industrial strike action was explored, as the scenarios saw police dealing with minor disorder albeit 120 people were temporarily contained, and a police officer had been injured by a lorry driven through a picket line.

Transport issues repeatedly came to the fore. The scenarios saw an HGV lorry involved in a collision, which closed both lanes of an important main road. Its trailer was on fire, and driver trapped while petrol leaked from the vehicle. Unsurprisingly, this inspired the participants to mobilize police, ambulance and the fire brigades. Another breaking incident saw a training run by Italian Olympic cyclists force a car off the road, resulting in severe injuries to the driver. Heavy rainfall and flooding brought delays to travelling spectators driving to an Olympic venue. A member of the British royal family meanwhile was rushed to hospital; the crowds that gathered outside inadvertently blocked part of the Olympic Route Network. Meanwhile, an unmarked police vehicle stolen from outside a property in South West London was discovered to hold accreditation to enter Olympic venues.

These simulated scenarios were designed to ensure that participants considered a wide range of incidents that might occur, and how these would be dealt with 'on the spot' by different levels of command. The participant discussions centred on three wider, highly important themes which, in our analysis, were of major significance for police, emergency and security services planning to host other major events.

First, a recurring comment by the participants at all of the 'Table Tops' was that London 2012 would, for those tasked with policing it, be 'business as usual'. That is, while the London 2012 Olympics was an extraordinary occasion, the actual policing of the event would involve incidents, planning and practices that were, or might be, evident in the capital at many other times. In this sense, 'normal' policing would be in place; and, by implication, the police would be able to respond effectively, or to 'adapt and overcome' with respect to whatever challenge presented itself. As one MPS Commander in charge on the first day stated: 'Nothing will happen that doesn't happen at any other day of year – we deal already with all that could happen' [3]

Second, 'actuarial policing' was to the fore in the discussions. The participants assessed each incident, the associated risks, and their professional responsibilities. The crucial questions during such discussions were: 'Whose issue is it?', and 'Who has the responsibility to deal with it?'. Where appropriate, participants then 'underwrote' that risk, through statements such as: 'I'll take responsibility'; 'The Olympic Command take the risk; 'It's a borough issue not specialist Olympic response'; and, 'That's for LOCOG Last Mile people' for a specific problem, for example, relating to a significant traffic accident, or a crime in the Olympic Village. The principle of the discussion was encapsulated in what we identify as the four 'R's of Olympic policing – Risk, Responsibility, Response and Resourcing – and all were integral to police talk.

Third, a crucial question which arose related to the definition of 'Olympic crime'. This issue was vital as it should, in principle, provide the basis for the allocation of key responsibilities: Olympic crime should fall to the 'Olympic deployment' of police, whereas non-Olympic crime would be the responsibility of other units and forces. But clarity regarding Olympic crime was elusive. A 'restricted document' circulated during the day offered a definition for Olympic crime, as: 'Any crime that has or may have an impact upon the effective delivery or image of the Games'. This vague definition failed to satisfy anyone on the Newham police table as, if tested, the consequences of any fallout could arrive on the desks of Newham police managers. Eventually, the North East Commander with control of the six MPS boroughs in North East London agreed that greater clarity was needed. This raised further questions in terms of: who was responsible for defining whether an incident is 'Olympic' or not? Who was responsible for what was considered unequivocally to be an Olympic crime? And, who must be informed of 'Olympic crimes'? Ultimately, there was no agreed answer to these questions by the end of the day.

The recognition that these ambiguities regarding definition would be reflected on the ground was summed up by the North East Commander who stated: 'Crimes outside (Olympic) venues and at events "policed" by Olympic staff will fall to us (borough policing)'. The fuzzy nature of the physical borders between the Olympic and non-Olympic areas was a complicating factor. For example, scenarios might involve Olympic competitors training in locations well away from the recognized Olympic zones; or, encountering criminal activity in relation to Olympic vehicles, which might be located outside of the Olympic zones, but which could still be considered Olympic-related. In many ways, the definition of 'Olympic-related crime' was up to whoever held the power to demarcate and classify routine crime. As one senior officer also told us, those tasked with delivering the Olympics could define 'Olympic-related crime' in any way that they wanted.

To conclude, the event highlighted a number of critical areas for those planning security around major sporting events, and personalized the roles and responsibilities to be performed during 'Games Time'. It facilitated face-to-face encounters and a degree of ensuing collegiality amongst the participants and their respective units or agencies; suddenly, there was a name and face behind the office and rank of any police officer who attended. Such personalized interactions built links and interdependencies between units and agencies. The event also highlighted the major themes of 'business as usual' within the Olympic context of 'actuarial policing', against a background of increasing ambiguity regarding the meaning of 'Olympic crime'.

While much of this risk assessment was focused on the iconic Olympic Park and stadium, the south of the borough was not being totally ignored. Those responsible for Olympic safety and security at the ExCel Centre in the south of Newham met for the first time at Forest Gate Police Station in January 2012. The ExCel venue was to host seven Olympic and six Paralympic events, which equated to 143 Olympic and 94 Paralympic sessions and 82 Olympic Gold medals, making it the biggest gold medal venue in the history of the Olympics. The venue had an 8,000-strong Games Time workforce including 325 LOCOG paid staff and 3,500 LOCOG volunteers. During the Games 70,000 would enter ExCel daily, and at any one time the maximum spectator numbers would be 30,000. The Last Mile of the approach to the ExCel venue contained all routes for ExCel's three delivery hubs, Canning Town underground and two DLR stations. All visitors to ExCel would progress along a boulevard containing takeaway food concessions and street furniture. Internal ExCel security would be managed by EVS, a private company who already had the security contract.

Security at ExCel was to be directed by LOCOG and involved a fusion of EVS security, G4S, 614 unarmed military personnel and LOCOG volunteers. All vehicles entering ExCel would be subject to a search at one of the two vehicle stops. Pedestrians would be searched by G4S and military. BJ, the LOCOG employee in charge of security in and around the venue explained: 'The army wanted their own command structure but they answer to LOCOG. There's a military liaison officer who works to me and I work to a LOCOG line manager'. This was all news to the Newham police.

Two issues concerned the local police, and both centred on search regimes. A senior Newham officer asked whether vehicles entering the Royal Dock Hotel – located well within the Last Mile – would be subject to searches. The answer was 'no' as no agreement had been made with the hotel. Furthermore the LOCOG rep explained that whilst he was aware that in theory LOCOG was responsible for all security and safety in the Last Mile, in practise commercial premises adjacent to the stadium within the Last Mile circumference would be going about their daily business. Consequently, LOCOG could not secure all Last Mile issues.

There were other issues LOCOG could not secure. The vehicle search regimes LOCOG were working with had a 'safety distance' of just 28 metres. The police in the shape of the Chief Inspector pointed out that they, the MPS, had written CT recommendations that procedures for large trucks had to be, ideally, 400 metres from any public buildings. BJ's response hardly inspired confidence in the ability of LOCOG to contribute effectively to the security of ExCel: 'I'm only four months into this job . . . I've got issues around staffing and you can ask a lot of questions about protocol . . . who agreed what? Well, he's gone – it's changed . . . People are leaving this project like rats off a sinking ship . . . The Venue Security Plan is 1,100 pages long.'

Two final issues that LOCOG had to deal with concerned child safety and responsibility for the waterways. Newham police were concerned that those carrying out searches were CRB-cleared?[4] The response confirmed that the soldiers were certainly not, and the best BJ could offer was that the other security personnel would have undergone Security Industry Accreditation training that required 'disclosure checks'. It was pointed out that venues on Marina Central and the Royal Docks were licensed to serve alcohol until 06.00 hours, and there would be 'all-day drinking for the boating fraternity . . .' a reference to the anticipated arrival of the super yachts of the global rich rumoured at one time to be some 30 vessels.[5] LOCOG had two 'patrol boats' of its own looking to 'share tasks and integrate' with the MPS Marine Unit.

There would be constant negotiations between the Centre and Newham police regarding the prioritization of police resources. The Sergeant employed by the Centre's Olympic Planning Department explained that a council estate in Newham adjacent to the venue would not be policed by dedicated Olympic policing units; they were to be the responsibility of the borough, as would a number of Games-related events and sites.[6] Inside ExCel, the police team would consist of: one Inspector, three Sergeants and 18 officers. The police command structure would see a dedicated (i.e. 24-hour) Superintendent, and two Inspectors and another Inspector (also from Newham) as the equivalent outside of the venue. In addition were the demands made on the MPS (and indeed the UK Government) by the IOC and its proxy LOCOG, as well as the Newham Mayor, the British Transport Police, the Olympic Route Network and the Westfield Mall management. Newham Olympic venues also had their own management and security regimes, and risk of terrorist attack was exacerbated by the imminent arrival of a large delegation of the USA Olympic Squad that would in Games Time be housed in the south of the borough at the University of East London campus, where a Newham Inspector would be posted. The US contingent of 350 training/coaching/admin staff supporting the US athletes would be arriving early in July 2012. Representatives from the USOC (United States Olympic Committee) had conducted a campus survey as early as April 2010, and it emerged that the US Government would not pay for the required police protection. This resulted in a 'vulnerability survey' involving personnel from the [Olympic] Venue Security Development Board and chaired by the Home Office. The Home Office response was that 'user pays'. The main issue for the US officials was response time to a site that was predicted to be the target of disruption and anti-US protests. For the duration of Games Time the US presence at the University of East London was seldom mentioned, and despite the fears of the Americans there were no recorded incidents of 'extremism' directed toward the USA Olympic contingent.

Over a 24-hour period, the ExCel venue would have 70 dedicated MPS officers, and the increasingly chaotic sounding demarcation of policing around ExCel was further compounded by the revelation that the MPS had between 12 and 14 officers in 'RIBs'[7] as an 'overt armed presence' between the hours of 06.00 and 13.00, but they 'couldn't shoot out into the Thames – they're for the docks only'. Inside the venues, LOCOG and the MPS were to have different control rooms in ExCel, which had 350 'internal and external' CCTV cameras; a further 72 had been installed for the Games to be operated by G4S. However, ExCel officers would be using 23 radio channels, and the number of personnel had made it physically impossible for all to share the same control room. With 180 days to the Opening Ceremony, the ExCel-dedicated Newham officer admitted to the researcher that: 'Months ago it was all theirs [LOCOG] . . . now it seems they don't want it, we've got to get protocols sorted out . . . and we need five-ton concrete barriers at vehicle check points to prevent a build-up of speed and a bomb attack'.

The meeting heard that air samples were now regularly being taken in ExCel and at Pontoon Dock as a potential chemical weapons attack on the Games had to be considered. The Games were inspiring imaginative worst case scenarios, and at a Table Top simulation exercise in January 2012, these imaginaries exposed both interagency and internecine tensions.

Table Top 2: riverside exercises

The title of the January 2012 afternoon schedule projected onto the screen of the room in Scotland Yard was 'A Really Bad Day in the River Zone'. This simulation exercise commenced with a scenario involving an armed robber under court escort by G4S being sprung from custody by three armed men who crash their getaway car into a temporary footbridge that connected Greenwich Riverside with Greenwich Park.

The subsequent discussion brought out disputes over: responsibility and ownership, what was considered to be 'local' (i.e. Newham policing) and what was 'LOCOG'. Communications, notably radio frequency, were also an issue, in particular whether one radio frequency would override all others; and protocols, for instance whose helicopters could hover over an incident, and whether MPS helicopters could land in Olympic venues. The latter question raised some consternation when a LOCOG representative explained that some of the venues contained 'temporary structures and 8,000 tons of sand'. The implication was that a helicopter merely in proximity to these venues could be somewhat problematic.

Also unwelcome at Olympic venues was 'guerrilla marketing', in which businesses that were sponsors of neither the London 2012 Olympics nor the IOC would still seek to advertize themselves in relation to the event. Through UK legislation that was passed in 2006, such activity was criminalized but led Newham police to ask why the MPS should carry out LOCOG's 'dirty work'. The group discussion laid bare disputes over 'ownership' of the problem – a recurrent theme in Olympic-related policing – with police officers claiming: 'It's a civil matter – it's not for the police', while LOCOG were understood to be suggesting that this was the responsibility of the local council. For the police, the deliberately vague Public Order Act, was always a fall-back position, to deal with the entire range of crowd disorder, but when the Chair asked ' who would carry out forceful removal from ExCel?', the answer from LOCOG revealed a clear public relations sensitivity: 'The EVS (private security) personnel would be the first but they might then pass it on to LOCOG security, who are military personnel, who would pass it to our police colleagues . . . we don't need footage of students being assaulted by soldiers'. Eventually it was agreed that with regard to 'guerrilla marketing', 'The final call is the Venue Manager', LOCOG would control the imagery emerging from the Games. A maverick comment then came from another MPS Inspector who asked 'What happens if one of the official sponsors sends dozens of people in all wearing the same t- shirt with their logo on it?'. No one knew the answer to that. No one offered an opinion either.

The meeting continued with various scenarios that included medical emergencies, translation facilities, and vulnerable and missing persons. The issue of ownership and responsibility within a contested and confused Olympic domain continued to dominate discussions. For instance, who had the authority to decide what constituted an Olympic 'misper' (missing person)? A suggestion by one MPS officer to place wrist tags on children bearing their name and a contact phone number should they become parted was shot down by one of the LOCOG representatives as 'culturally inappropriate for Arabic and Far East children and families'. Waffling somewhat, he spoke of 'different concepts of child care', and bafflingly cited the Queen of Jordan. It was suspected that his real concern was that search regimes and entry speeds would be completely compromised as a result of the tagging of children.

Table Top 3: riverside channels of responsibility

Entitled 'Readiness Testing and Exercising', the test event for the Riverside Zone, hosted in mid-May in Canary Wharf, attracted over 70 participants and was chaired by a Chief Superintendent from SO3.[8] The aim of the meeting was to clarify roles and responsibilities regarding incident management and multi-event possibilities. The big players in the room, alongside the Chair, were MW (Riverside Gold) and BB (MPS Olympic Gold) and Col. MOD (head of the military personnel deployed to the Games). Both Newham Council personnel and Newham police were present alongside ten officers from other police specialist units. Also present were ten members of LOCOG, and private security companies from ExCel Security, North Greenwich Arena, and Greenwich Park. The Chair explained that the day's purpose was also to remind all of the '3-C' structure of command/co-ordination/communication and concomitant information flows: 'there are 20–30 organisations here today all under different command and control structures'. A variety of simulations followed.

The first scenario addressed the possibility of transport failure that raised the spectre of large numbers of would-be spectators wandering into a local council estate and becoming the victims of crime. The scenario reflected the growing perception in policing circles that particular locals residing in council housing, notably in the south of the borough, may be a feral threat to the Games.

The meeting then turned to military deployments. All Olympic venues except North Greenwich Arena and Lords Cricket Ground would have a 'military contingency force' presence. At its peak this would see 1,000 soldiers located in Greenwich under the orders of the MOD. What came out of the ensuing brief debate was that an Olympic venue could request a military presence, and this request would be considered by the MOD. The matter would then go to COBRA[9] who would in turn pass the matter to MPS Olympic Gold which 'owns the resource'. The only military figure in the room, with the rank of colonel, added what he knew: 'We're doing perimeter security and "rapid search" and we've now got the Olympic Park. I may – or may not – have to attend other Olympic venues. If deployed the soldiers would be subject to military command'. That observation seemed to contradict the assumed supremacy of MPS Olympic Gold.

Another scenario involved a plane crash at City Airport, which initially inspired a well-rehearsed emergency response, but control over this Last Mile incident was further complicated by the possibility of terrorist involvement. This would impact upon London generally, with the possibility of contamination and the viability of ongoing events at ExCel in the light of a large portion of the 'Last Mile' being designated as a crime scene. Towards the end of the day, in response to a question from the floor, one Newham Superintendent made it clear they would be relying substantially on those who already controlled the venues in a most definitive manner: 'The venue manager is God . . . he knows more about the venue than anyone else'.

Table Top 4: riverside at New Scotland Yard

The formal hierarchy of Olympic security was further emphasized at a riverside Table Top in early May 2012, where with 79 days to go before the Opening Ceremony, the Olympic Gold Command met for the last time for a simulation exercise in New Scotland Yard. The ExCel venue had a multiplicity of security managers. One was BJ, LOCOG's head of ExCel Security. Below him were managers representing G4S, the MOD and others. 373 soldiers were to be dedicated to ExCel, hired by LOCOG to conduct searching duties. An ExCel duty manager would also be a permanent presence. An agreement between ExCel and LOCOG meant that staff of the former managed what was termed 'the estate', which meant the six hotels and their 1,500 residents and commercial tenants including restaurants and bars in the ExCel perimeter. This area also 'belonged' to ExCel security who had a dedicated CCTV system,[10] a year-round Counter Terrorism response model, and 80 dedicated security staff tasked in Games Time to support the LOCOG enterprise.

There was some concern in the meeting about the role of soldiers. BJ revealed that there had been a 'unique agreement' between LOCOG and the MOD. Soldiers would be led by two Majors supported by officers holding the rank of Captain and would be effectively working for LOCOG under the instruction of BJ who had ultimate responsibility for the venue. The military would ultimately answer to the General of London who would instruct on a daily basis. The military remit was around vehicle and perimeter security. Soldiers would not be searching pedestrians. As BJ explained, 'It's a living beast. The plans changed three times in the past two weeks. We're working on it. Ideally it's a military and not G4S task, it still needs fine tuning'.

The ExCel Manager stated that 'LOCOG have documents that we've bought into', which in turn provoked an MPS Chief Inspector to state that the MPS 'have had no sight of this'. The LOCOG Manager responded with the news that 'Memos of understanding have been drafted for all venues . . . If there's a serious incident we'll remove the stewards from harm and hand over to the police'. LOCOG were emerging as the ultimate pragmatists.

At this late date responsibilities were still being debated. If transport was disrupted who would control the foot flow both entering and exiting ExCel? Would the task of controlling the flow of Olympic visitors be left to the command of the British Transport Police (BTP)? Would it be a Last Mile issue? The answer from a Newham-based BTP Chief Inspector was that his force and the Docklands Light Railway (DLR) Management had negotiated a demarcation between problems concerning 'flow of people' or 'public safety'. Citing the potential drama that could present itself should people seeking refuge from crushing enter the rail tracks, whom, the Chair asked, would assume responsibility?

The answer from the BTP officer was that his organization would take this on in conjunction with the borough police. The Chair then raised the rhetorical question as to what happens in the event of serious public order: 'At what time do the MPS take over decision-making?' The single answer came from the Newham Chief Inspector who specified, 'When it's a risk to life'. This left a huge range of possible serious scenarios where the MPS would remain subservient to other agencies. Communications were also contentious, as ExCel were using 23 different channels with a maximum of 30 people able to tune in on each frequency. On top of this there would be 951 radios used in the venue and 16 dedicated communications operators.

There were also issues regarding who had the power to check the safety and security of Olympic venues, and to cancel Olympic events if these were considered dangerous. Even this crucial area was ambiguous and subject to a surprising amount of negotiation. Evacuating an Olympic venue would be a big decision, as at full capacity in Games Time the ExCel venue would host 40,000 spectators and staff. One of the ExCel venue managers argued that such a decision had to be taken by ExCel staff as they were the venue license holder. Whilst no one challenged this possibility, the realization of what an evacuation might entail provoked one voice to consider that public space outside the venue would have difficulty accommodating these numbers. One MPS officer deployed to Olympic Venue Planning was particularly concerned about a hotel located within the ExCel's boundary that had a 02.00 bar for residents but with no dedicated security. He considered the spectators for Tai-kwondo, judo, wrestling and boxing as possessing the potential for public order issues, both during and after the event.

The Chair had obviously made some pre-meeting calculations around the venue and revealed now that four Police Support Units (120 police) would be deployed daily to each of the three ExCel zones. One MPS representative responded stating that many police at the venue would be providing Mutual Aid, and therefore would be unfamiliar to London. For him, this situation had 'the potential for disaster . . . I think it could kick off and there's no one around to control it'. The Chair listened and recommended that he would talk 'off-line' to the LOCOG security representative alongside LOCOG venue security and the LBN Chief Inspector. We left the meeting concluding that LOCOG were, yet again, driving much of the security agenda of the 2012 Games.

Table Top 5: The Empress, the bomb and the Last Mile

The final Table Top for the MPS Bronze Command took place in May 2012 in Central London. The main purpose of the day was to analyze Major Incident Training (MIT), and was both a 'major incident refresher' and 'a reminder of the template to work off'. It was also a 'chance to get the Bronze Commands at each venue to get familiar with the procedures and each other'. The Table Top was essentially one story with a few twists. Before the simulation commenced, the room was reminded that the current UK terrorist threat was 'substantial' (i.e. a terrorist attack was a strong possibility), downgraded earlier in the year from 'severe'. The rolling and ever-changing hypothetical scenario concerned a car chase and an abandoned car which provoked a debate, yet again, about the nature of the Last Mile. Crucially nearly all of the London Olympic venues had a working/living population within their Last Mile and so could not be policed as if they were sterile areas. What became clear was that considerable confusion and ambiguity remained over who could do what within Newham's two Last Miles.

According to the scenario, the imaginary car, which had now morphed into a bomb threat, had been abandoned in the Last Mile. As Olympic Park and ExCel venues both had LOCOG and Venue Security Managers, the meeting could not agree upon who had the authority to throw a security cordon over the area when the Games are in play. One Table Top participant queried whether, in many instances, LOCOG were merely 'tenants' to venues that were owned and managed by a variety of companies, and as a consequence may have limited powers.

A significant issue centred on rendezvous points (RVPs) that were to be activated should venues need to be evacuated. A Chief Superintendent explained that everyone should familiarize themselves with a document titled the 'Multi-Agency Template Document', which had a restricted circulation. However, he did not want anyone to take it outside of police premises because: 'It'll get left on a train . . . LOCOG have already lost 10 to 20 laptops with important stuff on them even if none of them have made for a big story yet'.

The bleakness of the Table Top scenario was continued by the speaker explaining the ideal distances that people needed to be from various sizes of explosions. For instance: small object (briefcase/rucksack) 100 metres; medium object (suitcase/cars) 200 metres; large objects (vans /lorries) 400 metees. Present in the room representing Newham were a Chief Inspector and an Inspector. Moments later they were presented by the speaker with a map of the ExCel venue with three concentric squares in red superimposed on the south of the borough from Canning Town to Custom House. The realization of how many homes and businesses were within the 400 metres of the Last Mile left them speechless and shaking their heads slowly while the meeting then considered the emergency response to the car exploding.

Concluding simulations

We have discussed these Table Top simulations in order to present the reader with some of the complexities considered by the MPS in the run-up to the Olympics. The assemblage of control mentioned in the previous chapter is of course still evident, albeit with some different players and agencies and commercial entities. In some of these simulations the Newham public emerge as a threat to the Games, not only as in the case of Westfield where gangs were presented as a major problem requiring special multi-agency measures, but in the southern part of the borough entire estates were regarded as problematic to the multiple reputations hanging on the event's success, as well as to the wellbeing of Olympic visitors. This perception of Newham residents as feral predators who threatened the greatest show on earth, stood in stark contrast to more official representations, such as the 'Saris, samosas and steel bands' (Younge, 2005) that were celebrated on various corporate videos, or the LBN public relations exercises that valorized the inclusion of smiley-faced local residents. Jack London's 'Terrible East' of the early 20th century clearly had been relocated into a 21st-century five-ringed circus.

In so many of these hypothetical scenarios the police, who have responsibility for the safety and security of the civilian population, appeared to be subservient to the needs and requirements of representatives of multifarious Olympic interests, and in particular their accompanying commercial concerns. The police also appeared to come into the frame as a last resort for decision-making and responsibility when the ambiguity of the imagined situation became extreme.

The position of the vocal, media savvy LOCOG, particularly with reference to the no-longer mythical Last Mile, became more of an issue as Games Time crept over the horizon. Responsibility for this strategic space, as we saw in the case of Westfield, was contested by LOCOG and multiple police agencies and squads. Here, and in the case of ExCel, the consequence of making mistakes in the face of a whole range of dreadful scenarios was a daunting prospect. The unspoken conclusion was that while various branches of the commercial security industry, the military, and multiple specialist policing units had designated roles to play in various possible scenarios, gaps in responsibility were inevitable. These interstices were expected to be filled by non-specialist Newham officers.

The traditional hierarchical nature of police work, when faced with the multiple and ever-changing hypothetical scenarios of the Table Top simulation exercises, appeared at times to be both brittle and imprecise and rigid. There were serious question marks over the fitness for purpose of the conglomeration of police units and specialisms coming together for this extraordinary event. As Games Time edged ever closer, these Table Top simulations exposed enormous problems regarding communications, territorial ownership, and of course territorial and agency responsibility. Resolutions were often impossible to achieve. Fingers were being crossed. But in the last resort, it was expected that responsibility would fall to local Newham police.

While local conditions were being exacerbated by new institutions and sites, in common with the expectations generated by police organizational cultures at global level, frontline police officers in Newham were convinced of the inherent criminogenic nature of both the territory and the populace that they were tasked to control. With the Olympics now imminent, these assumptions were being reinforced by incoming police and security agencies. The population of Newham was increasingly regarded as comprised of gang members, thieves, and terrorists: the Olympics were expected to confirm these assumptions and much more. However, beyond the numerous apocalyptic utterances that threatened to build to a summer crescendo, annual leave, parking, shift patterns, and getting to work were not hypothetical concerns, but indicative of a policing *realpolitik* that was evolving as increasingly fraught.

Notes

1 See https://www.gov.uk/emergency-planning-and-preparedness-exercises-and-training.
2 The Olympic route network (ORN) and the Paralympic route network (PRN) is a network of roads linking venues and other key sites in the host city during Games Time. The network features 'games lanes' which are reserved for accredited games and emergency vehicles. For the 2012 Games, the network came into effect under the London Olympic Games and Paralympic Games Act 2006 which gave the Olympic Delivery Authority temporary powers over traffic management measures during the Olympics.
3 It is also worth noting the connotations of the word 'business' here; the police were themselves keen to showcase the world-class standards of 'British Policing PLC' at the Olympics (*Financial Times*, 17 July 2011).
4 CRB refers to the Criminal Records Bureau. All adults working in occupations bringing them into contact with children were required to possess a certificate confirming that the police had checked that they had no record of criminal behaviour that would bar them from working with children.
5 In Games Time vessels which might be considered 'super' actually numbered no more than eight.
6 For instance, the *Pleasure Garden* was an enterprise created specifically for the Games and was partly funded by Newham Council. Located on the site of the long-abandoned dock across the water from the ExCel Centre, it was planned to promote a number of events before and during Games Time. Shortly before the Games began the company that partnered the Council in this venture went into liquidation.
7 Rigid Inflatable Boats.
8 Scenes of Crime Branch/Directorate of Forensic Services.
9 COBRA refers to the crisis response committee set up to co-ordinate the actions of bodies within the UK government in response to national or regional crises, or to events occuring abroad that have major implications for the UK.
10 The venue had 75 perimeter cameras, in addition to 350 cameras inside the building.

6 Policing the boundaries
The heart of the Olympics in Newham

During Games Time, Newham police had their shifts changed, and for the most part policing specialisms were subsumed to the greater good of policing the Games. The major policing fears throughout this period related to the OCZ and the Stratford railway hub, and focused at one end of the scale upon the spectacular, in the shape of a terrorist atrocity, and at the other end of the scale on youth 'gangs', and the management of Olympic spectators. In between these extremes was a vast array of 'unknowns'.

In this chapter, we examine the Olympic-related planning, preparations and activities of Newham police within the immediate Olympic environs of Stratford. In effect, the police approach involved the creation of a distinctive zone of policing within the context of the wider borough of Newham. Our discussion focuses particularly on the prospective risks, problems, and challenges faced by Newham police at the Games. We examine, for example, the Olympic-centred police management of theft and counter-terrorism strategies, the fallout from the farcical collapse of private security provision for the Games (see Chapter 4), possible criminal acts within the Athletes' Village, potential failures of public transport, and the perceived need to police military personnel who provided emergency security cover throughout the event. A recurring issue concerned the often complex and uncertain question as to the demarcation of responsibilities amongst police units for specific incidents.

The borough within a borough

Throughout the Games both the Olympic Park and the Olympic Village had dedicated policing teams with their own command structures, and required accreditation for anyone to enter. Outside of these locations was the OCZ, which was a 'police borough within the borough of Newham': a ring around a mile in circumference around the Olympic Park with its own accredited personnel and command structure, and where responsibilities for policing were effectively removed from the borough police during the Olympics. The task of the officers working within the OCZ was to police the Last Mile around the Olympic Park and their remit covered Westfield Mall and Meridian Square. The OCZ consisted of 140 MPS police officers working a two shift pattern of

06.00–14.00 and 14.00–22.00. The most senior officer was a Superintendent who a year previously had held the post of Acting Chief Superintendent in Newham. His team, effectively the Senior Management Team of the OCZ, was supplemented by an officer from Westfield Mall, and LOCOG's Last Mile non-police 'Event Management Experts'. Although the land belonged to LBN, Meridian Square was under the control of Transport for London (TfL), and a recently retired mid-ranking MPS officer now employed by TfL joined the Senior Management Team. There was a huge amount of ambiguity regarding roles, responsibilities, and managerial hierarchies, inspiring the following rather confusing utterance from the OCZ Superintendent: 'Olympic Bronze has control over non-specialist units at all incidents, and at borough level Olympic Bronze trumps a borough Chief Superintendent; but it shouldn't come to that'.

We were none the wiser. But what became clear as the Games proceeded was that decision-making regarding the management of policing in the OCZ, although appearing to be rigidly codified, was actually relatively fluid and situational, and relied on interpersonal relationships. Decisions were made by an informal group working under the 'Gold' management umbrella, what the Superintendent later called 'A coven of trusted people subordinate to me . . . They'll work at my behest and do what I ask them to do. I've told them their roles and responsibilities and I'm prepared to take pressure off them to keep them from being re-deployed . . . All calls will be directed into a dedicated communication and command system. The "borough" (OCZ) will have an Impact Assessment written to ensure quality provision to the local community. It has a profile of four boroughs so all police working here know what they are dealing with. We'll also have a performance league – same as a borough. Effectively it's a territorial policing response to what is primarily a public order tasking. It's never been done before . . . well, to a lesser degree at [Notting Hill] Carnival, but never done around so many issues and for such duration'.

Negotiations for where the actual boundary of the OCZ ended went on until very late in the day. With only three weeks to go Stratford Park was taken away from the OCZ and passed to Newham Borough police. The two live sites in the borough (Stratford Park and West Ham Park) would be policed on the inside by the centrally organised CO11 (Public Order Operational Command Unit), alongside local officers. A 100-metre footbridge linking Meridian Square to Westfield, once the remit of the British Transport Police (BTP), had been the subject of lengthy negotiations which resulted in it becoming part of the OCZ. Although as part of the Last Mile it was LOCOG's, eventually the OCZ made it their own. Eight days before the Opening Ceremony the Superintendent was able to explain how the OCZ would work and his personal remit: 'Things will go wrong. But we've planned for it. We've got flexibility combined with a set of principles and agreements with partners . . . I've got six boroughs, and I've spent 18 months detailing the policing response for deployment and risk'.

The borough within a borough would have a Games Time remit which would begin at 05.00 hours on July 25 and last until September 10, 2012. The number of police was based on the following calculation: 'Eighteen months ago they asked me what I needed. No one knew then what the demand would be and they don't know now. I thought of a figure and simply added 25 per cent more on top!'. Immediately below the Superintendent were two MPS Chief Inspectors. One he knew well from working with him in Newham, the other whose usual posting was in Central London was barely known to him. In addition there was a Sergeant, highly rated by the Superintendent on account of his capacity to be socially capable and astute about police priorities in pressure situations: 'He can do "relationships"'.

Westfield was a clear bone of contention. With 850 CCTV cameras, its own security personnel and a dedicated Olympic Security Manager, the Mall, as we show in Chapter 4, was taking Olympic-related matters very seriously. Throughout 2012, the mall had attained the status of the highest counter-terrorism risk in the UK, and the Superintendent admitted that Westfield management were 'getting twitchy'. The issues that concerned the dedicated Westfield police were two-fold. First, on the sponsorship of the Olympics by Dow Chemical, a demonstration was planned for 27 July, opposing the role this company was preparing to play in sponsoring a shroud around the Olympic Stadium structure.[1] Second, on the potential for anarchist direct action, as the Superintendent explained: 'One group recently scoped Westfield out and we heard they were looking at throwing furniture around'.

Potential problems varied from terrorists seeking to cause multiple deaths, to those who might spoil the experience of Olympic visitors and spectators, or in some way embarrass the events' organizers or its backers. There were so many unknowns: for instance who might be the intended target of any potential act of terrorism? The Olympic Movement? Some of the 151 Heads of State expected to attend the Stadium in the course of the 17 days? Corporate VIPs? The athletes and implicitly the nations they represented? The potential range of 'at risk' individuals and groups seemed limitless.

Searching questions

There were, however, issues that neither the Superintendent nor anyone else had foreseen. The biggest was the deployment of British Army personnel called up to the Games at a very late stage to operate the search regimes to the Olympic Park. On March 30 2011 the world's largest private security firm, G4S, announced on its website that it had been appointed by LOCOG as the Official Security Services Provider of the London Games. The firm proudly declared it would be 'responsible for recruiting, training and managing the 10,000-strong security workforce tasked with securing the Games alongside police colleagues and local authority personnel across all London competition and non-competition venues'. However, just two weeks before the beginning of the Games, it was announced that because of the shortage of adequately trained G4S staff, 13,500 members of the British Armed Forces would be deployed at various Olympic venues.

Facing a Home Affairs Select Committee in mid-July 2012, G4S Chief Executive Nick Buckles apologized for the debacle and expressed his regret at having committed to the Olympic contract. He also agreed that his company would pay bonuses to the members of the armed forces who made up for the shortfall in G4S staff. This ineptitude cost the firm dearly as the £284 million contract had been projected to glean a £10 million profit. However, in the face of pressure from MPs, Buckles reported that the contract would in fact result in an £88 million loss (Plimmer & Moules 2013). The LOCOG Chair, Lord Coe laid the blame squarely on the shoulders of G4S, arguing 'we were consistently assured they would deliver' (Travis & Gibson 2012). The Chair of the Home Affairs Select Committee, Keith Vaz MP, suggested Coe and LOCOG may have been more attentive to the findings of two reports carried out by Her Majesty's Inspector of Constabulary in the lead up to the Games, one of which had noted that LOCOG's security programme was behind schedule and 'may put aspects of security at the Games at risk' (ibid).[2]

The military were not perceived as a problem; the Superintendent considered them as another level of reassurance for Olympic visitors. They knew their task and were trained in lines of command: 'They've had a very detailed briefing from Olympic Bronze. We've got liaison officers, but time will tell. I've got a list of their pay-days and when they're likely to be out on the piss . . . but I have to say I see them only as a big benefit to what we are trying to achieve'. The task of protecting VIPs and members of the Royal family added to the Superintendent's woes: 'Only at peak times will I be told who might be arriving or in the areas. It's a "Need-to-Know System". I'm fine with that'. There would be diplomatic protection around the gates of the Olympic Park, and police snipers on roofs. Armed support units were always available.[3] Not all police personnel would be visible in the OCZ: 'There'll be a variety of surveillance ops . . . on Romanian pickpockets, East European drug runners, credit card fraudsters, ticket touting'. During the pre-Olympic period the phantom of a foreign criminal threat was never far away.

The Olympics provided an opportunity for various diaspora to air their disputes, potentially before a global audience. A demonstration by members of the UK's Tamil community was planned for West Ham Park on the Sunday following the Friday Opening Ceremony. After a march to Stratford, one of the Tamils had vowed to commence a hunger strike for the duration of the Games. A space for their protest immediately opposite Stratford High Street DLR Station had been identified by Newham Council, and the hunger striker and fellow protestors were to be housed in tents. The march attracted 146 individuals, and as expected, passed off peacefully.

A week before the Opening Ceremony the OCZ Superintendent learned that the UK Prime Minister wanted a room in the Westfield complex for the Cabinet for the duration of the Games. This would bring extra, unplanned security dilemmas. In addition, the Opening Ceremony would involve the arrival of 120 Heads of State, alongside a host of lesser dignitaries travelling to the Olympic Stadium in a fleet of coaches.

In the weeks preceding the beginning of the Games, we spoke with members of the OCZ police about what they feared. Their responses might best be compressed into the following issues:

- Search regimes: could everyone entering the Olympic Park really be searched? If searching was discriminatory what were 'spotters' looking for?
- Vehicle searches: all OCZ officers indicated that total vehicle search regimes would be impossible given the volume of Olympic-accredited vehicles that were to enter the Westfield car park.
- Terrorist attack: all of our respondents stressed that Newham 'had an Islamic footprint'. Some also considered that the potential for an attack from Irish Republican sympathizers was a possibility.[4]
- Bored athletes: From day one of the Olympics an average of 380 athletes a day would be eliminated from competition.Police wondered what the athletes would be doing during the period that remained before they returned home.

There was intelligence that at least ten groups were planning protests around the Opening Ceremony. Some were members of migrant diasporas protesting against the presence at the Games of their home nations' rulers. Others were domestic protest groups unhappy about London hosting the Games. One example of the latter was a group with the title 'Anonymous'. On YouTube, this group posted images featuring a face concealed with a Guy Fawkes mask, otherwise made famous by the Occupy movement, and accompanied by the motto: 'We do not forgive, we do not forget'. A social movement protesting against the global corporatism of the Olympics, their YouTube broadcast invited sympathizers to gather on the day of the Opening Ceremony in West Ham Park from where they threatened to march to the gates of the Olympic Park. However, if they did turn up, they were not noticed and were subsumed by the tens of thousands of Olympic visitors; certainly, we heard no more about them in police circles.

There were others to consider as possibly a public order threat or at least a public nuisance. These were 'ticket touts', whose activities had been rendered illegal by the London Olympic Games and Paralympic Games Act 2006. The Games had not sold out, but some 'blue ribbon' Olympic events were ripe for the touts. The touts' selling sites were expected to be both online and at street level, and the locations with the highest Olympic visitor footfall were likely to be Meridian Square and the Westfield Mall steps.

Jugglers on the Greenway: Olympic transport

This was to be the first-ever public transport Games, and the Olympic Park could lay claim to be the best-ever connected Olympic arena. The venue would daily host up to 345,000 spectators, 270,000 of whom were expected to arrive via overground rail and underground. At its peak the transport system would carry 240,000 passengers per hour, with trains arriving every 13.5 seconds, and to accommodate Games Time demand, there had been a huge investment in the local rail infrastructure. The DLR had three new stations built and made major improvements to three others. There were extensions to the East London Line, and improvements also made to the North London overground line. fifty-eight per cent of Olympic visitors were expected to enter Newham via Stratford Regional Station and

42 per cent would arrive via Stratford International and West Ham tube stations. The *Javelin* train service between St Pancras International and Stratford International would take 25,000 passengers per hour on a journey of just seven minutes. Most significantly, a number of Olympic venues, including ExCel and the cluster on the Olympic Park, relied heavily on the Jubilee Line which was coming to the end of a two-year long upgrade. Overall, the impressive transport infrastructure into which the 2012 Games were embedded carried massive potential for disruption.[5]

The challenge of Olympic-related transport policing was set out by the Chief Constable of the British Transport Police (BTP) at a conference held at the Queen Elizabeth II Conference Centre, and terrorism rather than more mundane system malfunctions were, understandably, his priority. He stated that between 1991 and 2001 there were 60 'terrorist incidents' on the British railway infrastructure, the most notable being the attacks of 7 July and 21 July 2005, before claiming that 'The railway remains the number one terrorist target'. Terrorist threats, the Chief Constable explained, required a proactive response, which could be based on technology or 'police instinct'. The BTP's Pro-Active Counter-Terrorism Unit, with its firearms capability and armed patrols, held a remit to 'deter, reassure and respond', and this would be utilized alongside the Behaviour Analysis Screening System (BAS) that sought out suspicious individuals.[6] However, the police chief later suggested that the most effective tactic was 'Gut reaction of experienced police officers, but putting some science into it . . . looking for clues, unusual behaviour'.[7] The BTP's all year round 'pre-terrorist reconnaissance' and targeted surveillance of individuals had a legal footing, as explained to us by a senior BTP officer: 'Section 47 gives us power to search anyone without reason. We use it more than anyone in the UK and get few complaints'. Ten additional sniffer dogs were to be utilized, increasing the number from 30 to 42. The ramping up of police resources in the build-up to the Olympics was significant and, as noted earlier, a willingness to be proactive, particularly in using intrusive police powers was marked. However, the comparative lack of restraint in dealing with the travelling public was not apparent when it came to protecting commercial interests: 'In the event of an incident the Home Office will shut the motorways; we [BTP] don't do that. We always seek to keep the impact down, because we're aware of the commercial pressures to keep transport systems open'.

The pre-Olympic week was not kind to London train passengers travelling east. On Sunday the North London overground line was temporarily closed. On Monday the Central Line and Jubilee Line were partially closed. On Wednesday there was a Jubilee Line signal failure. Just to add to the general feeling of incompetence, the newly-opened cable car system from Greenwich peninsula to Royal Dock was closed because a wind-sensor had tripped the system. The possibility of transport disruption had produced some 'out of the box' thinking which provoked a degree of ridicule from the BTP Inspector who worked at Stratford: 'The Jubilee Line will fuck up – probably daily. Did you notice it was not advertized as a line to travel to the Games on? The stress on the public is for them to take the District Line to West Ham. The idea is you go there and walk along the Greenway. This idea caused concern during test events – people didn't want to walk the Greenway for various reasons so they've had to "incentivize" the idea. There's plans to have street performers and jugglers on the route, but there's problems with this idea because when the events are over we want people leaving the area as quickly as possible not standing around watching a fuckin' magician'.

During the Games the Stratford transport hub would be policed by one Inspector, three Sergeants and 21 PCs from the BTP. Stratford Station came under the control of the Strategic Command Group led by a BTP Superintendent responsible to the BTP Chief Superintendent who was Head of Operations. In the case of a Games Time emergency in Newham, be it on the DLR or London Underground, the Olympic Bronze Command would make a risk assessment, the most likely outcome of which was 'station control', which was not the same as closing the station but would involve 'filtering' of passengers at various points to clear trains. One month before the opening ceremony a BTP Inspector was very keen to talk about the Last Mile: 'We've had to work hard with the LOCOG Last Mile people. Well, it's 400 metres really, not a mile. They got it in the neck at the test event a few months ago when they were found to be not capable of doing what they're employed to do. They have their own command structure. It's not enough standing around with a sign with a pointy foam hand . . . What we've said is that during the Games we're not doing crowd control in and around the stadium. We've had no input into their training – we weren't asked. That said we obviously have crowd control measures – based on three criteria. If we look along a walking area and can only see above waist-height that's "busy" and of some concern. But if we can only see heads that's "dangerous"'.

Adding to the risky transport context, a crime wave had plagued the South East rail network, and it had Olympic implications. In 2010–2011, the overground and underground railway networks had been disrupted by over 1,000 incidents of theft of signalling cable. While a BTP national metal theft taskforce had seen incidents of theft drop to just 43 instances in 2012, the Olympics had created other opportunities for theft, some of which could be linked to terrorism.

Theft, terror and LOCOG

The LOCOG Uniform Distribution and Accreditation Centre (UDAC) immediately opposite the Star Lane DLR station began its Olympic-related operations in April 2012. During the summer of 2012, LOCOG was responsible for 'approximately 9,000 employees, 70,000 volunteers and indirectly over 150,000 contractors' (Wood, 2013). Everyone working on the Games was required to visit the large warehouse in order to receive their official ID and accreditation bearing a hologram and photo image. Olympic volunteers had to pick up Adidas training shoes, LOCOG- and Adidas-branded T-shirts and waterproofs as well as an Oyster card (enabling London public transport) with up to £300 of travel credit. TfL travel cards to the value of £90 million would be kept on the site. For Newham police, the site was a potential CT target, as well as a possible target for thieves, and despite the presence of several hundred CCTV cameras and 13 G4S security guards on duty 24 hours each day, a large number of laptops had already been stolen. It is open to speculation as to whether these crimes were tagged as 'Olympic related'.

The site was one of over 20 that were visited thrice daily by the CT 'bomb car' that routinely showed up at all Newham locations identified as potential terrorist targets. Although BTP deployed two officers to Star Lane for the first two weeks of the Games, Newham police felt that LOCOG were lax with regard to the CT and crime potential of the site, refusing both to deploy staff at nearby stations to direct future Olympic staff, and to pay £400 per day for a dedicated police officer for the area.

The other indigenous Newham threat

In contradiction to some of the gossip and rumour circulating within Newham police, CT did not believe that Newham's Muslim population in general considered the Games to be problematic. Over the course of their year-long intelligence gathering, just two features of note were found, both on Islamist websites. One site complained that the presence of the Games during Ramadan was an insult to those fasting, while another site viewed the Olympic mascot as insulting. However CT officers retained the belief that 'Newham is the top counter-terrorist interest in the UK'. While the only evidence offered was somewhat thin, and referred to vague associations with crimes, incidents, and investigations beyond Newham, there remained a clear belief that a potential threat to the Games emanated from the local Muslim population.

The fear expressed informally by CT officers was not collective behaviour, but 'susceptible individuals', the lone wolf 'doing a Roshonara Choudhry or an Omar Brookes'.[8] Added to this fear of the 'lone nutter', was that of a Mumbai-style suicide attack involving an armed group storming a building and attempting to kill as many people as possible before being killed by security forces.

Despite these concerns, the culture of constant reorganization within the MPS would have a direct impact on CT planning and expertise within the force. Shortly before the Games, the Newham MPS lead on CT issues learned that he was to be moved from his post in order to lead shifts on normal beat policing. To his chagrin the CT lead's job was being downgraded to a 0.5 position and would be going to an Inspector with less service and no background in CT. The new arrival had also been given another Olympic role, which included the security of LOCOG's Uniform Distribution and Accreditation Centre (UDAC) and negotiations around the security of the post-Games Olympic Park. She had no working knowledge of the borough and would have to learn quickly, for the flow of terrorist-based information was arriving very rapidly.

Local terror

In the build up to the Olympics, CT in Newham consisted of a perplexing array of organizations and units. Meanwhile, the flows of information linked to a number of dedicated operations were hampered by the MPS Specialist Counter-Terrorist Command (SO15) losing experienced officers to retirement in the 18 months prior to the Games. In addition, there was a perception that despite the deluge of CT personnel, the resulting Intel was not being properly shared, and that Central CT interest in Newham would be very temporary. As one Inspector involved in CT explained, 'The OSD [Olympic Security Directorate] get CT information but we [Newham] don't get to know about it. Stuff goes on in this borough . . . which we don't know about. The same will happen in and around the Olympics. Raids will happen. People will get lifted [arrested]. Days after the Closing Ceremony they'll [Specialists CT] be gone..

Newham's counter-terrorist effort was 11-strong; in addition there were SO15 officers in Newham managed by Scotland Yard who submitted their research and intelligence to J-TAC (Joint Terrorist Analysis Centre) who were jointly managed by MI5 and the MPS. Newham was the only London borough with borough-based *Prevent* officers tasked with dealing with the 'pre-criminal' phase of extremism.[9] In 2011 the 'Community Resilience Team' employed two full-time staff funded by Newham Council until the CT specialists of SO15 took over funding in 2012. In 2012 the *Prevent* database consisted of 2000 suspects, 9 per cent of whom were based in Newham. Clearly there was a strong perception within the MPS that there was a significant terrorist 'footprint' in the London Borough of Newham.

Alongside *Prevent*, there was the *Protect* scheme consisting of two Sergeants and two PCs under the command of Scotland Yard's SO20 (Counter Terrorism Protective Security Command), designed to find safe spaces for those withdrawing from their previous involvement in radical activities; *Prepare,* offering contingency planning in relation to worst-case scenarios; and *Channel*, an ACPO forum funded by the Home Office consisting of police and a variety of other mainly public-sector agencies whose remit was 'extremism and radicalization', and people considered 'pre-crim'. Individuals who were profiled by *Channel* in Newham were primarily males understood to be involved in Islamist activity; women and non-Muslims were rarities.[10]

CT operations had been intense and multi-faceted. The most public operation resulted in a house in Stratford being raided shortly before the Games as part of an operation across London where properties in East, West and North London were searched and six people arrested. Three men were arrested in the Stratford raid, and understandably much was made in the media concerning one of the men who was a former Police Community Support Officer who had worked at Stratford police station.[11] Eventually, three British citizens were convicted of planning an attack on the Wiltshire town of Royal Wootton Bassett – a town strongly associated with the British Armed Forces, particularly the repatriation of the bodies of those killed in Afghanistan and Iraq. The long-running operation against the three men was only revealed to senior Newham officers two days before the raid. One Newham-based CT officer explained the tactics and the timing using the following logic: 'They'll say it isn't "Olympic-related" 'cos the Olympics don't want to be spoken of in the same sentence as "terrorism" – but no one believes that . . . Anyway, it's useful. They (the suspects) are in custody and will be for the Games'.

Many local people had been subject to discreet police inquiries. As one Borough CT officer explained, 'There's been extensive vetting of shop staff [in Westfield] . . . Three operations will take place, one later today in fact. There'll be 20–30 people in all held in what is essentially preventive custody. It's an extension of the CT *Disrupt* programme. It's saying "we know you're up to something and whilst we might not get the whole picture we'll take away what we've got" . . . There's been a ramping up around this issue'. In the week preceding the Opening Ceremony, Westfield shoppers were accompanied by uniformed police with semi-automatic rifles in what constituted a clear intensification of armed police deployment in the UK. As one senior officer at SO15 explained, 'We might write a piece that will go in a local or evening newspaper. It'll be about the security guard at Westfield and what his job entails . . . it also tells the "would-be" that there's a number of plain clothes police looking out for unusual behaviour . . . We tested out the deployment of uniformed officers in the Westfield Mall carrying automatic rifles. People see this at airports and are used to it. We didn't know what reaction this would provoke in a shopping mall . . . I deliberately walked 20 metres behind the pair with guns to "clock" the reaction of those they were walking into. I can honestly say no one reacted or seemed to care in the least'.

The British armed services would also have a role. HMS Ocean and HMS Bulwood would be moored in the Thames Estuary; RAF deployments in Weymouth and in RAF Northholt would be on stand-by; and, as a final response to unidentified aircraft approaching restricted zones around Olympic sites, four Rapier missile defence systems and two high-velocity missile systems were to be set up on the roofs of buildings on the periphery of the Olympic Park. Alongside these capabilities were radar systems, specialist observers and military helicopters.

However, when we spoke to one of the MPS Olympic communities liaison officers, a rather more complex tale of Olympic command and control emerged: 'The MOD didn't chat with us [MPS] and they don't "do" petitions or even pretend to talk to protesters. What's not been revealed is the "agreement" between various councils and the MOD. Monies have changed hands and the councils are happy with the deals. It could be argued that such a deployment needs 28 days' notice under planning permission law. What the MOD are going to do is ride over this and at the end of the day they'll say, "Shucks . . . we were wrong; we won't do it again!" . . . The Rapier missiles involve military personnel from both the Army and RAF, but . . . the Command is down to Chris Allison [Olympic Gold]. That said, if it all went wrong and troops were deployed on the streets then we could see the troops subject to an Army Command'.

The day before the Opening Ceremony RAF Tornado jets were scrambled to intercept a plane above London skies that was not communicating with air traffic control. The plane was deemed 'suspicious' and the fighter planes were directed to 'buzz' it (i.e. accompany it and make contact with the captain). The suspicious plane turned out to be a Cook charter flight with either a faulty communications system or a pilot slow to respond to radio requests. Two days before the Opening Ceremony a story spread throughout the Olympic police which was true but 'not to be accredited'. A pilot in one of the MPS helicopters on a night training mission had communicated his frustration at being unable to use the helicopter's sophisticated system to get a 'lock' on a suspicious object in the sky. After a few minutes he realized that he was trying to lock on to the North Star.

Suspicious people: terrorist shadows

Suspicious people on transport of another kind set the tone in the weeks before the Opening Ceremony. Police and the security services were jittery. A passenger coach on the M62 in Lancashire was stopped and surrounded by armed police. The suspects were two young Asian men who had become suspects after their conversation was overheard by a fellow passenger who contacted the police on a mobile phone. The response closed the motorway for three hours. The two males were arrested and later released without charge. In the weeks preceding the Opening Ceremony the ExCel Centre had twice been closed and evacuated because of bomb scares, as had nearby Canary Wharf, the DLR, and other parts of the London Transport system. In addition, there had, according to one CT Sergeant, been 'dozens of examples' of hostile reconnaissance of the Westfield Mall in the course of the past 12 months. But what constituted 'hostile reconnaissance'? 'Taking too great an interest in things which doesn't make sense . . . Why go to a mall with a camera? What do you take images of? . . . Why would you take footage of the CCTV cameras? Or the fire escape? Or the car park? There was a classic one . . . a man hugging the concrete structure whilst his mate took a picture. What's that really about? Sent to those who have other intentions this image indicates the thickness or strength of the structures. Quite useful knowledge if you want to blow it up'.

With 24 hours to go before the Opening Ceremony the police, who as the quote above indicates were getting nervous, felt that everything that could have been done in relation to CT had been done. However, the message from the Newham CT Sergeant had not changed significantly over the previous 18 months: although a 'big one' was not anticipated, the actions of an unknown 'lone wolf' attacker were difficult to predict or counter.

The Army

One new concern for CT police arose when thousands of soldiers, some fresh from active service in the Afghan and Iraqi theatres of war, arrived in Newham. The G4S debacle had required LOCOG and the UK Government to re-deploy military personnel to shore up the search regimes that G4S had recently surrendered. Consequently, in and around the Olympic Park in Games Time there would be some 13,500 British military personnel, mostly in uniform, performing static duties related to Olympic searches.

The military on Olympic duties were mostly billeted outside of Newham. Some were in Tower Hamlets whilst the majority were on the London–Essex borders. Newham had relatively few soldiers staying in its boundaries. What the borough housed, however, was quite strategic. 250 soldiers, billeted at the West Ham Territorial Army HQ consisted of 'the Command Team, Parachute Regiments and Special Forces . . .'. While members of the parachute regiment had general duties, and were highly visible in their uniforms with distinctive berets, the latter were, as explained by the CT officer, a specialist tasking: 'Let's just say that armed responses in and around the Park and Westfield may be given to others as well as the Olympic police . . . Such people make it their job to fit into their surroundings'.

The behaviour of the military when off-duty was the concern of the Royal Military Police (RMP), as the Newham CT Sergeant explained, 'Some have just – and I mean just 48 hours – returned from Afghanistan. They fought daily, maybe lost a buddy and are in the middle of London in a carnival atmosphere and they've just got six month's wages. That means some are carrying £6–8,000 on them. The majority are single, not from London in many instances, and out to get wrecked on alcohol and shag anything they can get their hands on . . . Those based in "white Essex" aren't an issue. They've gone out in Romford, took over a couple of pubs and fitted in . . . that's not going to be so easy in Newham'.

Consequently a degree of 'cultural awareness' for the newly arrived was considered necessary. To this end Newham police met with an Army Major to establish 'a military point of contact should things go wrong', as well as to arrange a seminar for the soldiers on matters of cultural awareness. In evaluating what could go wrong, familiar bogeymen were cited: 'There's soldiers as potential victims don't forget. A squaddie goes to Westfield, gets pissed and trying to find his way to barracks walks through Stratford Park and the Portuguese Mafia see an opportunity to rob him. We'll tell the soldiers to travel in groups and don't leave a mate behind no matter what'.

Certain areas of the borough were to be made 'out of bounds' to the soldiers: 'The safe areas are Stratford and Westfield. There's lots of pubs and people are out and about. We've told them to avoid Green Street . . . I've walked from Upton Park to Forest Gate and in that journey been the only white male on the street . . . don't forget it's the middle of Ramadan . . . Picture it – 8–9 squaddies, short hair, tattoos, bit lairy . . . For many young Asian Muslims they look like the EDL [English Defence League].[12] They could attract comments and that could escalate'.

The issue of ethnicity was not a one-way process. The British military contained officers of Asian origin, and the Sergeant stated that they faced hostile comments from local Asian youths: 'You know "traitor to your faith" and "turn coat"'. If disorder did occur, the Sergeant had a formulaic agreement with the military: 'Army fighting Army equals RMP. Public assault on the Army is an MPS matter. Army assault on a member of police is also MPS. To mitigate such scenarios joint patrols have been carried out in Romford between the RMP and MPS'.

Conclusion

As we have shown in this chapter, Newham police were faced with a variety of shifting challenges and risks in and around Olympic Park. These had multiple potential sources, ranging from local petty criminals, terrorist bombers, disorderly military personnel, visiting athletes, fragilities in public transport systems, and a failing private security company. In both anticipation and response modes, policing strategies and tactics in and around the Olympic Park were required to be adaptable and mobile, as different police units and agencies were designated responsibility for dealing with specific episodes or incidents. Often, these situations were complex, intertwined with multiple interpersonal and institutional protocols that had few, if any, precedents. An array of potential problems were faced by the police responsible for the smooth running of London's transport infrastructure, primarily the railways. The BTP operated in an expensively renovated underground and overground system whose vulnerabilities to routine breakdown were all too obvious to London's commuters, while the network's vulnerability to attack had been made all too apparent in July 2005.

To make sense of the exceptional circumstances relating to the immediate Olympic context, Newham police created a 'borough within a borough', where a mix of police and, as we shall see, private security personnel, worked to interact with a public whose intentions were, on the whole, benign. At the very heart of this operation was Meridian Square, which, on the opening night of the 2012 Olympics, proved to be a significant focus for public and private folly, and for good practice. However, with just a few weeks to spare those concerned with a trouble free Games were reminded of a local and all too tangible threat.

Murder in the mall

Thirty days before the 2012 Opening Ceremony, a 24-year-old man was stabbed to death outside the *Hugo Boss* shop in the Westfield Mall. A resident of the E15 Foyer, the deceased was born and raised in Newham and according to the extensive databases held by both the MPS and local police, he was not a gang member. Shortly before his death he had been celebrating his birthday in the mall when he and three friends encountered three youths standing adjacent to a yoghurt franchise and a verbal altercation ensued that quickly escalated. A carton of yoghurt was thrown followed by glasses and metal stools, before Liam Woodards was stabbed in the chest, staggered out of the mall and died on the street.

The three youths fled, but were found at Stratford Station by seven friends of Woodards who had been shopping in the mall and had learned of the stabbing via mobile phone calls. A fight ensued, two youths were stabbed, and the three sought refuge in the tube system before British Transport Police arrived and made arrests. Dozens of uniformed police and Westfield security personnel descended on the site of the killing where they clashed with friends of Woodards, resulting in two further arrests.

The following day, a Superintendent from the OCD attended a meeting with Newham police, indicating that the killing was considered to have implications for the Games. According to borough police the murder was a consequence of a dispute between Newham and Waltham Forest youths who had links with the Tottenham-based Grey Gang, and the immediate priority was to disrupt any planned retaliation. The chief suspect had an alibi, while seven Newham youths with addresses across the entire borough, were arrested and charged with violent disorder. Five of these young men were remanded in custody, and two bailed to an address in Essex. Only two were on the Gang Matrix.

For Westfield, the killing confirmed the presence of the gang spectre, and the Head of Westfield Security focussed upon the deviant nature of 'gang-style brands' sold in the mall. Westfield were also concerned that publicity regarding the murder would lead to shoppers ignoring Stratford and turning to rival shopping centres. However, the security manager rejected suggestions from the Westfield hierarchy that his staff be issued with stab vests, but did call in additional private security in an attempt to quell any attempted revenge attack in the mall.

The Borough Commander had no reservations concerning the appropriate response: 'Step up reassurance and a Westfield presence. We'll have overt filming of known gang members in the vicinity of Westfield. Step up diversion on known gang members for the next few weeks . . . Target the suspects for the next three days then bring them in if they are doing something that is a threat to the Olympics. They're trying to take over Westfield and that's a reassurance risk to the Olympics'.

Although there was no evidence to support this claim, the GFU Inspector was also adamant: 'This is a gang-related incident with one dead and two stabbings'. Trawls of CCTV revealed what was interpreted as 'Green Gang hand signs', and remarks such as 'this is ours', and 'you're off your patch' were allegedly heard by witnesses. Gang talk was in full flow: 'Woodgrange are disparate and "underground". Warrior Square are organized and can be focussed on'. There were echoes way beyond Newham. In prison on remand, a cousin of Woodards and three other inmates from Newham obtained access to a wing of the prison they were hitherto prohibited from entering and stabbed a youth from Waltham Forest. All four were arrested and placed in segregation.

Police officers from Waltham Forest reported some vague 'Intel' regarding 30 youths gathering to travel to Stratford on the evening of the murder. However, 'They didn't get off there. We don't know what happened'. A Newham Chief Inspector bullishly proclaimed 'We're going on the offensive to prevent revenge and giving reassurance around E15 . . . There's a veiled threat from the PGM to take over other gangs'. The GFU Sergeant laid out a previously unheard of scenario regarding inter-gang co-operation that was reminiscent of the 1979 film *Warriors*: 'After the stabbing all the Green Gang went to Stratford Park. There's cross-gang friendships with the PGM. We believe the PGM direct the Green Gang youngsters to rob. They enter Westfield in groups of two to three . . . Then rendezvous. We're giving Westfield security up-to-date images of suspects for their facial recognition system'. However, while the Intel/Collation Officer tempered the emerging conspiracy theory by explaining 'We've no Intel about retaliation from the PGM', this was not going to hinder the Borough Commander: 'Whether it's drugs, robbery or handling we'll get information for disruption. The TSGs can do warrants. We've got to get it through that the warrant is really about violence and it's got to stop'.

Four days after Woodards' murder the killing was declared by Homicide Command as being unrelated to gangs. Both interviews with the suspects and CCTV evidence suggested that the death was the result of a chance meeting between two groups who were visiting the mall with entirely legitimate motives.

Yet a senior local councillor was insistent: 'It's a gang-related dispute . . . It's another bunch of idiots having a fight . . . My kids won't even go in Westfield'. This view was echoed by the Borough Commander who was unequivocal in maintaining the momentum that had been building against gangs: 'It's damning to the reputation of LBN and Westfield. So . . . let's make sure we are certain as we can be to prevent something like this happening again . . . I'm all for an assertive effort against the Green Gang . . . As we build up to 2012 we don't need this again'.

All of the fears and fantasies regarding gangs as an Olympic threat were confirmed by the murder in the mall. Despite a lack of evidence, the killing triggered a frenzy of anti-gang activity that took the very real problem of youth violence and exaggerated the collaborative potential of local youth groups. As we acknowledge in chapter three, a small number of these collaborations do carry the flag of a named territorial gang, but these, along with other more loose-knit groups, were now badged as a threat to the 2012 Olympics. And that could only be bad for business.

The Westfield security manager had the bit between his teeth, the gang footprint had to be erased: 'We've got the *Evening Standard* ringing us asking if Westfield's a safe place to visit'. This was also a task for public relations professionals, and Newham Council's Communications Officer was keen to step up: 'We've got to represent it (Westfield) as a neutral zone'. But like so many he remained somewhat bemused as to the nature of the problem: 'Anyway what constitutes a "gang"?'.[13]

Notes

1 The protesters considered that it was inappropriate for the company responsible for the Bhopal disaster, where over 15,000 people died, to be an Olympic sponsor. (Pearce & Tombs, 1993. Lapierre & Moro, 2002).

2 The contract with LOCOG included the manning of 1,110 x-ray machines, 1,500 search arches, 300 (plus) 'trace detectors'. The contract included the provision of training modules for both private security and military personnel.

3 There were also at least seven luxury yachts expected to be mooring in the borough's docks, along with two cruise ships moored as floating accommodation for Olympic staff.

4 Automatic number plate registration (ANPR) had been recently installed on the A13 between Dagenham and Canning Town. We were told by a source in Newham Police that the CCTV cameras were to monitor 'average speeds' and not give out tickets for speeding. Together these measures suggest that they had been implemented primarily as a tool for CT vehicle surveillance.

5 The Opening Ceremony would be served by 'an enhanced New Year's Eve service', and the subsequent 18 Games days would see the underground system running an hour later into the night than normal. All officers employed by the BTP had received training which would allow them to go onto the rail tracks in an emergency. Another

350 officers drawn from Mutual Aid would undergo Track Safety Awareness Training, allowing them to go onto rail tracks accompanied by BTP officers.

6 This system was based upon an Israeli model that had been devised to detect potential suicide bombers. For a critique of BASS see Silke (2011: 7).

7 The potential for the disruption of the rail network was enormous. The BTP response model worked with bomb threats at Category 1 level which would see the closure and evacuation of the station. The Category 2 response would not result in closure. As a consequence of a 2012 £14 million upgrade, 33,000 CCTV cameras were installed for the benefit of 16 rail operators.

8 The former, was a 20-year-old Bengali-born woman living in Tower Hamlets, East London who in 2010 entered the surgery of Tower Hamlets MP Stephen Timms and stabbed him. Omar Brookes (Abu Izzadeen) a resident of Hackney, received prison sentences for terrorist fund-raising and for inciting terrorism overseas. (*BBC News*, 17 April 2008).

9 *Prevent* began in 2007 in response to the 7/7 (2005) bombing of the London Transport system. Government Officers for London (GOL) was responsible for the delivery of CT programmes under the Labour Government up until 2010. The subsequent Coalition government from 2015 changed this arrangement, and the Minister for London tasked local authorities to deliver their *Prevent* programme according to local sensitivities. What was known as *Prevent* II began in May 2011, and involved liaising with various agencies – schools, universities, social services, prisons and police – to discuss, and if need be intervene and engage in various ways with individuals and groups who were considered 'extremists'.

10 This was not the case outside of Newham where *Channel* interventions were used for white teenagers associating with the Far Right.

11 See the story headlined 'Former PCSO among six arrested in anti-terror raids across London', (the *Independent*, 5 July 2012).

12 An anti-Muslim social movement which had held demonstrations in English cities (Garland & Treadwell, 2012).

13 In April 2014, after a three-month retrial, a 19-year-old Hackney man was convicted of Liam Woodards murder and sentenced to a minimum of 18 years in prison.

References

Garland, J. & Treadwell, J. (2012) 'The New Politics of Hate? An Assessment of the Appeal of the English Defence League Amongst Disadvantaged White Working- Class Communities in England', *Journal of Hate Studies*, *10*(1): 99–122.

Lapierre, D. & Moro, J. (2002) *Five Past Midnight at Bhopal.* New York: Warner Bros.

Pearce, F. & Tombs, S. (1993) '*US Capital versus the Third World: Union Carbide and Bhopal*', in Pearce, F. & Woodiwiss, M. (eds) *Global Crime Connections.* London: Macmillan.

Plimmer, G. & Moules, J. (2013) 'G4S takes £88m hit for Olympics fiasco', *Financial Times*, February.

Silke, A. (2011) 'The Psychology of Counter-Terrorism: Critical Issues and Challenges', in Silke, A (ed) *The Psychology of Counter-Terrorism.* Abingdon: Routledge.

Travis, A. & Gibson, O. (2012) 'G4S failed to understand size of Olympic job, says Lord Coe', The *Guardian*, September 11.

Wood, N. (2013) 'Where did LOCOG go?', *Management Today*, September 6.

7 The Opening Ceremony
Police strategies

Outside of Stratford Park on the night of the Opening Ceremony, a member of Newham Council's Enforcement Team excitedly approached a senior officer and loudly informed him that according to a radio message just transmitted: 'The Portuguese Mafia have just got on a bus in East Ham and are heading for Stratford'. The officer smiled, and politely thanked the breathless officer before returning to his task of overseeing the only significant crowds that Stratford Park would see during Games Time.

In July 2012, the public geography of Stratford changed complexion. Whilst construction workers put in 13-hour shifts to rectify 'slippage', local businesses were anticipating a lucrative Olympics. In the previous ten weeks Turkish and Lebanese restaurants had opened on the High Street, and in the Stratford Mall a shop that once sold cheap women's clothes re-opened in late June as a coffee outlet complete with roped-off *al fresco* areas. Meridian Square was being cleared of its commercial occupants, and in May 2012 the council instructed the 'Tuk-Tuk' coffee seller to relocate to the rear doors of the Stratford Mall, while the burger and flower stalls were also told to move. Immovable structures were superficially transformed. The bridge linking Meridian Square to Westfield Mall was covered in its entire length with corporate images of the Coca Cola Company, concealing, through its previously clear window panels, views of Stratford and the immediate neighbourhood. The monstrous 16-storey Morgan House that overlooked Meridian Square was similarly concealed top to bottom by advertisements for BMW. A 20-storey council housing block had its gable end covered in a huge advert for Gillette, whilst an Adidas advertisement graced another similar building. A 50-piece titanium sculpture known as *The Shoal* was wrapped around the façade of the Stratford Mall, making the view from the Westfield stairs onto 'old Stratford' a frankly surreal experience.

Elsewhere, changes in the Square had been subtle, but purposeful. A steam engine monument had been moved to fit in with 70 cylindrical metal barriers and bound stone structures which were accompanied by 50 standing stone structures. This 'street furniture' would channel and facilitate the foot-fall of Olympic visitors, and also serve as obstacles to any attempt at a vehicle-born terrorist attack in the Square.[1]

The morning of the Opening Ceremony brought heavy rain showers, and Westfield was host to dozens of camera crews as athletes wandered the mall in full national squad livery pretending not to be noticed. From midday onwards police who were deployed in groups in Meridian Square were constantly distracted by tourist requests for joint photographs, the half-dozen mounted officers being particularly popular. At around 17.00 hours, 22 MPS officers carrying semi-automatic rifles exited Westfield into the Square where they dispersed to a variety of pre-arranged deployments.

By late afternoon the square had been colonized by a dozen religious and other groups. At one time a stall selling memorabilia for the *Help for Heroes* British Military war-wounded stood adjacent to six men in Islamic robes from 'Team Silver'. By 17.00, leaflets were being distributed by a middle-aged African man carrying a large wooden cross, and by two Catholic Benedictine monks wearing cassocks. A twenty-strong group of female American Evangelists sang while distributing bibles.

Less than a mile away Stratford Park was being prepared for an anticipated 6,000 crowd to watch the Opening Ceremony on a large TV screen. Private security guards searched everyone entering the park, while uniformed MPS officers stood by. A temporary 12-foot-high metal barrier had been erected inside the park's perimeter fencing, and a 10-foot-wide 'moat' was positioned between the fence and the park's perimeter wall and railings in an attempt to prevent anyone attempting to gain entrance other than by the heavily guarded gates. Days earlier some rather incongruous banners were attached to the park railings by Newham Council workers: 'Free school meals for Newham Primary schools', 'Free swimming for Under-16s and Over-60s', and 'Free Bulk Item Collection'. School pupils were by now on their summer holidays; the last swimming pool in Newham had recently been closed down as part of nationwide cutbacks on public services; and, the disposal of redundant refrigerators and mattresses may not have been high on the list of priorities of those seeking Olympic thrills.

Crowds began to accumulate in Meridian Square from 16.00hrs, and by 18.00 there were three groups of singers accompanied by drummers. Some would-be spectators wandered the square, seeking to buy tickets for the Opening Ceremony. Four Pearly Kings and Queens – in the carnival dress of a long-gone white, working-class London – appeared in full sequined splendour.[2] At the crossing between Stratford Mall and Meridian Square sat a middle-aged African man with a homemade placard proclaiming: 'McQueen Killed by Freemasons: Royal Head Freemason'.

Opening Ceremony: the countdown

The Opening Ceremony briefing for the various police units had taken place in public at the foot of the Westfield Mall stairway in the late afternoon. The thousands leaving or entering the mall saw a huddle of PSU lead officers, most with the rank of Sergeant, and some Inspectors from both MPS and Mutual Aid forces. Close by was the heavy-set personnel of Mc-A private security who, employed by

TfL, formed a cordon across the foot of the stairway to act as a 'filter' for the crush of crowds going up and down the stairs. The officers who surrounded the OCZ Chief Inspector were quickly briefed on the five locations that required special attention; issues of risk in general, and risk in relation to reputations, were deeply embedded in these instructions.

1   Bow flyover: 0.5 miles from the briefing was the road junction where those classified as 'VVIP' would be travelling under police escort. This was where the boundary of the Newham borough began and where half a dozen PSU units were deployed. The instruction was simple: 'Lose it [control of access] and there's a lot lost . . . there are contingencies to re-route the convoys if need be'.
2   Stratford Bus Garage: While the policing presence on this location was very obvious, the volume of passengers on the 134 buses an hour that passed through it meant that more police would always be useful. The instruction was: 'High visibility at the back end of the station' – where the bus terminus met the railway station.
3   Angel Lane to the bus garage: The threat here was specifically terrorism – 'The area required high-vis counter-terrorist mitigation. Anyone wheels up with a bike and leaves it . . . anyone drops something there get onto it'.
4   Westfield stairs to first mezzanine: The issue here was stopping protest – 'Private security and Westfield security will stop people without accreditation. But if someone gets in and wants to create public disorder – maybe Fathers for Justice - deal with it'.
5   Public disorder (Westfield): A PSU was deployed on the Westfield Bridge as a 'mobile patrol'.

There were four additional issues that the Inspector brought to the briefing group's attention, again with a particular emphasis on risk and reputation:

a   Protest (what to permit, what to use): 'Gold have instructed that as long as it's peaceful and lawful we facilitate it and don't get involved. If it interferes with procedures we'll make that decision . . . Record what you do. Paint the picture of who did what and what we did. Protect ourselves and our reputation . . . Remember this: the decision you make around this might come back to you in two years' time. Act responsibly tonight because what you considered "reasonable" in the middle of an Opening Ceremony – in the cold light of day at a Tribunal in two years – might be considered differently'.
b   Bump-out (the emptying of the Olympic Stadium and Park): 'There are three ways off the park and these lead to two conduits for trains and taxis. Get out there at this time, be visible and reassure. The "pulse" will be controlled by the Last Mile people . . . This didn't work as planned on Wednesday night [the second test event] but they [the audience] were nice people and took it in their stride. It could be raining tonight' (suggesting inclement weather would dampen the mood).

c   Contingencies (around both space and personnel): 'If things go wrong we block the road (Stratford Circus) at both ends. That's obviously a last resort. We'd create a sterile area. Then we can open the gates to Angel Lane and if needs be can hold 5,000 people behind in the land behind the taxi rank. Another contingency – if there's a Westfield issue . . . Mutual Aid- PSU are halfway up the stairs and across the bridge. The other side of the mall will be taken by the Met'.

d   Charge/srrest (demarcations of classification): 'If you arrest anyone you report it. You'll be asked whether it's a "local issue" or an "Olympic-related" one. Depending on your answer you'll be directed as to where to take him'.

A final plea came from the Chief Inspector: 'Remember, this will never happen again. Tonight is history – the biggest UK police operation in history. You are part of it, you are making it. Be visible, be polite, keep to what you've been told. It's what we do best – understated efficiency'.

Stairs and lights: powers and procedures

By 1800 hours the square contained a few thousand revellers, most of whom stood around waiting for something to happen, while the adjacent bus terminal and train station disgorged hundreds of business-as-usual commuters and Olympic visitors every few minutes. A key police task inside the OCZ included securing the Westfield stairway, an undertaking that involved 70 police officers in addition to Westfield Security (20 plus), British Transport Police (20 plus), LOCOG Last Mile Security (20 plus), McKenzie-Anderson (Mc-A) Private Security (24), and Council Enforcement officers (10 plus). There were no shortages of personnel ready to control any aberrant behaviour.

For the duration of the Games, the Olympic Park was the most heavily policed area in the UK. On the Westfield stairs were six agencies 'policing' the entrance to the mall and implicitly the entrance of some 70 per cent of Olympic visitors to the park and the Opening Ceremony. One individual working for Westfield Mall held a megaphone and, addressing the crowd in the square, told them repeatedly to 'Leave the area . . . it will be very busy later'. No one left. As the crowds got bigger the tannoy exhortations to leave got louder and more repetitive. No one was leaving, but no one was sure what there was to see. Police intelligence via radio meanwhile revealed at 19.00 hours that a 'flash mob' (origin and purpose not specified) might attempt to enter the mall via the stairs. Those in the OCZ responsible for the stairs, while chatting informally, agreed that if they – whoever they were – appeared they were not to get onto the steps and would be 'beaten back' if they attempted to do so. The flash mob never appeared. But, for its protectors, the Westfield stairs had clearly acquired a symbolic significance. The atmosphere was tense.

The Opening Ceremony was to begin at 20.00 hours and with two hours to go the OCZ police had not been fully informed as to who should be entering Westfield. Even before 16.00 hours those with tickets for the Opening Ceremony had begun to arrive. Some were renowned ex-athletes, and some were celebrities. Others attending were less recognizable; all were formally dressed. The OCZ police were understandably confused as nobody seemed to have been tasked with checking Olympic accreditation. The police claimed that this was not a task for them. Apparently neither was it a job for BTP, or for Westfield security. It was an Olympic event within LOCOG's Last Mile. But the LOCOG staff were not checking tickets. Consequently, any exclusionary 'policing' was somewhat arbitrary. This situation was compounded by Stratford Underground Station disgorging hundreds of train passengers every few minutes who then walked to Meridian Square, and up the Westfield steps and into the mall. Some had tickets for the Opening Ceremony, others did not. Meanwhile, at the other end of the mall, Stratford International Station was also delivering ticket holders, non-ticket holders, curious tourists, homeward-bound commuters and other passengers every few minutes. Most of these also made their way into the mall, where some of the businesses remained open.

Most shops had been instructed by Westfield Management to close for business at 16.00 hours. This instruction was not well received. However, by 16.15 hours, although most of the shops had closed, the food outlets, both fast-food and high-end bars, ignored the instruction and in the case of the latter were honouring table bookings made months previously from people who were to attend the Opening Ceremony. A further problem was that Westfield mall had two hotels (with 2,000 beds) and a 24-hour casino-nightclub. How could people, many of them Olympic visitors and indeed Olympic officials, be denied access to facilities that they had paid for? Another problem was that whilst the retail stores had closed, staff were in many instances kept on for stock taking. Ideally, from a policing point of view, all staff would have gone home by 16.30 hours, but thousands remained in situ and left via the mall at various times throughout the evening. Some left work only to call into Westfield bars and restaurants.

Five days after the Opening Ceremony the confusion over whether Westfield should have been off-limits to the public that evening was discussed in the OCZ 'Morning Prayers' (daily police unit meeting). The conversation was instigated by a mid-ranking CT officer who admitted that he had received a 'bollocking' from his line management in the Centre who were adamant that their instructions stated that the mall should be closed to the public and only those with Opening Ceremony tickets be admitted. The meeting discussed how thousands had entered the mall on their way to the Olympic Stadium, but also to enter the hotels, the dozens of restaurants and the casino in the Westfield complex. The meeting surmized that commercial considerations generated by many Westfield businesses, the LOCOG hospitality events in the mall and hotels had produced a change of policy, which in turn had led to a decision to over-ride the police (Fussey, 2014: 11). However, no one had sought to convey the decision to the officers in the OCZ who were tasked with controlling the Last Mile.

Securing the Opening Ceremony

The policing issues were: Who could decide who were 'accredited'[3] and 'appropriate' guests permitted to go up the stairs, and who should not be allowed to take this route? The two dozen private security personnel from Mc-A, each working a 12-hour shift, proved integral to both the Opening Ceremony and the subsequent 17 days of the Olympics. Contracted by TfL and taking instruction from a former MPS officer, who had recently retired from the police and now worked for TfL, the men (and two women) from Mc-A were the most muscular of all security in the area. When not involved in Olympic duties they were, in the words of the person who hired them, 'pub bouncers and cage fighters'. Obviously glad of the work, which saw them dealing with a pleasant, mainly sober and compliant public, they took responsibility for deciding who could enter. We witnessed no one seriously challenge any decision made by the Mc-A staff. Those displaying Olympic accreditation were directed by Mc-A staff to three supervisor colleagues standing at the bottom of the escalator from Meridian Square to the top of the stairs. This 'channel of access' saw the three check the accreditation, and direct the carrier up the Westfield stairway escalator. In case anyone unwanted slipped through, the top of the escalator was manned by MPS personnel. Yoko Ono, Jackie Chan, Peter Gabriel and other 'celebrities' all followed this route. The Mc-A staff also took control of the pedestrian crossing, which was part of the Olympic Route Network (and therefore officially a LOCOG duty) thereby making the passage of the thousands of vehicles and tens of thousands of pedestrians per hour unproblematic. The Mc-A personnel carried out this task for the duration of the Games, and during the course of the Games their numbers employed in Meridian Square doubled.

The Square received unexpected visitors at 20.30 hours, arriving mostly on bicycles with a few on skateboards. Numbering over 200, this gathering of the cycling movement Critical Mass approached at speed and with some members broadcasting music from speakers strapped to their cycles,[4] while dozens of others were blowing whistles. Entering the bus station they completed a lap of its platforms then left to re-join the Stratford Circus dual carriageway. They then performed another lap of the bus station before leaving. Their arrival received applause and whoops of appreciation from those assembled in the square, but minutes later, half a mile from Stratford, and just outside the OCZ, the cyclists were corralled into a side street by 14 police vans. 182 were arrested, and just four were subsequently charged.[5] The intervention attracted widespread coverage across the UK media, which highlighted in part the low numbers of those charged, while some cyclists and onlookers were quick to upload videos of the episode.[6]

Those attending the Opening Ceremony were all in their seats by 21.00 hours. The thousands in the square however did not disperse. After five hours the megaphone was still being employed, imploring people to leave the densely packed square. Near the bottom of Westfield steps was a large electronic billboard. Owned and controlled by Westfield, its messages were pre-programmed and focused upon promoting the mall and the Games' sponsors, as well as providing Games information. Many waiting in the square wrongly believed that the screen would soon show the Opening Ceremony. The OCZ police were concerned about the size of the growing crowd and wanted either a message telling the crowd to disperse to be broadcast or for the screen to be switched off in its entirety.

A series of conversations ensued on the steps involving the OCZ, Westfield Security, BTP, and others for some 15 minutes. There was concern that, if the screen was turned off, Westfield or the Games' sponsors would sue the MPS. Any message telling the crowd to disperse had to be agreed with Westfield, and it was doubtful that anyone with the appropriate authority or expertise was available. Even if such a facility was available, what was the message to be? As a commercial entity, would the mall want people to leave the area? Was there really the capacity at the local live sites for thousands of late arrivals? Finally came some logistical questions. Who had the authority to utilize the facility? How could that person be contacted?

The Head of the council-funded Enforcement Team, having listened to the cluster of officers and officials discussing the matter, stepped away from the group, opened his mobile and, speaking directly to the Westfield Head of Olympic Security, asked him for a favour. The latter knew the caller who similarly had retired after a 30-year MPS police career, and the favour was to turn the screen off. The request was agreed without further discussion and the screen went blank. The crowd dispersed, and religious groups dominated Meridian Square for the remainder of the 2012 Olympic Games.

Conclusion

In liminal and 'threshold' spaces such as Meridian Square, it is difficult for those charged with social control to predict behaviour. The day of the Opening Ceremony provided senior officers with an opportunity to set out how they anticipated the policing of the 2012 Games would be played out. Public order was clearly a concern, and apart from the sheer density of the public and the issue of checking Olympic accreditation, the major social activity within the square, which fell within the Olympic regulations, centred on this unanticipated proliferation of diverse religious groups singing, leafleting, and discoursing on their respective faiths. We would suggest that, in these liminal spaces at sport mega-events, the police, while continuing to 'plan for the worst', need to address more everyday activities, while allowing for the unexpected such as the presence of diverse faith groups or the sudden appearance of a large group of cyclists. The mass arrests of participants in 'Critical Mass' was a huge public relations mistake, not to mention a facile over-reaction that exposed some of the tensions amongst the police. Commercial interests were not shy in flexing their muscles, and LOCOG were yet again an ambiguous presence whose Last Mile responsibilities were largely swerved. The night of the Opening Ceremony was tense. Nobody was sure how the policing of the Games would unfold.

Notes

1 In and around Meridian Square during Games Time there were also hundreds of Olympic Ambassadors, most wearing uniforms of beige trousers and maroon T-shirts, and all festooned with official accreditation including a photograph of the wearer and their

name on a laminated card which hung around the neck. The ribbon that the card hung on also contained the 2012 motif and the name of its sponsor – ATOS. This French-based company had over the previous two years worked on a UK Government contract to reduce the number of people claiming sickness and invalidity benefits. Various campaign groups – including disability rights groups – were to point in particular to the Orwellian irony of having ATOS as a sponsor of the Paralympics.

2 Pearly Kings and Queens are men and women dressed in traditional Costermonger attire. They are prominent charity fundraisers in the London area.

3 'Accredited' meant those residing in the Westfield hotels, those with Olympic Park passes, and those with tickets for the Opening Ceremony.

4 Critical Mass are an informal social gathering of cyclists who meet in London in order to cycle an unplanned route in relative safety; earlier police attempts to closely regulate and potentially to ban these gatherings were rejected by the courts on the grounds that the rides are a 'customary' rather than 'planned' procession (The *Guardian*, 26 November 2008).

5 See the *Independent* (29 July 2012). 48 hours later it emerged that the cyclists had almost blocked the Bow flyover and delayed the arrival at the Opening Ceremony of the Queen. This was relayed to us as a justification for the mass arrests. Informally many Newham police summed the arrests as being an example of 'the Met going over the top'.

6 See for example the *Guardian* (30 July 2012), The *Independent* (29 July 2012).

Reference

Fussey, P. (2014) 'Command, Control and Contestation: negotiating security at the London 2012 Olympics', *The Geographical Journal*, advance publication DOI: 10.1111/geoj.12058.

8 Stratford's big sports day
The Games

In the words of one Newham police officer the Olympics were, 'the revenge of middle England' after the 2011 riots. Despite the presence of thousands of overseas visitors the spectators who flocked to the 2012 Games were largely white, well-behaved, patient and mildly excited. Aside for the odd sight of a middle-aged male in a tight-fitting onesie in patriotic colours, any sense of carnival was limited to the waving of Union Jack flags and wearing heavily logoed official merchandise. Spectators came into contact with uniformed Games volunteers at transport hubs around London who directed them to the various event venues. For months Londoners had been warned by the government to avoid the capital during Games Time, although London Mayor Boris Johnson, in a booming recorded address that echoed across the capital's overground stations, was keen to keep the city working:

> Hi folks! This is the Mayor here. This is the greatest moment in the life of London for 50 years. We're welcoming more than a million people a day to our city and there is going to be huge pressure on the transport network. Don't get caught out. Get online and plan your journey at GetAheadoftheGames.com.

Many Londoners got out of town, took time off, worked from home and generally avoided a city that was expected to break down due to overcrowding.[1] Consequently, during Games Time the centre of London resembled three weeks of Sundays. It was empty, quiet and a little bewildered as spectators travelled in to mainline stations, caught the underground to the venue and repeated the trip in reverse when their ticketed event was completed. Incredibly, the transport system worked efficiently and effectively, and crowds whose class, ethnicity and demeanour resembled that found at the All England tennis tournament at Wimbledon, arrived at their destinations to be greeted by still more smiling Olympic volunteers. The 70,000 'Games Makers' bore the brunt of directing, cajoling and welcoming these visitors across the 34 separate Olympic venues, but also were involved in transporting athletes, helping out behind the scenes in the technology team and making sure that results were displayed quickly and accurately. One poor soul, resplendent in his purple and red uniform, spent an inordinate amount of Games Time in the public lavatory at Waterloo station distributing change for the turnstile.

At West Ham Station the foam-finger-wearing volunteers channelled spectators onto the Greenway and along to the stadium. Police presence was minimal in one of the few sites where spectators could sample local culture in the form of a couple of grateful shops opposite the station. At Stratford, most spectators were filtered through Westfield to the Olympic Park and never set foot onto the streets of Newham. After opening night, few even entered the Stratford Mall, to the cost and chagrin of shopkeepers and stallholders who had prepared for a bonanza.

> I was told to treat the three weeks of the Olympics like the three weeks leading up to Christmas. I had extra staff, arranged overtime and longer opening. Waste of time, look at it. Dead. I am closing early, sending people home.
>
> (Manager, national chain store)

> A lot of regular customers have gone on holiday, stayed away because of the Olympics. That's all you heard about, crowds, and crush and that. Nobody here.
>
> (Stallholder)

> I reckon two thirds of my trade is people who commute here (Stratford) to work. They come out at lunchtime and during the day to do a bit of shopping. They have all gone on holiday to avoid the crowds. Business is shot.
>
> (Stallholder)

Few spectators had any interest in venturing beyond the Olympic Park, and those who did seldom got further than Meridian Square, where the cacophony of religious enthusiasts touting their wares tended to drive them back to Westfield and the delights of the crowded food hall.

The Olympic faith-off

During the Olympics, Meridian Square was a very busy and complex public space located in-between the inner and outer Olympic areas: not inside the Olympic Park, Westfield Mall or Stratford station, but very much at the policing centre of the OCZ. The square was where thousands of Olympic visitors, and many media people, accredited Olympic officials, as well as the manifold police and security personnel, would interact before drifting off, heading into Westfield and, for many, into the Olympic Park.

Falling under OCZ regulations, the square also involved strict restrictions on the advertizing or sale of goods and services. There were a number of well-ordered demonstrations (Fussey, 2014: 8), but religious proselytizing was in full flow, peaking at some 46 different faith groups during the Games. The overwhelming majority were Christian Evangelical and Pentecostal followed by more orthodox Christians (Catholic and Protestant), followed by Islamic groups, Buddhists and those of Judaic persuasion. Mormons and Hare Krishna followers also made an appearance. Spoken messages and leaflets exhorted all to reconsider their relationship with their God, to consult websites and attend future meetings. The groups were respectful of each other and did not engage in inter-faith arguments or contests.

The police did not anticipate the arrival of these faith-related groups at the Games. Such a possibility was never discussed in any pre-Olympic meetings. Some groups had become a well-established daily pre-Olympic presence in the square and nearby mall. The Games (and their audiences) exacerbated the levels of preaching (one group hired a shop unit in Stratford), but most were there because of the exceptional flow of people in a significant pedestrian bottleneck.

Some groups had musical instruments, while some Christian groups stood still and could barely force a smile as they promoted a not very attractive salvation in the next life. Some wore t-shirts with slogans and others wore clothing that indicated a more sombre religious approach. The preaching usually began around midday and lasted until the early evening. Invariably orderly and good natured the message was at times delivered by an individual and at other times by groups numbering up to two dozen. At times the pamphlets were slick and commercially produced, while at other times the document was clearly homemade and photocopied.

Not everyone was happy with the situation in Meridian Square, and Westfield Management sought reassurance from the OCZ that no faith group would be tolerated on the bridge. The police meanwhile 'higher than Bronze' ignored a request from one very senior officer in Newham Council (police would not reveal the source) to clear the area of Islamic groups. To do so, the MPS argued, would be discriminatory.

Olympic threat or dancing priest?

This spirit of toleration on behalf of the police, if not the council, was tested further when Meridian Square hosted the notorious Father Horan. Horan was, according to the MPS Olympic Intelligence Team, a potential threat to the Games, carrying the potential to disrupt. Consequently, they had visited his London home ahead of the Games and negotiated with him; while banned from the Olympic Stadium, he was free to visit Stratford. On the day he was to visit, his movements were known as soon as he left his home, uniformed OCZ police met him at Stratford Station, and a Chief Inspector made it his business to become acquainted.

Horan was a defrocked Irish-born Roman Catholic Priest notorious for his disruption of sporting events. Ordained in 1973, he belonged to the Apostolic Fellowship of Christ,[2] believing that Jesus would return to rule from Jerusalem in a world where 'there will be two classes of people: "immortal saints", who will rule a world government for 1,000 years from Jerusalem, and "mortal citizens", who will become "adopted Jews" and live for 900 years'. More importantly, Horan was attracted to sporting mega-events. On July 20, 2003, he ran onto the Formula 1 British Grand Prix track at Silverstone, waving a banner and forcing several drivers to swerve to avoid him on the 200mph Hangar Straight, for which he received a two-month custodial sentence. A year later Horan visited the Athens

Olympics, and at the 22-mile point of the men's marathon he bundled into the race leader, depriving him of the lead, and as a consequence was given a 12-month suspended sentence. Later that year, Horan was defrocked from the priesthood shortly after being found not guilty of a sexual offence involving a 7-year-old child. His disruptive behaviour continued in Germany in the build-up to the 2006 World Cup Final, and during the birth of the royal baby in 2013, Horan was distributing business cards outside St Mary's Hospital London with the tag-line: 'My mission in life is to help prepare the world for the Second Coming' (Miller, 2013). The same message was printed on the business cards that he handed out at the Olympics.[3]

In Stratford, Horan was accompanied by a black-clad well-built white male aged in his 30s, wearing reflector sun shades and wheeling a sack barrow upon which sat a speaker and various advertizing materials. Looking like a professional bodyguard, the man stayed silent and in close proximity to Horan. The OCZ police informed Horan that he should set up the speaker adjacent to the bus terminal railings. He then disrobed to reveal his dancing garb. Father Horan wore a green beret on top of his long curly hair, large spectacles and a thick beard. A green tabard over a white loose-fitting shirt, and a short brown skirt, yellow tights, and brown socks was complimented by a rosette proclaiming the West Ireland County of Kerry, and a shoulder wallet which bore the symbol of the Star of David. Horan's dancing was described by one incredulous onlooker as 'Irish Traditional or even *Riverdance*', and involved Horan skipping in a small circle before spinning on his heels. He did this for 15 minutes before distributing calling cards and leaflets.

Quite what Father Horan was promoting or promulgating was difficult to ascertain. The stickers on his speaker proclaimed 'Human Rights', another promoted 'Technology For All'. The Olympics seemed to be an excuse for him to dance. Returning to his dance routines, Horan negotiated with watching PCs to move away from the railing to a more central location. A deal was struck. The square was relatively empty; he could move as long as he did not obstruct the free-flow of pedestrians. He did so and left 20 minutes later. Father Horan had danced to mild exhaustion, onlookers took photographs and moved on. This ostensible threat to the Games packed his show away and was gone less than an hour after arriving.

The good weather that typified the Games from Day 5 undoubtedly helped the event's success, and the tension and nervousness in and around Meridian Square on opening night had faded. It was replaced by a regime where a combination of Olympic Volunteers and Mc-A bouncers managed the crowds, while police officers generally relaxed. Local officers in particular never lost their cynicism regarding key aspects of the games, and in particular the constant references in the media to 'legacy'. Provincial police officers reported to us that this was the easiest duty of their careers: their main tasks seemed to be posing for photographs and giving directions. One of the iconic photographs to emerge from the 2012 Games was of a group of South Wales police officers striking sprinter Usain Bolt's trademark stance while on duty inside Westfield. The image went viral, and although they were told that senior officers were not happy with such triviality, there is little denying that similar PR stunts had been common at the Notting Hill carnival for decades.

OCZ Chiefs had become highly irritated as out of boredom Mutual Aid officers in particular were leaving fixed deployments around Meridian Square, and mobbing up to chat with colleagues. This was seen as unacceptable, and resulted in daily reminders being issued to line management. But there was little to do, and the sight of expensive police resources gathering together around Stratford occasionally having their photographs taken with tourists remained a bugbear of police managers throughout the Games. Other officers were kept busy by travelling in vans on a two-hour round trip to Chelsea where they were fed. Police canteens in Newham were closed.

There was not enough for the mass ranks of provincial police officers to do, but when they were confronted with a mundane policing matter, they found themselves to be part of an extraordinary, unfamiliar and quite unique assemblage of social control. When a middle-aged man reported to a LBN Enforcement Officer that someone had attempted to pick his pocket while crossing the A118, a favourite spot for 'dippers', the officer took the alleged offender to a bouncer who was working the Westfield steps as part of the Mc-A security team. The offender was handed over to a member of one northern force who took him to a senior MPS officer who made a decision to charge the man. A member of another provincial force took a statement from the victim and, accompanied by a local PC driver, took the prisoner to Plaistow Police Station where he was interviewed before being released on bail. This was not designated as an 'Olympic-related crime', despite taking place a few feet away from the Westfield steps and involving Olympic-wide UK policing resources.

Operational issues and the OCZ

The OCZ met daily at 08.00 hours in a dedicated office in the Westfield Management Suite. Chaired by one of the two OCZ Chief Inspectors, those who sat in on the 'Morning Prayers' daily meeting were drawn from Counter Terrorism, Westfield police, Newham Safer Neighbourhood Team, Westfield Management, London Ambulance Service, London Fire Brigade, BTP, Transport for London and various offices of Newham Council. These meetings never took more than 40 minutes, and were held in an air-conditioned room with a large screen TV broadcasting 24-hour Sky News.

The OCZ meetings always opened with a discussion of Intel via a telephone link to Olympic Silver. In the first week the Chair politely asked non-police to leave the room. By week two nobody was being asked to leave. Familiarity with many of those in attendance, coupled with some considerable confusion regarding who represented what agency and organization as the audience changed on a daily basis, meant that valid membership of the group along with issues around shared intelligence were rather complicated. All knew that the focus was the Last Mile, but nobody had a working definition of what defined 'Olympic crime'. All assumed that the final 'score' would be compiled by 'the Centre', and that some 'filtering out' would take place to reduce whatever figure might be the 'truth'.

The daily concerns of the OCZ meetings were varied. For instance an Olympic Event was scheduled involving the Hungarian water polo team. Two days previously, handball supporters of Hungary were noted asking passers-by for tickets. Furthermore, some had been doing so whilst drinking. Although no specific intelligence existed to indicate planned disorder by Hungarian supporters, such a possibility was enough to merit a closer policing intervention. Those with a long-running campaign were a concern, and an individual notorious for his publicity stunts to publicize the cause of *Fathers 4 Justice*, an activist group focused on divorced fathers' legal rights, was known to have four tickets for the Olympic Stadium. These seats were located and a 'policing plan' was implemented. Two days previously the same individual had entered – alone – another Olympic venue. But he, 'Got turned over . . . he had his F4J t-shirt on under his shirt'.

Elsewhere in the OCZ routine problems continued to occur. 'Two assaults in a chicken shop in Stratford in the early hours of this morning . . . One cut finger, no suspects . . . who wants it?'. One response was: 'It's whoever wants it' (meaning it could be an OCZ or borough crime statistic) which elicited the supplementary question: 'So . . . Who manages the secondary inquiry?'. On the same day an altercation outside a Stratford pub between two Lithuanians resulted in one assault charge and two arrests. The Lithuanians were not part of their nation's Olympic delegation, but had lived in Newham for years. Furthermore, a man was in hospital following an altercation outside McDonald's in Stratford at 02.00 the same morning. His assailants ('drunken idiots') had just left a nearby public house. Days later it emerged that although the assault had occurred within the OCZ, responsibility had been shifted to the borough's Violent Crime Unit, and thus, at a stroke, was divested of any possibility of being tagged as an 'Olympic-related' offence.

Calculations, the OCZ and the notion of Olympic crime

The crowds attending the Games brought statistics that the OCZ did not welcome, the most notable being theft from person. However when reports came through of theft of wallets from persons in the Westfield Mall a cynicism arose as to whether the OCZ should 'take' the crime. The issue began in the first 24 hours of the Games. The Newham Crime Analyst explained: 'Saturday saw 32 dipping/touting offences occur in the OCZ – the biggest number yet in Games Time. The former seemed to be happening at the road crossing between Meridian Square and Burger King where crowd density is at a premium and where "bumping" is almost legitimized by the opening and closing of the opportunity to cross the road'. This figure had prompted emails of consternation from 'Central', which provoked the OCZ Inspector: 'Private security control that procedure . . . and in truth there's very little we can do with "dipping" . . . Another thing is that they can get dipped anywhere on their journey, but it's only when they go to get their wallets and purses out in Westfield that they realize they've been robbed . . . but the crime becomes the OCZ's'.

A Westfield-based MPS officer offered his response to what he believed was a criticism of OCZ policing deployments: 'In the course of Saturday and Sunday, maybe 400,000 people went through Westfield . . . and a few dozen lost their purse. That figure is what you'd expect in a city of 400,000 . . . plus on top of that we've a borough population of over 300,000 . . . They've been all over fuckin' London and get into the OCZ then realize it's gone and we get the crime . . . It should be a crime recorded at the victim's home address'.

What was new was that some of the thefts were 'bag slashings', i.e. cutting off bag straps with a sharp instrument. There were, the meeting assumed, professionals at large. At which point, the Chair of the OCZ meeting made a decision: 'Deploy a Westfield PSU to stand around Meridian Square . . . and for the rest of the week I want a 24-hour-a-day tasking on the road crossing'. Further contestations around classification arose a week later. Some seven days after the Opening Ceremony the Crime Analyst revealed: '147 so-called "Olympic offences" for theft of unattended bags. There were four on Westfield steps yesterday'. The issue here was whether the crime belonged to routine shoppers, or represented a crime against those who might be considered 'Olympic-related victims'. The cold statistic could not differentiate between these two victim types.

At one level the issue was procedural. One officer from the Westfield policing team expanded on the five reported thefts and ended stating not all had been 'filtered' through his team. As such he had discovered that some of the claims regarding lost or stolen mobiles were logged onto the police system because the complainants had told an officer that without a crime sheet reference number the insurance company would not pay compensation. Although this produced a crime statistic, police surmized that the person may have actually lost the device; or equally they may be seeking to upgrade the device by false reporting. Further provoked, the CI explained: 'I've told the PSUs and their supervisors every day that they pass all Westfield crimes through the Westfield's team . . . I can't get through to them. Reports are going straight to CRIB [Crime Recording and Investigation Bureau] and not Westfield . . . I know why. They can do CRIB electronically and quickly. They don't have to phone Westfield and explain the report. It's all over in minutes . . . But some reports are not crimes so we're deploying (officers) to address non-existent crime problems'.

No one wanted the crime stats that were being generated. The borough was also receiving crimes they claimed were not 'theirs'. As the CI explained: 'I've got the Newham SMT raving and hysterical about the borough getting hit . . . Areas of Newham have gone 'red' with displacement and those doing business – as usual – are spitting feathers . . . In the OCZ there's been ten residential [burglaries] and a non-res [non-residential burglary] in two weeks . . . Right, from today all burglary and robbery crimes have to be reported to the OCZ in person by the officer taking the crime'.

The OCZ believed some statistics were a product of too many police on Olympic duties not having a defined role: 'There's 70 cops every minute of the day from the Constabularies roaming the borough bringing us 25 prisoners in the past 24 hours: drink-drivers, street drunks and low-level public disorder and they leave us to deal with it'.

Specialist operations were also generating crimes and moans. Operating within the OCZ were plain clothes police with Olympic-related remits. They brought hundreds of arrests for ticket-touting. On Day 10 the OCZ Chief Inspector chairing Morning Prayers read the arrest statistics regarding ticket touting with incredulity stating: 'This is not a professional racket. You know blokes who want to unload cos' their missus can't get here . . . That's not 'touting'. Tell the Podium lot to leave off . . . They're nicking the wrong people'.[4]

The Chair then informed those present that police from Operation Podium would be working the Westfield Food Court on a targeted operation against theft which provoked the same person to ask rhetorically 'I thought they were ticket touting?'. Elucidation was provided by the CT officer who offered the following explanation: 'They sit at a table with a mobile on it waiting for a snatch then run after them'. This provoked a terse 'News to me' from the Chair. There were a few other procedures that were new to experienced police officers.

Olympic crime: athlete issues

Although the Olympic Park and Olympic Village had their own dedicated police personnel and Command, some of their issues could impact on the OCZ and certainly held the potential to constitute an 'Olympic-related' crime. A few incidents in the Olympic Park made national news. One concerned a drunken Lithuanian making a Nazi salute. Another concerned a drunk, middle-aged, white UK citizen throwing a plastic drink container at the starting line-up of a sprint heat. He was arrested and charged. Due to appear at Stratford Magistrate Court, his case, intended for August, was adjourned until the autumn much to the relief of the Chair of the OCZ. The media scrum that his court appearance would attract was considered detrimental to the image of the Games.

There were crimes that carried political baggage and were never made public. A female cleaner on the Olympic Village was sexually assaulted by an Olympic competitor. Towards the end of the Games an Olympic gold medallist was detained by Westfield security staff accused of shoplifting items to the value of £100 from a department store. Within 12 hours the store had withdrawn its statement and the man 'de-arrested' by the MPS. A statement was required by the store from police to legitimize the withdrawal of the accusation. This provoked a few cynical questions around the OCZ room.

- 'So what's the difference between him and some cockney tea-leaf [thief]? He's leaving the UK in two days . . . Is that it?'.
- 'The store didn't want to proceed . . . yet a lot of the time they'd [the same store) pursue shoplifters down the civil recovery route . . . Was he in his country's regalia when nicked? Did he have Olympic accreditation to "blag" it [avoid apprehension]?'.

- 'How can we justify that from a police point of view? How can we explain it? Olympic athletes commit offences and get off with it we're told the law applies to everyone'.

No one in any senior position in the OCZ could answer these questions.

With the Games coming to a close, one of the PCs on Olympic duty asked the OCZ Superintendent what athletes were permitted to take from the Olympic Village, adding: 'There's some with duvets under their arms and we had a plasma TV . . . What's acceptable? What do we do if we see them carrying stuff out?'. No one knew the answer to this. Eventually the Superintendent stated: 'An authorization form is needed for any stuff carried out of the Olympic Park . . . We'll follow the guidelines that governed the building of the Olympic sites'.

The whereabouts of some Olympic athletes created confusion. Seven male Cameroonian athletes left the Olympic Village and were reported missing by their Olympic Committee. Missing Persons Reports had been issued for all of them. The OCZ Chair revealed that the Newham Borough Commander had been contacted by the national media to comment on this situation. He then discovered that the seven were known to have visas to remain in the UK until November 2012. This was not good news for the Chair who raged: 'I've spent three hours this morning arguing with a variety of people as to who these Cameroons belong to. Bronze (the Superintendent) said it goes to the borough, they're 'mispers' (missing persons) and there's a set of procedures: you search their last place they were seen at – their home. But we're not allowed in the Olympic Park! Then you de-brief the informant – in this case it's the Cameroon Chef de Mission. You apparently ask: "What might be the issue? What political situation there might be? Are they potentially seeking refugee status?" Then you'd talk to their fellow athletes or try to find out who knows what. Four fuckin' hours it took me, eventually Crime Investigation Olympic Village said he'll take it'.

One incident in the Olympic Village involved an allegation of stalking. A female athlete was being followed around the Olympic Village by a coach from a Middle East country. This resulted in five 'embedded cops' in the Olympic Village being deployed to 'man-mark' the athlete to reassure her she was at no risk of harm from her stalker. 'This had gone high up. It's now a "Diplomatic Incident". It's very sensitive because of where he comes from. He's been warned very firmly about his behaviour. There is the possibility of deportation . . . but it's "political"' (Superintendent).

Considering the continual references made by police to Newham's problematic Islamic or terrorist 'footprint' the Games were remarkably free of Islamic-related controversy[5], and we observed an Islamic-centred demonstration handled very sensitively by the OCZ. Those CT issues that had arisen had proved to be either false or based on vague information. A report had been received of an Asian male overheard in a Westfield coffee bar stating his belief that a bomb would explode at the Closing Ceremony. His reasoning was that the 'the Illuminati' would be present in numbers at the ceremony. This report provoked a CT officer to state 'We hear this all the time – "Don't go shopping this Saturday" or "Avoid this place or that". There's no specific Intel on this. We've passed it on to SO15 . . . Some people read too much Dan Brown'. Another report had been made to police of an Asian male asking Air Force personnel involved in the Olympic Park search regime about their shift patterns. 'This is more worrying. We don't have any description, but we've asked for a CCTV trawl of the ticket office area to get an image'. This 'Intel', like so many truths, half-truths and incidents during the Games, came to nothing.

Whereas the first OCZ meeting had 24 attendees in attendance, by the end of the Games there were just seven in a room listening to the Chair mocking himself while echoing the fatigue they were all suffering: 'Intel? Fuck all. Footfall? Fuck all. Incidents of note? Fuck all. Interest? Fuck all'. Things were winding down.

Closing: for sport and peace

The Sunday evening Closing Ceremony posed similar policing problems to that of the Opening Ceremony. A specially invited audience had to be facilitated at the same time as the mall was open. At 15.00 hours there was some consternation in the OCZ control room when they heard of a major fire in a recycling plant some seven miles away being attended by 40 fire fighters. Spoken of as the largest fire in London for seven years, the conflagration was not going to threaten the Olympic Park, but one officer did remind those listening that if Westfield 'went up' tonight there would not be much by way of a fire brigade response to dampen the flames.

The Westfield Mall closed at 16.00 hours. This closure had ostensibly been 'agreed' between the businesses, the Westfield Management and the MPS. Why 300 businesses would willingly close their doors on the afternoon and evening of the Closing Ceremony was not a question anyone in the OCZ room could answer. It had happened; someone had brokered or demanded it. Police could now operate on the mall steps and in the mall unconditionally. Ideally, the only people entering or walking in the mall post 16.00 hours would bear accreditation and be on their way to the Closing Ceremony. By 16.30 hours the mall was empty and the shop staff gone; police had secured all doors, and were in large numbers throughout Meridian Square where a crowd of some 1,000 had gathered. The religious affiliates and small groups of Africans and South Americans sang and danced. Police chatted with tourists and the OCZ Superintendent looked on this from the top of the steps and reflected ruefully: 'Public order policing is changing . . . five years ago the Met would have cleared the square'. The implications were that the MPS now tolerated more than they once had. However, as representatives of the world's media were present in and around Stratford, this assertion was never likely to be tested.

Considering the demography of Newham, there was a relative dearth of Muslim leaflets given out in Meridian Square. The two Muslim organizations that were evident daily were London-based, while another that appeared more fitfully appeared to have its origins in Pakistan. These leaflets did not hold any content suggestive of promoting or preaching extremism, and one produced by 'Muslims for Peace' was an organization proclaiming itself as being devoted to promoting non-violence. At 17.45 hours on the final day a group of 60 Muslim protesters had gathered in a supermarket car park a half a mile away before approaching Meridian Square. Within minutes police near to the gathering announced over the police radio that this group were led by a man who had 'been of concern' to Counter-Terrorism police for years. The OCZ police deployed mobile units to the supermarket rendezvous, traffic police were instructed to block two roads to facilitate their movement;, and the OCZ Chief Inspector advised the Sergeant and Inspector on the Westfield steps: 'They're protesting about something about the Games. There's hundreds of journalists in here and you can see dozens of photographers . . . For two weeks there's been no issues. We don't want to give them a story. So stay smart, politic, alert. Do what needs to be done without being noticed. Don't fuck it up in this final minute'. The OCZ Superintendent listened and then explained the issue more brutally: 'With a few hours to go we don't want tomorrow's front page showing Imams in police headlocks . . . We have to police this carefully. These occasions can come back and bite you on the arse'.

At 18.45 hours, the group, 60 strong, arrived in the square under a 100-strong police escort. The square was very busy, people were preoccupied by preachers and singers and were admiring the dozen mounted police. The two most senior officers of the OCZ stood atop the Westfield stairs looking onto the newly arrived. One stated: 'Keep 'em sweet . . . but they can't do nothing "inciting". We've no specific Intel on their aims . . . If they attempt to come up stop them and if they persist we'll baton them back down the stairs. Proportionality'.

The protestors were dressed all in white robes. Some carried banners. Some distributed leaflets. One headline *'Exposing Teams of Terror'* explained their cause. The issue was *'Atrocities against Muslims'* perpetrated by China, the US and the UK. They had an Olympic relevance: 'those who proclaim unity and peace and who currently top the medals table, also top the medals table when it comes to the oppression of Muslims, occupation of Muslim land, torture, abuse, murder and mayhem'. Some of the placards contained pictures of corpses in war-zones, and in the supermarket car park a deal had been struck between the protestors and police – placards could be carried and displayed but the images of the dead had to be removed. The dead bodies were crudely cut out of three colour pictures. Other placards carried the following messages: 'See who wins medals in crimes committed against Muslims/See Evilolympics.com/Exposing Teams of Terror/ Stop the Bloodshed'.

Assembled in three rows by a railing at the rear of Meridian Square, the protesters were addressed by various speakers, including one who spoke of the 'triviality' of the Olympic entertainment and dismissed the achievements of Usain Bolt as epitomizing the futility of 'the Western world'. The group attracted a few dozen curious onlookers. Most tourists however looked elsewhere, in particular to two very tall soldiers in the full regalia of the Parachute Regiment who just happened to be passing through the square. More photographs were taken of these two individuals than of the protesters. Halfway through the protest at the top of the Westfield steps appeared four uniformed officers with automatic rifles. A couple of elderly white men in the square walked towards the protesters and voiced their fury at their presence before being politely, but firmly, ushered away by uniformed police. A muscular, shaven-headed, heavily tattooed man in his early 40s stood close to the Muslims shouting abuse, and as a consequence was 'man-marked' by two uniformed police. He was not arrested. Minutes later a white male, aged in his late 50s, walked down the Westfield steps, and while smoking a small cigar, became somewhat 'over attentive' towards the movements of groups of police officers. An officer from SO15 broadcast his whereabouts to uniformed colleagues, who allowed him to join his shaven-headed colleague close to the protestors. The pair now kept their hostilities limited to stares whilst police engaged them in conversation. One told an officer that in 30 minutes '200 EDL' would be in Stratford. When this was relayed by radio to senior officers, they laughed and dismissed the man's claim as unfeasible.

A message came over the police radio that a member of the public had called 999 claiming that the chant being used by the demonstrators was 'Jihad, Jihad, Jihad'. None of the police present had heard such a chant, but the claim was relayed to the OCZ who did not respond to the message or deploy officers. Their logic was that the demonstrators were orderly and they were contained on three sides by uniformed police. The group prayed, and then after 40 minutes returned in an orderly and dignified manner to their vehicles. In a striking juxtaposition of different religious observances and the mind boggling diversity of this micro-cosm of multicultural London, this exclusively male procession, under police escort, passed by rows of mainly female, African evangelical Christians, joyously shaking tambourines, proclaiming the coming of the Lord, and singing 'Jesus wants me for a sunbeam'.

Before and during the final of the men's 100 metres, the campaigning organi-zation *War on Want* projected a 65 foot-high image onto the façade of Denning Point, a high-rise council block overlooking the Olympic Park, replacing the word 'Adidas' with 'Exploitation' and the sub-sentence 'Not OK Anywhere'. Earlier in the evening the activists had been challenged by council-employed security guards who had naively believed the story given to them that they were a 'news TV crew'.[6]

At 20.00 hours of the final day, Mc-A Security spread itself across the foot of the Westfield steps. No one was allowed up the stairs without Olympic Stadium accreditation, and a Westfield security officer armed with a tannoy demanded that both the Westfield steps and the square be cleared by 21.00 hours. As crowds drifted away, the OCZ Superintendent and Chief Inspector chatted about what had been an uneventful evening, and indeed a quiet Games. The Superintendent reflected: 'Where we are right now and what we've policed for 17 days is, in terms of policing and ownership, the most complex piece of land in the UK. Unknown to most people these past couple of hours were a nightmare . . . But the crowds have gone home and in a few hours the Olympics are over . . . Who won, eh?'.

By 21.30 hours the square contained fewer than 300 people who did not seem to know why they were there. The Closing Ceremony was underway but neither visible nor audible, and the Mc-A security good-naturedly went about their task, the finishing line in sight. A few minutes later, the tranquillity of a Westfield hotel bar was interrupted by the arrival of 14 uniformed police officers each carrying an automatic rifle. The guns were placed upright between the furniture as the officers relaxed in comfy chairs, and over coffee enjoyed the TV broadcast of the Closing Ceremony. Job done. The Games had remained the story.

Conclusion

By the final day, the police had refined a system of low-key consensual containment that stood in stark contrast to the heavy-handed reaction briefly shown at the Opening Ceremony. Indeed by the Closing Ceremony, essentially informal and ad hoc techniques of public order control and, crucially, news avoidance, had become the norm. This was of course after three weeks of a steadily declining expectation of a major incident, where the prospect of terrorism had faded with every day, and the temper of the spectators had matched the balmy weather.

Meanwhile, the rest of Newham needed policing. While local youth were unlikely to make an appearance during Games Time in an environment dominated by so many uniformed police officers looking for something to do, they continued to feature strongly in the policing of Newham beyond the OCZ, where for most Newham residents the Olympics were a distant irrelevance to everyday life.

Notes

1 See Giulianotti et al. (2015) on the mobility issues surrounding London 2012.
2 The Apostolic Fellowship of Christ believe in the infallibility of the bible, and await the return of Jesus Christ.
3 The card also advertized his availability for weddings, birthday parties and bar mitzvahs.
4 Operation Podium were a dedicated team within the MPS Specialist Crime and Operations Directorate, whose role was to prevent and investigate a range of serious and organized crime affecting the Olympic economy.
5 During the Games there was some considerable scaremongering by UK newspapers concerning 'Islamic terrorism'. See, for example, the story headed, 'London 2012 Olympics: terrorists plotting cyanide poison hand cream attack' (the *Telegraph*, 26 March 2012).
6 The campaign focused on factory conditions in Sri Lanka, China, Indonesia and the Philippines. Claiming that workers were forced to work excessive overtime and were paid as little as 34p per hour, the campaign contrasted this with the £529 million profits made by Adidas in 2011 (see www.notokanywhere.org).

References

Fussey, P. (2014) 'Command, Control and Contestation: Negotiating Security at the London 2012 Olympics', *The Geographical Journal*, advance publication DOI: 10.1111/geoj.12058.
Giulianotti, R., Armstrong,G. Hales, G. & Hobbs, D. (2015) 'Global Sport and the Politics of Mobility: The Case of the London 2012 Olympics', *British Journal of Sociology*, 66(1): 118–140.
Miller, N. (2013) 'Royal Baby Delay as Media Eats Itself in "Great Kate Wait"', *The Age*. Retrieved March 27 2014, from http://www.theage.com.au/world/royal-baby-delay-as-media-eats-itself-in-great-kate-wait-20130719-2q8ig.html?skin=text-only.

9 Policing the Olympic borough during Games Time

In the previous two chapters, we examined the policing of the Olympic 'Last Mile', within the OCZ and more specifically Meridian Square. In this chapter we consider the Olympic-related policing that occurred away from the Last Mile, within the wider Newham area, and out of sight of Olympic visitors. Our focus is on the everyday world of policing in Games Time, centring on police strategies, tactics, and operational activities for engaging with young males in particular. The Games enhanced MPS manpower as officers from across the UK converged on London, offering the potential for 'payback time' in dealing with local 'folk devils'. We also examine here the work of the Newham Monitoring Project: the one 'community organization' to pursue an extensive, critical monitoring of police activity during the Olympics.

The void

In Games Time, beyond Stratford Broadway, it was hard to discern that a global sporting event was taking place. The borough was much quieter than usual, appearing oddly like an Olympic void. Various attempts to spread the wealth being generated by the Games beyond Stratford proved to be in vain as Olympic tourists ignored Newham. A food market established specifically for the Games close to Canning Town station closed down early into the Games due to lack of trade, as did a similar venture in Leytonstone. The food outlets in Stratford Park, just one bus stop away from the Olympic Park, also closed after a few days due to lack of custom. Most notably, the company running London Pleasure Gardens, who took over a derelict site near to the ExCel Centre in order to develop 'a cultural quarter and party venue for visitors to the Olympics and local residents', went into administration after visitor numbers were much lower than expected, and an event was cancelled due to safety concerns. The venture had benefited from the backing of Boris Johnson, and a £3 million loan from Newham Council.

Four hundred meters from the Olympic Park, on the day when the UK won three gold medals, the local pub had horse racing on the TV. It was mid-afternoon and a group of three men aged between early 40s and mid-60s discussed the Olympics. 'Waste of fucking time, not for us is it? I mean, if it was, all them flats they are building would go to local people. No chance that ain't going to happen. Fucking loved the rowing though. And the boxing. Looking forward to that. I am going to the table tennis. Pal of mine is getting me in. Promised me a UK team shirt'.

'It's a load of bollocks. You go down Stratford Broadway, fucking empty. Nobody comes here. And it won't make no difference in the long run'.

At which point the door of the pub opened and an enormous silhouette was framed against the blazing sunlight outside. The Olympic non-believers were transformed. The new arrival was Lawrence Okoye, the 6-foot 6-inch, 23-stone Team GB discus-thrower. He had arrived in vest, shorts and carrying a back pack, and was immediately swamped by the suddenly starstruck Olympic sceptics who insisted on several photographs being taken before the young man could speak to the pub's licensee, who had allowed him to park his car in the yard.

A week later and the same drinkers were becoming annoyed by a group of loud Americans whose USA tracksuits encased physiques forged in the pub rather than the gymnasium. When Terry complained to the pub licensee, he was told that the drinkers were connected to the USA shooting team. Terry turned to the Americans and loudly proclaimed, 'Oh yeah, shooting. Get Mickey down here, he's handy with a sawn-off'. The Americans left the pub.

Although there was a house in Corporation Street E15 with a picture of Mo Farah in the front window, for most Newham residents, if they did not watch the events on TV, it was easy to remain oblivious to the Games. For spectators, there was little reason to venture outside of the Olympic Park/Westfield bubble, and if they did, with the remarkable exception of Meridian Square, they would be hard pressed to locate anything approaching an Olympic effect.

From a policing perspective, the minimal social impacts of the Olympics on the local area were a huge benefit to maintaining everyday law and order. Indeed, in many ways, it was the ubiquitous presence of police that would have particular impacts on local crime. In the opinion of most local police officers, the over-resourcing of Olympic policing would displace crime out of the OCZ and Stratford area, and into the Newham area generally, or its adjacent boroughs. Beyond the OCZ boundary, Newham police attempted to be 'business-as-usual', a philosophy that was shared by locals involved in crime. Yet little happened beyond the OCZ that could fit the category of 'Olympic-related crime', and the fears expressed to us by senior officers at the Centre that predatory local youths would target Olympic visitors who were roaming the streets of Newham had proved to be ridiculously misplaced, as few of these visitors ventured beyond Meridian Square.

However, during the Games the principal target group for Newham MPS was the same as before the Games, the 30–40-strong group of young black males who met habitually in a local park, and were known to the police as the 'Portuguese Mafia' (PGM), as discussed in Chapter 3. Mutual Aid officers who were under-employed in the OCZ offered a considerable manpower boost for anti-gang operations in the wider borough, and in particular for stopping and searching young black men, the demographic identified in the pre-Olympic policing focus on 'serious youth violence' (SYV) and gangs.

In what follows, our discussion is divided into two main parts, as we examine first the Olympic-related policing of the PGM and wider everyday crime before and during the Games; and second, the work of the Newham Monitoring Project (NMP) in monitoring the activities of the police throughout the Games.

Policing gangs and crime in Olympic Newham

Displacement and location

In Newham, the Olympics brought an initial displacement and increase in crime. The evening of the Opening Ceremony produced seven thefts from persons and eight robberies. The latter, according to senior officers, were partly explained by the displacement of crime out of the immediate Olympic zone, as one explained: 'All borough "Tasking" (manpower) got sent to the Opening Ceremony. So the robbers went to East Ham and nicked four i-phones and four sets of gold jewellery from Asian women'. Subsequently, crime statistics for Newham indicated that, across the opening Olympic weekend (Friday evening through to Monday morning), as one Detective Inspector put it, '70 additional crimes' were committed in the borough. The data breakdown pointed to 14 'weapons offences' (consisting of items seized via the search regimes from people about to enter the Olympic Park), 25 thefts (20 in Westfield and five inside the Olympic Park), and 18 robberies. The Violent Crime Unit (VCU) Sergeant explained the context for the displacement, with reference to the mobility of offenders via London transport: 'In June robbery figures were down 34 per cent on last year's. Now it's just 15 per cent. They're doing it in East Ham and Upton Park 'cos police are all over Stratford. Over the weekend there were 12 in Upton Park, all within 400 metres of the tube station. In East Ham they're mostly within 50 metres of the Tube'.

The Detective Chief Inspector (DCI) who led the Robbery Task Force offered further explanation which focused on resourcing and procedures: 'We've no Robbery Task Force in Games Time. We've [Newham borough] got 111 officers displaced to Mutual Aid. In return we've a couple of "serials" [PSUs] but add their numbers up and they're less than a quarter of what we've lost . . . On an average weekend there might be seven or eight crime reports for the borough. This weekend there's 50 'cos there's so many "A" serials going back to their boroughs and putting Intel on our system . . . so we're getting the stats for the Olympic policing'.

Olympic Crime was clearly being played down at the expense of local crime statistics, yet behind these figures lay more complicated issues relating to the politics of police priorities and resources, and proactive local policing based on intelligence. For instance, the DCI had discovered that on the same days that the Centre had deployed extra manpower to Stratford, the boroughs of Wandsworth, Bromley and Hounslow had received more numerous police deployments than Newham. He angrily declared: 'It's political . . . They've [these boroughs] had to send personnel to Mutual Aid and then periodically they get something back to help their local problems. It's not based on reason. It's just to keep 'em happy'.

On the other hand, effective proactive policing faced challenges emanating from local youth violence. On the opening day of the Olympics, Newham police were informed of a threat to kill a local 'gang member', made by his Waltham Forest rivals. A search of the threatened man's home revealed a hand gun and 43 rounds of ammunition; one round was in the chamber. A PSU was deployed by the local Detective Inspector to cruise the border area between the two boroughs for the remainder of their shift.

The very usual suspects: policing the Portuguese Mafia

'It's all "Portuguese Mafia" this and "Portuguese Mafia" that. Someone told the Centre that they're going to come out and rob everyone during the Games. The DAC [Deputy Assistant Commissioner] and Commander then get on the phone demanding to know what the borough's going to do about them' (GFU Inspector).

In the opening week of the Games, the Newham Borough Commander reported that robberies had risen by 3 per cent over the years 2009/10–2010/11 and by 1 per cent over the years 2010/11–2011/12. The good news was that since mid-2011 Serious Youth Violence (SYV) was down 48 per cent and gun crime down 60 per cent. Robbery was now the borough's key reputational problem, and the group understood by local police to be behind much of these offences became the obvious focus of policing. The GFU Inspector was unambiguous about the policing of the PGM (see Chapter 3): 'They're a "robbery gang" if you want. At times they're 30-strong in Stratford Park – they intimidate and rob other youths of mobiles and money and target Asian women for gold jewellery . . . Intel from informants is that they will "up" their robbery to include Olympic tourists'.

Two weeks before the Opening Ceremony five youths assaulted a young man and stole his mobile telephone outside the reception of the E15 Foyer building. The victim made no complaint to police, but the incident was captured on CCTV. The film revealed that shortly before the robbery two females were talking with the victim. One of the women was a girlfriend of one of the assailants. The police had the identities of all involved; the assailants were charged with robbery and the women with conspiracy to rob. The five people arrested for assault were associated by police with the PGM, and consisted of three who lived in Newham and two who lived in nearby Ilford. The former were visited early morning by the GFU, accompanied by personnel from the Department of Work and Pensions (DWP) and the UK Border Agency (UKBA). The Ilford suspects were served with bail conditions barring them from entering Newham between the hours of 06.00 hours and 19.00 hours until after the Olympics. The GFU Inspector explained: 'Their [the Centre's] focus is the "border" of the Olympic Park and the "ring of streets" around it. The Stratford Dispersal Zone ends July 25th. We're looking to extend it after the Olympics – it'll happen. When we nick them, bail conditions will be set to last until after the Olympics'.[1][2]

In reality, the threat posed by the PGM to Olympic visitors was overplayed, as these young men proved indifferent to the Olympics. In any case, the vast majority of Olympic Park visitors did not venture anywhere near the wider

Stratford area, let alone the rest of Newham. Just a few hundred metres outside of Meridian Square, Olympic-related enthusiasm was rarely evident. With uniformed police always prominent, West Ham Lane was devoid of any significant activity. In midweek daytimes, only a handful of viewers watched the Olympic Live Screen in Stratford Park, and some street-food franchises within the park did not bother opening, while on most evenings the park closed at 21.00 instead of the scheduled midnight. During the day, viewers watching the Games on a giant TV screen were outnumbered by police and private security staff. On occasion, in the same park, up to 100 youths and children might be found watching an impromptu five-a-side football tournament or playing basketball on the park's two courts, while a handful of East Europeans would be performing pilates. More people were doing sport than watching it in the shadow of the Olympic Park, even on historic days for Team GB athletes. However, the absence of any obvious Olympics threat did not deter the police from refining their response to the PGM, who had become 'police property' (Reiner, 2010: 131) *par excellence.*

Targeting the PGM

With the GFU maintaining its focus upon gangs during Olympic time, and the PGM being increasing considered as a robbery threat, responsibility for their policing fell to uniformed officers patrolling in vans, occasionally assisted by members of the Violent Crime Unit (VCU) who were deployed to 'spot' the PGM for Mutual Aid officers who were unfamiliar with the PGM. The VCU Sergeant took a particular interest in the group: 'It's easy to get into the UK . . . For a start we don't do checks on who leaves the country – never have done. This means that a 13-or 15-year-old African boy can leave and within reason give his passport to another boy of similar age and there's a near impossibility that any facial differences will be picked up at any border check on a kid coming into the UK . . . Who are they? We don't know. They could be hardened criminals in Lisbon, but over here they're unknown'.

The Sergeant assumed that the PGM 'members', in most instances aged in their late teens/early 20s and having lived in Lisbon before moving to the UK, would likely be known to Portuguese police as teenage offenders. Ideally, as fellow EU members, the Portuguese would be able to supply the MPS with crime histories and details on whether the youths were 'Portuguese citizens' and eligible or not to remain in the UK. Of his own initiative, the Sergeant had discovered that Portuguese Residence cards carried as identity documents by some youths were not in themselves proof of Portuguese nationality; they were instead status documents given to Africans disembarking in Portugal but were not validations of citizenship. Drawing on the vogue for deportation as a form of crime management, exemplified by Operation Nexus,[3] the Sergeant had sent a list of ten names and dates of birth to Newham MPS Crime Administration, requesting that these details be sent to the Portuguese police to ascertain who was 'known'' and who was actually 'Portuguese'. His email included the statement: 'Have arrived in the last 18 months . . . we believe to target the Olympics'. Asked if this was really the case, the Sergeant laughed and replied 'Probably not, but that's what the MIB [Met Intel Bureau] told us recently so we'll use it, won't we?'.

The MIB document, dated 25 May 2012, entitled 'Portuguese Robbers' stated that the PGM were a group 'primarily involved in committing personal robberies in Newham . . . moving into dealing and supplying of cannabis and Class A ['hard drugs', such as heroin and cocaine]'. Different 'Intel' applied to different perceived PGM members: four were 'robbers', one was also a 'burglar', one was part of the Green Gang, one sold crack, one sold cannabis, and three had 'access to firearms'. Crucially, the document claimed that the PGM 'May well target visitors to the Olympic Games, committing robbery, theft and assault . . . as well as putting visitors at risk, they will tarnish the international reputation of London and the MPS'.

However, the two most notorious PGM associates were well known to the GFU, and their backgrounds did not fit the VCU Sergeant's proposal that they should be deported. One was British and of Jamaican heritage who lived with his grandmother and mother. Both of these women were articulate, employed, local citizens who when encountered by the GFU on home visits were considered to be distinctly 'pro-police'. The other main suspect was of Anglo-Portuguese nationality (and therefore eligible for UK citizenship) and came from a secure two-parent home. In the words of the GFU Sergeant, 'The home is spotless . . . so is his bedroom. There's furniture which might have come from Habitat and scatter cushions. It's all well thought out . . . unusual for this neighbourhood'. The stereotype of the foreign gangbanger infiltrating the UK in order to plunder its citizens (Hobbs, 2013) clearly did not fit.

The uncertainties surrounding the national identities, 'gang' status, and alleged criminal activities of the PGM were not the only youth-orientated problem for Newham police. A few days before the Opening Ceremony, one Newham youth had received a 16-year custodial sentence for a fatal stabbing. The incident had created bad feelings between youths from Custom House and the Maryland and Chadd Green districts. In the E15 neighbourhood, another incident during the first week of the Games saw a youth stabbed three times in an altercation involving, according to police, the Thatched House Thugs: an entity hitherto never before mentioned in GFU circles. Yet these events were presented at Olympic Time Parades (police team briefings which preceded each shift) as relatively minor events, and attention continued to centre on the PGM.

On the opening weekend of the Games a youth associated by the Newham police with PGM activity was suspected of robbing four Newham women in the street, and a further robbery of a local woman after he stayed overnight at her home. A search of his flat yielded a number of bullets, and he was arrested and put in custody on suspicion of the robbery offences, where he was joined by another PGM associate with previous robbery convictions.

The Violent Crime Unit (VCU) was based in Stratford Police Station, just across the road from the PGM's preferred gathering place in Stratford Park. As the PGM were regarded more and more as a robbery rather than gang threat, they took it upon themselves, mainly through the initiative of a long-serving

Sergeant, to sporadically launch offensives against the PGM. At times they would be plain clothes police working in tandem with uniformed officers doing stop and searches. At other times they would be proactive. Given the GFUs remit to deal with gangs, and the head of the GFU's firm belief that the PGM did not constitute a gang, (see Chapter 3) he was more than happy to pass responsibility for their policing to the VCU, who were increasingly irritated at their temporary disbandment during Games Time. The VCU felt that their knowledge of local 'faces' was largely rendered useless, and as a consequence Mutual Aid officers, often from forces where the notion of multiculturalism was a somewhat alien concept, were conducting unnecessary stops on innocent youths who were merely young and black and in proximity to the Olympics.

On Day 5 of the Games, the early evening 'parade' for the night shift was led by the VCU Sergeant. Importantly, his address was directed at both Newham uniformed officers and officers from two counties on Mutual Aid. For the benefit of the latter group, the Sergeant was setting the scene, explaining the key policing issues that they would face in the local area. He offered the following observations on the nature of the PGM: 'They've been coming here for the past 18 months to two years to target the Olympics. There's 40 or 50 of them. They're hostile to the police . . . insulting. They attack on bikes and do bag snatches and target women visiting the Olympics. They originate from Burkina Faso via Portugal, but think we're a soft touch compared to Lisbon. Get in their faces . . . they met their match the other day with Strathclyde [Scottish police force]'.

The final comment was an admiring reference to the Scottish force, also on Mutual Aid, when conducting stop and search. The PGM were apparently routinely hostile to MPS officers during searches, but had been shocked by the verbal threats from the Scottish police when they had voiced similar sentiments. The advice from the Sergeant drew further on the powers and resources available, some of which were irrelevant and some of which seemed contemptuous of due process: 'Use Stop and Search whenever you see them. Visit them at home. Let them know we know them . . . There are complaints from Ilford that our criminals are going on to their patch because of the poor sentencing they get if convicted. Look at _____'s record, look at _____. who's breached his ASBO (Anti-Social Behaviour Order) three times this year; the first two times he got a one-day sentence, the third time he got an 85-quid fine and a one month "confine". Yesterday he was nicked for robbery. Let's get him deported, we've checked with immigration, and it all depends on nationality and "propensity to commit crime and disorder"'.

Over the previous 12 weeks Newham had suffered 84 snatch robberies, and in Olympic Time there had been a rise in chain snatches in the East Ham area. These incidents usually occurred between 14.00 and 16.00 hours. The *modus operandi* was to 'hug' the victim, lowering them to the floor as accomplices snatched their jewellery. Without firm evidence, the VCU Sergeant opined that all of the robbery suspects were part of the PGM, and gave information and directions to the parade concerning three specific individuals: 'He's got an ASBO but no specific times attached for living or sleeping in the [Newham] address'. The second had an ASBO banning him from Newham as part of his bail conditions. The third had a 9–6 bail condition for an E12 (Manor Park) address where he had to be between early evening and mid-morning daily.

The following day another briefing allowed another Newham-based officer to identify the Olympic Time enemy for the benefit of police from out of town.

Escalating the war against the PGM: Operation Flame – crime and nationality

Reading from an electronic whiteboard, a Newham MPS Detective Chief Inspector informed the parade that according to police intelligence the PGM had moved their activities from Stratford to East Ham and Beckton. One individual in particular, a street robber known to carry weapons, was wanted for robbery and was to be arrested on sight, and his identity documents obtained so that UKBA might check his status to remain in the UK. To help identification, Newham Robbery Squad officers were tasked to ride in three Mutual Aid PSU vans 'spotting' the PGM for the Mutual Aid officers.

This was based upon an initiative that had not to-date been mentioned in the borough or in the OCZ, namely Operation Flame, which was based on Section 44 of the 2007 UK Border Act. This legislation gave police the right to ask anyone, regardless of the cause of arrest, for proof of nationality. As the DCI explained: 'It's a massive power rarely used. If they say "Lisbon" as their place of birth – don't accept it – it's the only place they've heard of in Portugal where they claim they're from. If they say "Angola" they might be eligible for deportation. And we can get a Section 18 and search their premises for evidence'.

The DCI then read an 'Intelligence Profile' written by a Newham-based Crime Analyst titled 'Olympic Tasks to Newham Borough in Relation to PM Gang'. According to this document, the PGM were now, officially, a 'gang'. Incredibly, the document claimed that the PGM were 'Up to 200 in number drawn from former Portuguese colonies on the West Coast of Africa. With an active, organized membership spread across MPS. And whilst not a "gang" in the traditional sense in that they fight other groups over post-codes, will use extreme levels of force and are very defiant towards SNT' (Safer Neighbourhood Team).

The report also claimed that the PGM had girlfriends in the E15 Focus building who moved drugs for them. Their violence was 'unnecessary punches to face and blows to the head', they were known to 'intimidate local shopkeepers' and known to follow off-duty police officers from Stratford Police Station and 'intimidate them'. They also wore identical dark clothing to make identification difficult. In recent weeks they had been 'active' around building societies and banks. The DCI stated he did not agree with the latter claim, but was forthright in observing 'MIB have finally recognized our problem with our gangs and especially the Portuguese Mafia . . .[4] They're always in the park playing basketball, tops off, ripped, thinking they own the place, fearing the life out of decent people . . . They're having an adverse effect on the Olympics'.

This marked an enormous escalation of the significance of the PGM. Further, the vagueness and ambiguity displayed by officers that we reported in Chapter 3 had been discarded entirely. The size of their membership, the extent and seriousness of their activities, their violence and importantly their status as a *bona fide* gang had all been hugely exaggerated, along with the tangible threat that they now posed to the Games. However, this exaggeration was not confined to the PGM, and the 'crime intelligence' that the Chief Inspector was referring to had more details on gangs. It told of 'tensions in East London' and how the 'Globe Town Massive' and 'Green Boys' gangs were planning to rob Olympic tourists. Furthermore, 'Cathall Street robbers were planning to descend on Westfield'. None of these groups were ever mentioned again in relation to the Olympics. The Globe Town Massive had never entered the conversation of the Newham GFU, nor were they mentioned again for at least a year afterwards. The 'Green Boys' may have been a reference to the Newham-based 'Green Gang', who had no history or intention of robbing tourists, and were already subject to the dedicated Games-Time attentions of the GFU under the aegis of Operation Slaytor.

During Games Time, while all other squads were subsumed into general CID duties, the GFU were the only specialist squad in Newham retained as a discrete unit. To keep his team together the GFU Inspector 'found' a dedicated police operation which targeted a Pakistani national in Plaistow who ran a drug-dealing business from his house. The DI justified the GFU running this operation by claiming that members of the Green Gang were involved, and although this was not true, Operation Slaytor was subsequently regarded by the police as a success and four people were convicted. None of those found guilty were connected to the 'Green Gang', or indeed to any of Newham's named territorial gangs.

Smart cops could manipulate Olympic-based gang hype to their advantage, and with pressure increasingly emanating from the Centre, these same officers sensed a conflation of two Olympic fears; gangs and robbery. The DI explained: 'CO20 [Territorial Support Group] have sent through a request and sent resourcing to the borough to target the PGM. They want Serials (police units) in Stratford and West Ham Lane . . . There's been some snatches and robberies over the weekend and they're wanting to sit on it . . . It pisses me off. They've panicked because there were a dozen or so robberies over the West-End around the Games' opening . . . So someone tells us what our problem is – as if we didn't know – and tells us how to deal with it. None of the victims over the weekend were Olympic tourists, which is what the Centre's scared of . . . but it shouldn't matter if it's jewellery from Asian women who live here or i-phones from young Newham kids . . . You know what this is about. We haven't got enough people throughout the year to have an effective Robbery Squad. We've got 150 away from the Borough on "AID" . . . They take one in seven of our strength then tell us we've a problem, and then they've sent 48 uniformed cops to sort it out for three nights. We've been asking for a year for this resourcing to sort the PGM out but we never get it. Then, all of a sudden, because of the Olympics, we get loads of men'.

Street robbery was a potential Olympic public relations disaster, and the PGM now became regarded as robbers, which was precisely what some of Newham's more astute police officers had been saying for some time: 'They have got fuck all and sit about with nothing to do. Somebody walks passed with a phone or a [gold] chain and they think "I'll have that". So they "nick it". That don't make them members of a gang'.

Jewels in the crown

The huge amount of effort directed at the PGM seemed to have borne fruit midway through the Games when two of their more notorious members were arrested in East Ham on suspicion of jewellery snatches. Their arrest was a consequence of both intelligence and good luck related to routine police patrol work. One Newham-based PCSO positioned himself in the vicinity of a Sikh Temple knowing that Indian women who often wore high-value jewellery were attending a service there. In the late morning police took a call reporting that three black youths had snatched gold chains from the necks of two Asian women in the vicinity of where the PCSO was situated. He chased two young men into the path of a van containing MPS officers that had been rented from a commercial vehicle hire company and had no police markings. The two men were arrested and it was discovered that one of the suspects had recently been placed at the top of the Newham Gang Matrix. Although no items of jewellery were found on either of the men, the former had a stamped envelope addressed to a Manchester pawn broker who paid cash for jewellery with 'no questions asked'. Customers had merely to package jewellery in the pre-paid envelope and post in the nearest mailbox. Hours later another PGM member handed himself in at Plaistow Police Station. The mobile phones of the original two arrested suspects revealed a 'selfie' of a youth holding a shotgun and a fan of £50 notes. The other phone contained a photo of bank notes totalling a few thousand pounds strewn across a staircase, and another image of £50 notes arranged to form the initials 'PGM'. In addition, officers were perturbed by some photos taken weeks earlier of uniformed colleagues patrolling in Stratford Park. Whilst police officers were delighted with the arrests, within an hour there was a further jewellery snatch in the borough.

That evening, the DCI leading the Parade, with the VCU Sergeant present, stated that officers should, 'Get to know the faces of the PGM . . . get a curfew on them'. The issue here was that, despite the efforts of police to combat the PGM there had been two snatches which constituted in the words of the VCU Sergeant, a 'growing cluster'. Tomorrow would see a Section 60 across the borough 'to deal with the robberies and with the perpetrators concealing their faces'.

Later that night the Mutual Aid provincial force that now patrolled Newham seeking the PGM came up with a drug dealer, but not a robber. An African born man in his early 20s, in jeans and t-shirt and riding a bike, was followed by the police van for half a mile. Realizing the police were on him, the cyclist threw his bike to the floor and spread himself over a short wall legs apart and arms over his head. Police searches were evidently familiar to him. The search revealed cannabis wraps in sufficient number for him to be taken into the van where he was subject to a (illegal) strip search which garnered three wraps of crack cocaine. The young man was arrested and taken into custody.

A few days later ten robberies were carried out across Newham over a 24-hour period: three on High Street North, two in Little Ilford, two in Westfield, one in Custom House, one in Canning Town and one in Forest Gate. In the view of Newham police officers, these locations confirmed that the massive Olympic police presence around Stratford had displaced crime to the East. The potential 'crime generator' for the robberies was alleged to be a flat above a shop on High Street North, where three leading PGM members were living.

However, the immediate problem for Newham police was attributing the High Street North robberies to the PGM. The gold-chain robberies were taking place at around 08.00 hours; the PGM usually committed crimes after mid-afternoon. Station gossip speculated whether 'crack heads' were behind the robberies. A female Inspector commented that she had frequently arrested one man for these types of robbery when stationed at a neighbouring borough. A decade earlier the man, now aged in his late 30s, had been a prolific offender with a long record for burglary and robbery with violence. On the morning of the robberies he had been seen riding a bike in the company of known burglars. However, as he was white and Scottish, he was not an obvious gang associate, and it was gangs that were the 'suitable enemy' of Olympic time police.

By the end of August five leading PGM members were in custody on remand, three for a post-Games (16 August) robbery in E15. Significantly however, during their detention, the previous Bank Holiday weekend had produced 19 robberies in Newham, not all of which targeted gold jewellery. This evidence suggested that the PGM were not responsible for most robberies in Newham. However, Olympic resourcing alongside policing from a Newham-based PCSO had resulted in the arrest of key PGM suspects in Games Time. Yet the problem continued to be obtaining evidence to convict. When the Olympic duty ended the borough still had robberies and snatches. Nothing had changed.

Murder in Games Time

Some of the 'serious youth violence' and gang activities during Games Time were related to perceived status challenges, and to robberies that victimized young men from adjacent neighbourhoods. From a police perspective these incidents were by their very nature highly situational, personal and impossible to anticipate or prevent.

An 18-year-old 'associate' of the Young Blood City (YBC) gang from the Alma Estate in Stratford was stabbed to death in the early hours of a morning during Games Time, some two miles from the Olympic Park in the Borough of Waltham Forest. Living with his mother, he had been attending a house party for his 16th birthday hosted at his father's home. The party was in full swing when ten youths living locally known as the Peanut Crew attempted to gain entry. The youth's father objected, and the late arrivals were told to leave. An argument over who had the right to remain developed into a street fight, and after striking one of the Peanut Crew over the head with a wooden stick, the youth received a single knife wound to the chest. He staggered to his home and died in front of his mother. The police response was two-fold: the most pressing issue was to find and charge the murderers, while a concomitant duty was to ensure that there was no revenge killing.

Within 24 hours four youths had been arrested. Surveillance cameras captured images of five youths assaulting the murdered youth. A knife, believed to be the murder weapon, had also been found. Whilst he was not a known gang member, the youth's death had the potential for retaliation and threats to kill in revenge had appeared from friends of the deceased on Facebook. The GFU claimed that there were 'tensions' between the Newham-based Green Gang and two Waltham Forest groups, the 'Clayhall Boys' and the 'Beaumont Crew'. The deceased was allegedly an associate of the latter, and it was rumoured that it was they who would be seeking revenge.

Speculation was rampant. One officer opined that the issue could be gang-related and that possibly the Green Gang had an alliance with the YBC against their Waltham Forest counterparts. The GFU visited the home of known YBC members, and the GFU Inspector advised: 'Hard stops all day on the YBC, execute any warrants on YBC/Maryland Gang over the next few days . . . Kick a few doors in if needs be. A Section 60 exists today throughout the borough'. For the next two weeks, uniformed PSUs drove around the neighbourhoods of both the deceased and the suspects, an area which covered much of the periphery of the Olympic Park. The Central Command Gangs Task Force were sent from the Centre.

The aftermath of the murder once again highlights the malleability of the 'gang' metaphor, as well as illustrating how 'gang' fears informed so much of Olympic police strategy. The reputation of the Games taking place just two miles away was not considered to be at risk, but the repercussions might bring trouble into Newham and into the proximity of the Olympic Park, as many of the YBC lived on a nearby estate. Initially, it might seem that the six-month pre-Olympic policing operation against the YBC had been futile. Yet the altercation that led to the murder was not part of a criminal conspiracy, but was instead a situational act of youth violence that was devoid of any prior incident or territorially based antagonisms.

Making sense of local 'gangs': police views on the ground

We have noted in previous chapters how the meaning of 'gangs' in the Olympic policing context, and more widely for the MPS, is opaque and highly malleable. The cases of the PGM and the tragic murder described above reveal serious flaws in the way that the police connect gangs to specific criminal acts, to particular types of criminal activity, and to specific individuals who live in inner-city, working-class locales. At the everyday level, police officers on the ground held far from uniform understandings of what gangs were, what they did, and who was or was not involved in these formations. This was exacerbated by the multiplicity of police forces, units and agencies of social control that converged on the 2012 Olympic borough. There were multiple attitudes and responses to the problem of gangs, and the desire of some officers to annoy, confront, antagonize, criminalize and even deport some of the young men of Newham was not a position that was universally held in police circles. Elements of the Newham MPS, particularly operational units, were at times realistic about the criminals in their midst and, as they saw it, the causes of criminal activity.

These diverse perspectives were highlighted at one Morning Prayers meeting of the OCZ during Games Time. The discussion was prompted by what seemed like the daily call to Newham police from a serial complainer, in this case on the subject of the PGM. As a resident in the council estate adjacent to the E15 building, the caller had made multiple complaints about the anti-social behaviour of youths living in the building. This had not changed during Games Time. A one-time Newham SNT officer listened as the complaint was read out by the OCZ Chair and wearily offered the following explanation: 'He calls daily. He lives next to the playground adjacent to the Focus building. His problem is that youths who live there stand outside smoking dope. He wants us to disperse them all day and night. There's 200 poor kids who live there. We've tried everything. He should move house! There's more police in Stratford than anywhere in the borough. When we appear they all run off and we're not doing foot-chasing . . . Anyway, it's not really a PGM issue. Really, there's just ten robbers in the PGM . . . and four of them live in High Street North not the Focus building'.

Some of the officers whose task it was to deal with the most recalcitrant young men of Newham on a daily basis held attitudes, and implemented tactics, that were more akin to social work than 'total policing'. They saw the value in intervention and diversion, and also understood the socio-political sub-text around the people and issues that were encountered. During the peak of the Games, six of the GFU were sitting in their dedicated office in Plaistow Police Station. Discussing one of their more notorious gang targets, one of the male members of the unit in his early 30s reflected on the changeable nature of this single individual: 'He's like many of them. On their own many are meek, articulate and respectful'. The brief silence was broken by a colleague some ten years older who added 'You wonder what chance they have . . . Many have useless families so the streets and mates become their family and might genuinely hold them with affection and even look out for them'. This provoked another with a similar number of years' service to add his wisdom: 'Hanging around with the big men for some is like having a personal bodyguard. They know no one will touch them – until they're found in the wrong place on their own'. The youngest members of the unit had her own take: 'They see some lad a few years older who can fight and who, for a time at least, has good gear on his back and girls around him. That does it for many youngsters – they want to be him'.

This resonated with the first speaker: 'But they don't know what "rich" or "wealthy" is. They've come from homes where a bottle of Lucozade is not affordable, so when they see someone a few years older with a roll of £20s they think he's a millionaire. He isn't; he's got just a few hundred quid to last all week and the roll is like an ornament he carries'. Some of their charges annoyed them, but their boasts were seen as hollow. As the GFU Sergeant explained: 'Some are arrogant and they'll say "Officer, I earn more a week than you do", which is bollocks. If they earn any money it's working every hour of the day and night and they spend their life looking over their shoulders for someone who wants to take it off them. Then they go home to a room in a council flat owned by their Mum'. The first speaker had a ready case study with which to illustrate his point: 'Kevin's a case in point. He told me he was offered a Country Line[5] to go to Woking or somewhere and stay in a flat or hotel room and sell crack. The hours of work were 09.00 to 13.00. For what he was getting paid he'd be better off working in Footlocker'. The notion of a 'gang career' was considered implausible because the GFU police believed the internal chaos evident in this culture was more effective in its own destruction than the actions of the police: 'It's a tragic circle. They pursue money and think it's easily obtainable and without consequences. Some of the older ones left street dealing and robbing, have tried 'project' robbery, you know hold-up on premises where there's tens of thousands of pounds . . . But this is only realizable if there's one with a good brain behind it all. Thankfully for us their chaos reflects on their projects and it all goes wrong and they go to jail'.

The first speaker admitted to a fascination with the scenarios he was employed to deal with: 'I thought of writing a film script about this gang stuff I deal with . . . I was gonna' call it "Spiderweb" cos' that's how I see it – all webs of connection without a centre,with the spider as the individual in the middle of all sorts of intrigue'. The female detective did not share the previous speaker's fascination, and returned to the social contexts of gang activity: 'They're mostly thick, impressionable, scared and don't want to be alone. At the same time many have had a shit deal in life, have weak Mums, no Dad and have little by way of possessions or income'.

There was a general agreement that gang involvement had an entrepreneurial basis in the drug trade and for participants in this economy such criminal enterprise required, at times, violent responses in order to deter predators. However: 'Our gaffers won't have it that the basis of all of this is drugs. I tried to have this with the Chief Superintendent, but he won't see that the drug economy sustains the violence'. Overall, these diverse perspectives on youth crime and policing around the Olympics highlight the relationship between policing, social context, and young people, which were also concerns of one community-based organization in Newham which was strongly active during the London Games.

Olympic Time resistance: the NMP

From an everyday operational standpoint the MPS were able to regard the Games as a success. The crowds were amiable, there had been no hint of public-order problems, the youths who had been singled out as a particular Olympic threat were conspicuous by their absence, and the overwhelming numbers of police officers milling around Stratford enabled an element of sensitivity to be employed in dealing with demonstrations and overt displays of religiosity. However, when subjected to close observation, some of the methods that enabled the organizational goals of the MPS to be achieved were far from unproblematic.

The Newham Monitoring Project (NMP) provided the sole day-to-day (non-state) organizational check on police activity in Newham during the Olympics (in effect, from the Opening Ceremony until the closure of the Paralympic Games). Founded in 1980 following the racist murder of an Asian youth, the NMP defined themselves as a Newham-based community organization with a mission to 'resist racism and defend civil rights in East London' through a mix of individual case work and community and outreach activity.[6] NMP's casework activity around the Games encompassed five of the main Olympic boroughs – Barking and Dagenham, Hackney, Newham, Tower Hamlets, Waltham Forest – as well as Redbridge. A key focus was on informing young people about their legal rights when subject to a police 'stop and search'. Whilst this policing tactic had been a significant issue in London for young people since at least the 1970s, it also reflected what NMP officials reported as a proportionately greater volume of 'racial harassment' in broader contexts, such as with local authorities.[7] The NMP were concerned *inter alia* that the police were engaging in racial profiling when conducting stop and search, targeting specific ethnic minorities.

For the NMP (2012) the Olympics harboured several major potential threats to civil liberties, including:

- the sheer scale of the police and security presence on local streets throughout the summer;
- the massive rise (by over 2,500 per cent) in the use of 'stop and search' in Newham from 2007 to 2010 (NMP, 2012: 3);
- the implementation of a large dispersal zone in the Stratford area during the Olympics, and its likely impact on ethnic minority youth;
- the possibility of racist mistreatment of people by police. After the 2011 riots the NMP had picked up a caseload of over 50 allegations from locals on racist mistreatment by police; one notorious incident, recorded on the mobile phone of an arrested youth, had been uploaded onto social media and attracted national attention (see Chapter 3).[8]

NMP's Olympic strategy centred on establishing a group of voluntary Community Legal Observers (CLOs), whose main roles would be to variously monitor policing in Newham; deter police misbehaviour; monitor and record details of arrests; examine accusations of assault by police; monitor police attempts to gain witnesses in relation to any incidents; and inform local people of their civil rights by distributing NMP's rights cards.

The plan to recruit volunteers went out through a comment piece in the *Guardian* newspaper. Subsequent calls were conveyed through social media, NMP's website and links to wider networks such as the Network for Police Monitoring and the Counter Olympics Network.[9]

Over 100 volunteers signed up for CLO training, which briefed participants on the role of CLOs, NMP's strategy for the Games, and key issues relating to human rights and legal matters regarding the Olympics, dispersal zones, stop and search, arrest and detention, and curfew powers. Volunteers were subsequently scheduled into different groups to walk or cycle around Stratford and adjacent areas where, according to local knowledge and subsequent information, police were understood to be most active, or where young ethnic minority groups might be expected to be located. NMP patrols each ran for three hours over 12-hour periods each day; the day's activity would usually conclude around 22.00, though at weekends some patrols operated later. The most active volunteers featured a strong gender mix (the clear majority were women), and were mainly comprised of white, London-based young people, particularly social-science graduates and students from a range of universities, such as Oxford, Cambridge, LSE, Goldsmith's, London Met, and Essex. Local people also comprised a sizeable proportion of partici-pants: most were young adults in their 20s and 30s, some were older, including a few over 50s; and, included a wider range of ethnicities, notably a good num-ber with South Asian and some with African-Caribbean backgrounds. The CLO teams soon became a familiar presence in the local area, attired in red high-visibility bibs provided by NMP, walking and cycling in and around Meridian Square, Stratford Centre and High Street, West Ham Park, Maryland, and Romford Road. Our research featured fieldwork with these CLO teams through-out the course of the Olympics, as well as individual and focus group interviews with NMP officials and CLOs before, during and after the Games.

The CLOs reported that, according to the broad categories used by NMP, the local policing and security atmosphere was almost always 'relaxed'. A large pro-portion of CLO time was spent talking to local residents and distributing over 7,000 rights cards. Many CLO patrols, especially those operating in weekday afternoons, had relatively little to report in terms of witnessing extended police–public interaction. Evenings offered CLO teams more opportunity to talk with young people, particularly local males, several of whom indicated they were una-ble to go into the Stratford area due to the possible activation of dispersal orders on them by police. NMP also received several reports of strip searches being conducted in the back of police vans, a policing practice that although illegal, was deemed preferable by many young people to the legal alternative of being taken into custody for the search to be conducted. Although they were unaware of the existence of the PGM, during the Olympics the CLOs came to recognize the Focus E15 area as a particularly important site for their activities, given that a large number of young people were based there, often accompanied by one or two police vans.

For the CLOs, behind the quiet atmosphere at the Olympics, there were more complex factors at play. Some CLOs were told by local people that policing prior to the Olympics had already been unusually intense. As Eve (CLO, student) explained, 'Local people weren't really able to see much of a contrast because they already recognize that they're heavily policed on a daily basis and they would just talk about, "Well, we get police through here all the time", or "I get stopped and searched all the time", or "The police say this to me, the police say that and it's just carrying on"'.

Several CLOs pointed to an apparent major contrast in policing styles according to location and public audience. As Jaz (CLO, local resident) observed,

'On one side of Stratford, on the Olympic Park side there seemed to be a kind of PR policing; "We're your mates", kind of thing. Then as soon as you headed away from the Stratford Centre into Newham it was the reverse. It was what I'd experienced in my life in general for the policing of inner London, in that it's quite confrontational, oppressive, discriminatory . . . The general public who were coming to the Olympics would see the one nice side and the people who live in the local areas would see the other side of it'.

One NMP official commented that the police appeared to have laid down early pre-Olympic markers through reports of stronger policing among local Muslim communities and the arrest of 182 cyclists on the first day of the Olympics (see chapter 7): 'I think both those things sent out a specific message to protest communities and the black community about the kind of policing that's possible with these resources'.

In broad terms, NMP's CLOs found that during the Olympics, police were widely using their stop and search powers. Some local males alleged assault on top of being stopped, and/or that they felt targeted in terms of being stopped and searched regularly or for no good reason. Others reported that police did not provide reasons for the conducting of searches. A regular concern was that police were failing to inform people of their right to a copy of the record of the search, to be issued either on the spot or when requested within a 12-month period.[10] Some CLOs reported that, when they were present at a police stop or stop and search, the police officers made an exaggerated show of issuing copies to people. Others reported that the official (private) security personnel at Stratford Park, as well as the police there, were systematically excluding local black youths due to potential 'gang' activity. Homeless people also reported that they were being stopped by police and being required to move on, often in ways that were experienced as aggressive (NMP, 2012). In the first week of the Olympics the NMP were concerned that forms of racial profiling might be occurring, with people of East European (notably Romanian) appearance being targeted for stop and search by uniformed officers.

In their reports from patrols during the Olympics, several CLOs stated that police officers were not displaying their officer numbers; when such officers were queried by the CLOs, they would often reply that the number was covered by another piece of clothing or equipment, or had just happened to 'come off'. Some CLOs filmed stop and searches; on one occasion an officer complained about this, stating that he lived locally and that he believed such recording might see his image posted on the internet. Police occasionally asked CLOs to act as supporting witnesses; CLOs firmly declined, stating that this was strictly not their role as legal observers. In one exceptional instance, CLOs did work with police to help a woman in severe distress. On several occasions, when members of the public had been stopped, some police asked CLOs to stand a few yards away in order to allow a 'private conversation' between the officer and individual concerned; the CLOs were still able to listen in, and to pass on rights cards and any further advice, after the individual had agreed to their being present. Overall, the CLOs gained the strong impression that, when they were present during police activity with local people, the latter were more likely to avoid arrest or for no further action to be taken.

Everyday relations between CLOs and police officers were generally distant, with minimal dialogue except when incidents were occurring with police and members of the public. In the first week, it was clear that many police officers, particularly those drawn from outside the MPS, had no idea who the NMP were, or had little prior training or experience of working with legal observers. In contrast, some local and other MPS instantly recognized NMP and, on occasion even offered sarcastic comments, to be heard by fellow officers and CLOs, on the status of the volunteers' legal training and local knowledge. The variability of police responses to the CLOs was summed up by Emily (CLO, local student), after monitoring police vehicle spot-checks on Romford Road: 'I think the inspector was trying to talk to us, he tried to shake my hand, and to explain, and to some extent they were being quite transparent, giving us the numbers of all the officers and accidentally giving us the map of the area. The inspector was trying to be nice and helpful but some of the other ones were much more aggressive really . . . So they haven't quite worked out what to do with legal monitors, they lack a coherent policy'.

At the same time, CLOs did not take a uniform view of the police. Some volunteers, such as Sheila, a local resident new to the position of CLO, took a sanguine view of police interaction, stating 'The police were fine, they were smiling, I'm very positive about them, I've no problems with them at all'. Others, such as Dave, a London-based student, took a pragmatic view of their broader contribution to police-community relations: 'What we're trying to do is improve relations and trust between local people and the police'. Some experienced CLOs indicated that both police and NMP maintained a very visible separation. For the NMP, this separation was important in order to retain the confidence of local people. They cautioned that, for the police, there was no such thing as a 'friendly chat': officers were always on duty and seeking to pick up information that might be used later. Some of these assessments of the police by CLOs (particularly local males) were backed up by stated experiences of being harassed (such as through verbal abuse, or stopped and searched for no credible reason), drawn into arguments that resulted in arrest, or assaulted by officers.

Several substantial episodes of interaction involving police and CLOs were observed during the research; three episodes are outlined here. First, on a midweek evening, several CLOs encountered 18 police officers at the entrance of West Ham Park conducting vehicle spot-checks. Across the road, officers pulled aside an Asian boy, aged 14, to inspect his pedal cycle. When he was slow to respond to questions, one officer placed handcuffs on him, stating he was being arrested for failing to give details. When the boy asked why he had been stopped, the officers stated that he was in a robbery hotspot; other officers stated to the watching CLOs that he had been swearing at police and cycling on the pavement. One CLO managed to get past police to hand the boy an NMP rights card. He was then released, with police stating that they would talk to his parents about his behaviour. As this went on, several onlooking local youths were joined by an Afro-Caribbean youth who advised them to 'watch what you're doing round here'. A CLO then crossed the road to ask the Sergeant about police activities.

In response the Sergeant questioned her legal training and criticized her lack of knowledge of NMP's history. Other CLOs meanwhile managed to pass rights cards through to drivers being stopped by police. After a while, the police shouted among themselves that they would be heading for Forest Lane, which the CLOs took to be a false steer to them, got into police vehicles, and drove off.

A second bit of CLO-police interaction occurred during a midweek evening at Upton Park tube station. A group of CLOs encountered a TSG unit, six of whom had gathered around a young Asian male on a motorbike. One CLO started to film the incident on his mobile phone, while the Sergeant appeared and, seeking to gain the initiative, stated to the youth: 'It's Newham Monitoring Project, do you want to tell them why you've been stopped?'. The youth explained that his bike, which had a flat tyre, had been stationary but was pointing the wrong way down a one-way street. Meanwhile, several other officers were talking to another CLO, asking her name, which she declined to give. After a short delay the youth was allowed to go and the police got back into their van. A verbal exchange then ensued between one CLO and some police officers in the van, leading to the Sergeant briefly alighting the vehicle; both sides then accused each other of being 'unprofessional' in regard to the language used (by the CLO) and general conduct (by the police). The van then left. The CLO stated to his colleague, 'The point is, that interaction demonstrates how the police operate, their antagonistic approach towards everyone . . . It always turns out like that. I've asked them a question and their response is like, "You think you're a smart arse, I'll be a smart arse." That kind of demonstrates what the police are like. Imagine you're a young person and you say "Well actually I don't have to give my name and address". "Well OK smart arse"'.

In a third instance, CLOs were present when an Islamist demonstration was staged on the evening of the Closing Ceremony. Around 60 demonstrators surrounded by police walked 500 metres from the Morrison's supermarket car park to Meridian Square and back. At the march's conclusion, a small group of police pulled over one demonstrator to check whether there was an arrest warrant for him. One NMP CLO sought to offer advice to the man, but an MPS officer tried to ease him away. This led to an argument over whether police were being 'patronizing' and preventing the CLO from witnessing what was taking place. During the argument, the protestor asked the CLO to calm down; comments which police reiterated to the CLO. The police check came up negative, and he was allowed to go. The CLO shook hands with the demonstrators, and commented later on the irony of his situation: on the one hand, he was observing police activity to safeguard the rights of the demonstrators; on the other hand, as a Shia Muslim, he believed that the Islamists on the demonstration would normally be shouting for him and his people to be killed.

The major institutional obstruction to NMP's work during the Olympics came not from the police but from Newham Council. A week into the Games, the official security personnel on council duty at Stratford Park had banned NMP's CLOs from entering on the alleged grounds that they were 'making it easy for criminals and giving them tips'. As a 'live' Olympic site, Stratford Park potentially afforded NMP CLOs with access to significant numbers of local people and visitors. When NMP protested to council officials, different explanations were given for their exclusion, including the possibility that NMP might generate 'litter' through the distribution of rights cards, and the event policy that banned organizations with a 'branded presence'. NMP viewed such explanations as absurd. A further ban on NMP's CLOs was imposed at Stratford bus station through the activation of a Transport for London bye-law.[11]

After the Games, NMP's CLOs offered varied reflections on police–community relations during the Olympics. A few, such as Janine (CLO, trainee teacher), considered that the minimal tensions had been a positive sign: 'I didn't see a lot of issues which would have raised tensions between the public and the police ... there was a lot of improvement with the relationship between the public and the police'. Others, such as Phillip (CLO, London student), expressed concerns about the potential normalization of blanket policing: 'To some extent by design, but I don't know to what extent, the fact that there were a lot of police meant that you got used to it'. One subsequent concern was that armed police became a normalized sight outside Stratford Station, and even a tourist attraction for some visitors who would pose for photographs with these officers. For some, the sheer number of police in the wider Newham area was viewed as offering more chances for harassment, as Alex (CLO, local resident) stated: 'The level of resources lent itself to harassment . . . On evenings you would find vans of police driving around . . . Some of the police who like that kind of thing probably felt quite happy that they had an opportunity to tackle groups of young people on late evenings. The police generally travel in patrols of two or three. I don't think two policemen would just stop like five, six, ten young people normally. I think those were the kind of differences you'd find'.

For some NMP officials and CLOs, the Olympics had highlighted some important missed opportunities on the part of the police in terms of building better relations with the local community. Some CLOs indicated that, while admittedly a time-consuming practice, the police should be fully consistent in issuing copies of records to people whom they had they stopped. Others commented that they had received reports from members of the public that, when arrested, the police had prevented them from calling NMP: a practice which had no legal basis. Several CLOs recognized that it would be too much to expect a single one-off event such as the Olympics to have a huge impact in transforming how the police were organized or conducted their business. But, some CLOs again highlighted the unduly different ways in which police presented themselves to different audiences, as Claire (NMP official, local resident) commented:, 'As they were presenting this very lovely "bobby on the beat" face at Westfield, there was also an opportunity to create a different relationship with the community in Newham . . . Seeing as that face was being presented at Westfield, why isn't that the face that's presented to everybody else all the time?'.

NMP CLOs commented that their main impacts and achievements centred on monitoring police activity, and in some cases gaining the strong impression that an NMP presence served to positively influence police conduct when interacting with local people. The CLOs also observed that, more widely, they had increased public awareness of civil rights, and the available support of NMP in the event of arrest or negative experiences with police.

The NMP's post-Olympic report highlighted several lessons that may be drawn from their experiences, which might be transferred into other situations where legal observers are established. These lessons included: the importance of strong local knowledge, so there is an immediate awareness of potential hotspots; recruiting a large volume of volunteer CLOs, in part to allow for varied availability and some attrition, while making full use of experienced CLOs at the outset; training CLOs to use 'observation and common sense'; use of cycle patrols to cover more ground; provision of good back-office support; regular volunteer feedback meetings; and post-event celebration of the work of CLOs. While Newham is highly unlikely to see a comparable mega-event occurring in the foreseeable future, these findings might be applied to other contexts when NMP or other organizations may bring together a mix of experienced and new CLO volunteers, such as for major public demonstrations or large-scale one-off sport events. On such occasions, more stringent and widespread policing will be to the fore, hence NMP and other civil rights organizations will be focused on examining the policing impacts and experiences of the local community.

Conclusion

In this chapter, we have examined policing and police–community relations during Games Time with respect to the core organizational participants: Newham borough policing (and colleagues on Mutual Aid) and the NMP. For the police, their main target 'gangs' were, particularly, but not exclusively, the PGM. Key criminal activities pursued by the police centred on robberies and serious youth violence, but although the murder of a youth during the Games just over the Newham border was not the borough's remit and did not a carry an Olympic foot-print, it was a reminder that the issue of SYV was never too far away. For the NMP, the massive police presence in Newham in Games Time required monitoring, particularly police interactions with young people of minority ethnic origins.

Games Time police–community relations in Newham featured three forma-tions that had different degrees of formal organization: first, the most stratified and institutionalized entity came in the shape of the police; second came the NMP, a long-standing community organization that relied particularly on the goodwill and availability of volunteer CLOs; and third was the PGM and other groups who were, despite their 'gang' label, amorphous, loosely constituted, and lacking any sense of a sustainable organization. One crucial issue for all of these formations concerned the extent to which they were able to draw on friends and allies to assist their respec-tive activities. Through the Mutual Aid initiative, Newham police received back-up from police forces across the UK. In order to implement their ambitious monitoring programme during the Olympics, NMP recruited, trained, and co-ordinated large numbers of volunteer CLOs, drawn in many instances from outside of the borough. They too had mobbed up. In marked contrast, the PGM did not appear to increase their presence in any way during the Games; indeed, through arrests or displace-ment they declined in numbers: the outrageous claims made by 'Intel' concerning their numbers being supplemented during Games Time, were predictably false.

Three key themes emerged from the everyday policing and police–community relations in Newham during Games Time: diversity, information and communica-tion. First, on diversity, it was clear that a wide range of views were held by police on gangs, youth and local crime. The same applies to views held by NMP CLOs on policing during the Games. As we discussed in Chapter 3, there were diverse meanings and definitions with regard to 'gangs'; in terms of what constituted a 'gang', who might be classified as a 'gang member', and in what criminal activity gangs were engaged. The case of the PGM provided a strong illustration of the multiple projections (and indeed non-projections) that can be imposed upon the 'gang'.

Secondly, police intelligence both from the Centre and from civilian analysts in Newham proved to be wide of the mark. Yet, the dissemination of Intel regarding gangs targeting Olympic visitors had a major influence on planning Olympic Time police strategies, both in the build-up to the Olympics and during Games Time itself. Speculation regarding PGM numbers and their Games Time activities were used by various police units and special squads in order to justify their activities, or support requests to the Centre for additional resourcing.

Thirdly, police intelligence on gangs, which ultimately shaped policing strategies, made relatively limited use of the stocks of knowledge and expertise that were held by specialist police units on the ground. For example, the views of officers within the GFU on gangs appeared to have little impact on overall police strategies, and a conspicuous remoteness from local communities, including those who constituted 'police property', were serious deficiencies that were particularly glaring with regard to the PGM. Without a reasonable level of knowledge and understanding as to who they were, and what they needed to lift them out of what was in many instances a very miserable existence typified by exclusion, there was little prospect of an effective long-term strategy in terms of moving away from police and criminal justice system solutions, towards alternative forms of intervention.

Given the distinctively mobile and fluid nature of an Olympic public who adhered to neither the local community nor its related territory (the locals were not present, while the visitors were merely passing through), it was left to police audiences to identify events as troubling, or signalling a weak social order. While the huge police presence around Stratford during the 2012 Olympic Games was a very visible symbol of social control (see Manning 1997, 2003), outside of the core Olympic zone, that symbol was less about reassuring the local public (see Jackson & Bradford, 2009), and more about providing forms of institutional reassurance for the wider police organization *per se*: making clear that professional risks were under control, and post-Olympic reputations would be protected if not burnished. To this end the police strategy was basically to loiter in anticipation of mass public-order problems, while making occasional forays into the hinterland to confront the usual suspects.

Notes

1 Shortly after this conversation, the GFU discovered a Kalashnikov rifle with one bullet in the magazine hidden in a park near a housing estate in Custom House.
2 For a discussion of Olympic-related bail conditions see Fussey (2014: 6–7).
3 'Operation Nexus is a joint Home Office and Police Service initiative to identify and remove or deport those who pose a risk to the public or who are not entitled to be in the UK. The most significant feature involves stationing Immigration Officers at police custody suites to identify immigration offenders and organise for them to be detained

pending their removal from the UK.' (an inspection of Immigration Enforcement activity in London and the West Midlands. Independent Chief Inspector of Borders and Immigration. December, 2014).

4 Interestingly the 2011 statement from the Centre that the term 'Mafia' should be replaced in policing circles by 'Robbers' was now forgotten. The Portuguese were once again a 'Mafia'.

5 Country Line was a very popular term used by police officers to describe drug-dealing activity by local youths carried out outside of Newham. Newham youths were being discovered as active beyond the borough, particularly in Essex, Surrey, Kingston, Bath and beyond. Rather than regard this as unremarkable evidence of the East End's long-established tradition of entrepreneurship, it was often described to us by police officers as an example of gang imperialism, an effort to expand their territory. However as a local entrepreneur explained to one of the research team many decades earlier, 'It's not the principle, it's the money'.

6 The victim, Akhtar Ali Baig, had been murdered on East Ham High Street in an attack later described by the trial judge as 'plainly motivated by racial hatred'. NMP's website reported that, in response, '150 Asian and Afro-Caribbean youths marched to Forest Gate Police Station, but police refused to release any information, claiming it was a "mugging". These youths formed the "Newham Youth Movement" and called for mass demonstrations, which led to several arrests . . . Newham Monitoring Project was born later that year out of the need for an organisation representative of all local constituencies active on the issue of racial discrimination.' (see http://www.nmp.org.uk/timeline/).

7 Interview with Elaine, NMP official, April 2012.

8 See, for example, http://www.theguardian.com/uk/2012/mar/30/police-racism-black-man-abuse.

9 The Counter Olympics Network was a network of groups and individuals linking critics of aspects of the 2012 Games.

10 According to the Police and Criminal Evidence Act 1984, Code A, 3.10.

11 The bye-law provisions stated *inter alia* that, in regard to areas such as TfL bus stations, 'no person on the premises shall . . . display anything for the purpose of advertising or publicity, or distribute anything' (technically, these provisions could encompass NMP's distribution of rights cards and promotion of their work). See https://www.tfl.gov.uk/cdn/static/cms/documents/road-transport-premises-byelaws.pdf.

References

Fussey, P. (2014) 'Command, Control and Contestation: Negotiating Security at the London 2012 Olympics', *The Geographical Journal,* advance publication DOI: 10.1111/geoj.12058.

Hobbs, D. (2013) *Lush Life: Constructing Organised Crime in the UK*. Oxford: Oxford University Press.

Jackson, J. & Bradford, B. (2009) 'Crime, Policing and Social Order: On the Expressive Nature of Public Confidence in Policing', *The British Journal of Sociology*, 60(3): 493–521.

Manning, P. K. (1997) *Police Work: The Social Organization of Policing*. Prospect Heights, IL: Waveland Press.

Manning, P. K. (2003) *Policing Contingencies*. Chicago: University of Chicago Press.

NMP (Newham Monitoring Project) (2012) *Monitoring Olympics Policing During the 2012 'Security Games'*. London: NMP.

Reiner, R. (2010) *The Politics of the Police*. Oxford: Oxford University Press.

10 Post-Olympic policing

Practice and legacy

The London 2012 Olympic Games came and went without major incident. There were no mass protests, no terrorist attacks, and the feared robberies of tourists by predatory local youths never materialized. The Table Top exercises had built lines of communication and forms of understanding across different blue-light agencies and hierarchies, but the worst-case scenarios under discussion had not occurred. Taking a strongly cautious, 'risk-averse' position, the police had sought to 'manage-out' anyone regarded as posing a potential challenge to commercial and governmental reputations, and to cleanse the Olympic neighbourhood, partly by removing 'offending' groups and unwanted businesses that did not fit with either the smooth running of the Games, or its legacy potential. During Games Time anyone constituting a perceived threat was excluded from the vicinity of the Olympic zone by both police and private security personnel. Any residual 'matter out of place' (Douglas, 1966) was carefully managed by local police, or swamped by the hordes of Olympic visitors (Chapter 8) who generally moved around without their public transport journeys being disrupted.[1]

The UK government guaranteed the IOC a safe and peaceful Games, and to this end some 50,000 people drawn from government, civil service, military, police, organizing committees and private security had delivered at a cost of £1.1 billion (Raine, 2014). Local risks with international implications saw an over-resourced intelligence capacity working alongside a massive uniformed presence of some 12,000 officers drawn via Mutual Aid from across the UK's police forces, as the police promoted and protected the symbolic economies of this often fractious entrepreneurial city. The governance of the Games was never vulnerable to challenge, and critical infrastructure was not disturbed. Hosting the Olympics marked an opportunity to leverage an unprecedented policing capacity (cf. Van Wynsberghe et al., 2012), but within police circles there was a general reluctance to apply too much diligence to the concept of 'Olympic-related crime', which stood at 276 arrests over the 22 days of the Games, comprising: one bomb hoax, 168 for ticket touting, 22 drug offences, 11 for theft, ten for fraud, five for robbery and two for burglary (Channel 4 News, 2012, cited by Fussey, 2014: 6).

Changing places: Olympic legacy

During our time working in the field there had been some remarkable changes regarding policing in the London Borough of Newham. For example, by 2013 we could note that Lithuanians were no longer commonly discussed amongst police ranks as a 'crime problem', and although we were presented with some inconclusive crime statistics suggesting that some Lithuanian men were fond of drinking alcohol and fighting each other, we gained the impression that this was a community beginning to mature, settling into London via a familiar mix of assimilation and retention of tradition that historically has defined so many immigrant flows. It is also significant that the Detective Inspector who took a close professional and personal interest in the plight of the Lithuanian community had from early 2012 been posted elsewhere in the MPS. Despite the increasing centralization of MPS police strategies, we would suggest that some individual officers do succeed in imposing a personal influence within an increasingly rigid, depersonalized organization; this influence, and its absence, will be reflected in the crime figures, and the DI's relationship with the Lithuanian community is a case in point. Additionally, both during and shortly after the Olympics, Newham's chicken shops were enthusiastically targeted by the borough's officers, particularly with regard to food- and health-related legislation, and as a consequence had ceased to be regarded by the police as 'crime generators'. Indeed, in post-Olympic Newham the location generating most concern with regard to crime and disorder became the 24-hour casino, which as part of the Westfield complex is integral to the 2012 Games legacy.

Policing: winners and losers

There was no Newham post-Olympic debriefing nor were there any Newham officers invited to the de-brief meetings held in Central London in the Autumn of 2012. Many senior officers considered the Games to have been 'just another event' which the MPS had taken in their stride and managed with quiet competence. The policing of the London Olympics was undoubtedly a 'win' – but no-one knew why.

According to Newham's OCZ Superintendent, this success was due to planning, procedure and providence: 'I'm not sure why it was a success! Some plots were disrupted, we had the right people in the right places'. There was also a commonly held belief that the MPS possessed a command structure that had coped competently with risk and stress. As the OCZ Superintendent explained, 'As a sub-bronze [and therefore part of a much larger command structure] I had lots of checks and balances which made risks easier to accept. The ones I thought were realistic I resourced for. I accepted more risk once I trusted people [in partner organizations]. In the first week we spent the whole time dealing with logistical problems, which prevented us assessing the competence of others . . . Three of four days out from the Closing Ceremony I started to relax'.

As an Olympic Bronze, the Superintendent received Olympic-related intelligence which he had to trust, but did so comforted by a massive potential response in the shape of the Olympic Reserve at his disposal. As he explained, 'You have to trust what [information] comes to you, even if it is sanitized to within an inch. The key is how it is corroborated. If it is single strand and uncorroborated then it gets a minimal response. During Games Time I had so many cops who could be deployed that I could respond to everything'. Risk calculations were informed by resources. The one interventionist strategy that the Superintendent admitted to related to crowds in Westfield on Day 1, which were not being particularly well managed; he acted: 'I got LOCOG and Westfield to come and see me. It wasn't my role, but I needed to get the operation working'. There were some decisions that had to be made. The Superintendent revealed that one man tasked with managing part of Meridian Square 'wanted it cleared out' [removing all of the religious groups] and another 'senior council' (LBN) figure was unsympathetic to the presence of the religious groups. Having taken counsel from his two Chief Inspectors, the Superintendent refused to move anyone from the Square, explaining: 'You have to keep checking yourself and remember that there are people here and a community to be policed. There's a right to protest. They [the two CI's] persuaded me to leave everyone where they were. It's the benefit of having local cops. We had all been to meetings and knew about the local "Cohesion" agenda. There were only pockets of people complaining about the religious groups, and there were no grounds for arrests. Maybe it tells us that we have to accept a degree of "criminality" for the sake of community harmony'.

When asked whether the Olympics had left a public-order policing legacy, the Superintendent replied, 'There are lots of [new] policies and procedures arising out of the Games. The role of the Protest Liaison Officers[2] was cemented during the Games; that allowed us to do smarter policing. Going forward, public order [policing] needs to be more sophisticated and more aware of the borough's needs'. And did the Olympics bring specific crime? A smile preceded his response: '"Olympic-related" was used by the Olympics [Command] to push crimes back onto the borough. Within the MPS there were tensions regarding Olympic remits: who investigates which crimes was an issue which, despite the plethora of pre-Olympic "Table- Tops", had to be constantly negotiated, especially around the OCZ whose personnel did not want "Olympic-related" crimes attributable to their "patch"'.[3] This ambiguity meant that the true extent of 'Olympic-related' crime was unknowable.

The Closing Ceremony inspired a degree of resentment amongst some Newham police officers, particularly those who had worked long hours in the OCZ. As one CI explained, 'A few at the top will get Queen's Medals. Those who have lived and breathed it, both in the years leading up and in the 17 days, will get a letter from Gold saying "Well done. Thanks for the 'hard work'" then that's it . . . The plaudits will be for LOCOG for delivering and the Army who came in late and who can do no wrong . . .[4] We just delivered and secured the whole damn thing. The heroes of the Olympics were those of us who held the perimeter'.

In addition, some colleagues were retiring after a rather comfortable final few years of duty, while others were leaving with lucrative Olympic-inspired post-retirement plans. As one Inspector commented, 'You watch . . . There'll be dozens of Olympic "security experts" and "consultants" in the phonebook by Christmas'. 'Dozens' was an exaggeration, but within a year a number of retired MPS officers were advisors to the 2016 Rio de Janeiro Olympics. While Olympic Park duty was considered as the easiest in the MPS, consisting of little more than standing around having photographs taken with Olympic visitors,[5] others who had enjoyed generally pleasant Olympic duties had a shock coming to them: 'They've had years in a Met Office working 9–5 getting to meet important people and celebrities . . . in September they're back on borough regular duties. They'll hate it . . . and some won't be liked by those who got left behind and missed the gravy train'. However, beyond these relatively minor, but we would argue culturally telling gripes and jealousies, the MPS had enjoyed a remarkable Games informed by a policing response utilizing unprecedented resources.

The formula for the management of policing the Games was unique in the history of the MPS. A distant Centre took control of disseminating and managing information, particularly in relation to interpretations of 'Olympic-related' crime. This ratcheting up of managerialism was not problem-free; tensions were apparent at the wider MPS level between conflicting portfolios of those pursuing the wholesale reform of territorial (borough) policing from late 2011, and those concerned specifically with the delivery of Olympic policing. In particular, the reform process was characterized by a lack of clarity about timescales and operating models, which during the first half of 2012 had seemed to be in a state of constant flux.

In Games Time, primacy was given to what might best be termed desk-based interpretations of local realities, and the status given to intelligence seemed to have no boundaries. The intelligence-handling capacity made available to Olympic Commanders proved to be four times over-resourced as a consequence of assumptions about the likely increase in intelligence: a calculation extrapolated from the wholly dissimilar context of the 2010 Vancouver Winter Olympics.[6] Intel sometimes emanated from unattributed rumour and gossip, but few were prepared to articulate their scepticism. Intel-led planning assumptions had layered one 'worst-case scenario' (most obviously, a terrorist attack) on top of another (such as a repeat of the 2011 riots), with the result that London had mustered an unprecedented number of centrally accountable public-order units which were ultimately surplus to Olympic policing requirements.

The interpretations of intelligence by a Centre lacking local insight and context were often not recognized at a local level, most notably during Games Time with regard to the PGM. Crucially, the Olympics demonstrated how parochial social problems, such as internecine violence between local youths, could assume major significance and associated individual and institutional reputational risks. Confronted with these risks, with a finite timescale and limited to a distinct locality, there was every incentive to take temporary, distinctly illiberal but pragmatic measures to enforce the separation of local and Olympic populations. Indeed, the routine use of tactics such as Section 60 stop and searches, as well as implementing dispersal powers directed at youths in public spaces, constituted a clear contradiction of any claims regarding 'intelligence-led policing'. The use of these tactics further undermined police legitimacy in the eyes of that all- important Newham demographic: young men in their teens and early 20s.

Policing legacies

According to Olympic Gold, the Games gave the disparate parts of the MPS a common purpose. Non borough resources were 'controlled centrally. Everyone agreed that this was a much fairer set-up than what we normally have . . . and thus developed a better, fairer way of running London, but it meant that bosses and fief-doms had to give up resources and control. The organization is not well equipped to give an accurate picture [of events and policing demand across London]. This has to be built from the bottom up, but the current system is too slow: crimes are reported, assessed by analysts, and fed in to local tasking processes, and this can take two weeks. My view is that boroughs need a "watchtower" model, where a central office can view events in real time and take decisions quickly . . . and if extra resources are required this can be referred upwards in fast time'. If the MPS were to take lessons from the Games, it is not inconceivable that London could be policed using the public-order Gold/Silver/Bronze model, with non-borough assets/resources managed centrally, with serious consequences for the autonomy of local borough policing. However, when we asked if the MPS might adopt this more centralized model, the rueful, soon to retire, officer replied, 'Probably not. We have the wrong people in the wrong roles. The Met will fall back on its com-fort zone – as it has been doing for the last 180 years'. However, despite this slice of seasoned occupational wisdom, our research has indicated to us that in the cur-rent climate of austerity, if a plan could save money, it is highly likely to find itself in the frame to be considered for implementation.

Crucially however, the much vaunted terrorist threat to the Games was never realized. Indeed, whether there had been a genuine/meaningful increase in 'hos-tile reconnaissance' around the Olympic Park and Westfield, we will never know. According to Silver, the detailed intelligence database compiled by the OCZ gave a 'very detailed picture' and it was believed that any major security threats would have been identified. Yet the threat of terrorism did produce an Olympic-related policing legacy in the form of the Counter-Terrorism Network, essentially an organizational partnership consisting of the security services, police intelligence units, and the national lead for domestic extremism. However, senior officers in Newham were unaware of the existence of either the partnership or the database that it generated, which severely limited the dissemination of Intel, and effectively hamstrung local officers. The contents of the database were searchable, but had not been copied onto the main intelligence database used by the MPS.

Borough policing: training for the future

Newham was a desirable posting for ambitious senior officers, and taking on an exceptionally diverse and statistically failing borough could considerably enhance future prospects. Career progression demanded 'evidence of impact' as indicated in crime league tables, and a constant churn of senior police personnel combined with an obsession with short-term (daily and fortnightly) crime statistics, produced a form of micro-management from the Centre which encouraged tick-box managerialism with never-ending references to 'assets', 'nominals', 'intelligence profiles', 'problem solving', ideas of 'proportionate' action and response, and, of course, risk, resourcing, resilience, and reassurance. The mission was 'priority crime types', 'performance targets', and 'Top 10 nominals' (be they robbers, burglars or gang members). Complexities were simplified and reduced to categories and then sub-divided to fit police structures. In the absence of an understanding of broader contexts, police relied on piece-meal intelligence and too often fell back on the clichéd notion of 'Mr Bigs' who need to be 'taken out'. The philosophy did not change even if the personnel did. By the end of our Olympic research the demographic of Newham's police managers had changed significantly: in two instances, they were Oxbridge-educated, some had flexible working conditions to accommodate child care; some cycled to work. They were the future of the MPS.

As we have shown earlier in this book, during the pre-Olympic years, the relationship between Newham police and Newham Council was often tense, and post-Olympics these strains did not ease. The council's hierarchy and subsequent line management was not as rigid or clear-cut as that of the police, and officers frequently denigrated council personnel and their abilities. It is worth noting that council employees were in some cases working with the spectre of redundancy, and in the course of our research several individuals involved in various forums lost their jobs. Conversely, council officials and politicians, and particularly the Mayor, were often critical of the police, in particular concerning SYV/Gangs, and a number of councillors demanded punitive action, which in turn was opposed by other councillors as well as a number of police officers. There was a reluctant, sometimes fractious working partnership, but money assured that the police and the council continued to work together. The council held discretionary funding from City Hall, for instance via the Mayor's Office for Policing and Crime (MOPAC), and therefore needed to be kept onside, and when extra resources became available, disagreements were accommodated. The council held the purse strings for the funding of both Total Enforcement, and to a degree the assistance given to the GFU via Section 92 policing funding (as explained in Chapter 3), and negotiations concerning the tasking of these sub-contracted officers were often fraught, particularly regarding the circumstances in which they could be recalled or deployed by the Borough Commander.[7] The 'Crime and Disorder Reduction Partnership' structure was ultimately concerned with the allocation of funding, often with regard to sub-contracting police services to either local authorities or to commercial entities, and this brought to the fore tensions regarding governance, ethics and intelligence-sharing protocols. A lot depended on trust.

The Olympics did not alter borough policing culture. Generally, as we suggest in Chapter 9, the concerns of Newham MPS in Games Time were the same as those of the preceding and succeeding years. Crime trends, particularly crime performance, were continuously scrutinized. Outcomes were described as 'acceptable', 'good' and 'not so good', and officers heading sub-specialist units became obsessed with criticism from their seniors regarding these metrics. For all levels of police management, the key issue was to equip themselves with a credible *narrative* to explain their performance, as represented by the crime statistics, to their superiors. Police narratives invariably claimed that falls in crime resulted from police efficacy, while rises were the result of external factors, such as the 2012 Olympic-related drain on borough resources. As in the pre-Olympic milieu, during Games Time and after, there was constant haggling over crime classification, most notably around the distinction between 'theft' and 'burglary', and 'gangs' and 'robbery'. Efforts were made at times to justify the 'no-criming' of allegations, and Fixed Penalty Notices (FPNs) were wielded against those accused of falsely claiming that they had been robbed of their phones.[8] Manipulating the metrics was given a very high priority.

Post-Olympics, this 'busy but not dangerous' borough remained a place where Newham-based officers chose not to live,[9] and the most ethnically diverse local authority in Britain was policed predominantly by white British-born men and women who commuted to work from the suburbs. The frequently bewildered police officers had little comprehension of the lives or cultures of a local population drawn largely from the global South and former Eastern Bloc states.[10] The vast majority of Newham's residents were law-abiding and busy with the task of making ends meet, and had limited engagement with the police. Consequently, post-Olympics 'public confidence' in the police remained exceptionally low in Newham, the borough coming last in a 'league table' of London's 32 boroughs.[11] However, in our years of research in the borough public confidence seldom merited substantive discussion in police circles, and our questions to the SMT on this matter were dismissed (see Stanko et al., 2012). However, when the Newham Borough Commander of two years duration departed in mid-2014 he was lauded for his role in restoring public confidence as interpreted by MPS-generated statistics, and his successor was also lauded for his role elsewhere in the MPS for policing SYV/Gangs.

Whitehall and County Hall

The MPS took comfort wherever it could in the post-Olympic milieu. Despite recorded crime levels continuously falling since the mid-1990s, the relationship between the Conservative Party and the police, cemented during the Miners' Strike of 1985/6 and the wider Thatcher era, was now strained to the point that the police union had taken to protesting on the streets, balloting their members to strike and taking every opportunity to publicly oppose the planned policing reforms that were pursued by the Conservative Home Secretary. These conflicts were manifested most clearly in the heckling of Home Secretary Theresa May during her speech to the Police Federation just two months before the Olympic Opening Ceremony. The successful delivery of London 2012 did not change this growing antagonism, and police learned shortly after the Games of a reduction in starting salaries and the requirement to contribute to their travel costs to work. In the summer of 2014, May unveiled measures to restrict the use of stop and search, declaring the practice 'an unacceptable affront to justice', an 'enormous waste of police time', and damaging to public–police relations. Introducing a voluntary scheme for 20 forces which would restrict searches when no suspicion was evident, chief police officers would henceforth need to deem it 'necessary' to authorize stop and search powers in the belief that violence 'will' (rather than 'may') take place. The Home Secretary also required forces to record the outcome of the searches in more detail, including whether any stops had led to arrests.

Less than a month after the Closing Ceremony a Conservative MP and Chief Whip, Andrew Mitchell, was involved in an altercation with a police officer whilst attempting to exit the main gate to Downing Street on his bicycle. According to an official police log, Mitchell responded angrily swearing at the officer and describing the police as 'fucking plebs' (Winnett, 2012). The following day the Government's Deputy Chief Whip received an email, apparently from a bystander, which corroborated the log's version of events. After the story went public, calls for Mitchell's resignation emanated from sections of the press, the Police Federation and his political opponents, and Mitchell (still denying using the p-word) resigned in late October 2012, However, in December 2012 Channel 4 News reported that the author of the email sent on September 20, which corroborated the police log's versions of events was actually a police officer. This was followed by the release of CCTV footage which seemed to support Mitchell's claims about the brevity of the exchange and the lack of witnesses. Eventually, misconduct charges were levelled against seven officers: one involving criminal conduct, three involving gross misconduct and three involving misconduct that did not warrant dismissal from the MPS. On 6 February 2014, an officer, facing charges of misconduct in a public office for sending the forged email, was sentenced to 12 months in prison. Former Director of Public Prosecutions, Lord MacDonald, criticized the MPS for the length of its inquiry (Siddique, 2013), while Home Secretary Teresa May cited the incident in her calls for reform of Britain's police forces (Kettle, 2014). The post- Olympic policing honeymoon was well and truly over. The whole episode concluded when Mitchell lost a libel action in November 2014 against the *Sun* newspaper, which had reported the original story, with a judge ruling that he probably had used the phrase 'plebs'; the insulted police officer later accepted damages of £80,000 from Mitchell, who was estimated to have lost up to £2 million in total costs (Evans, 2014).

Who actually ran the MPS became a post-Olympic issue. The Mayor of London, Boris Johnson, speaking in January 2014 urged the MPS to 'get Medieval' on those who caused public disorder in the Capital (Barrett, 2014). In June 2014, fearing a repeat of the 2011 riots, Johnson purchased three second-hand water cannon vehicles from the German federal government at a cost of £218,000. Senior officers in the MPS admitted to journalists that there were no plans to use the vehicles, which would be worthless in the built-up urban environment of London. The Home Secretary had not approved their purchase, and they were being phased out in Germany for safety reasons. Learning of the purchase, Newham-based officers shook their heads in disbelief as they remembered the inappropriateness of the attempted deployment of the six Junker bomb-proof and bullet-proof vehicles to Newham's narrow streets during the 2011 riots, and the judicious parking of these vehicles out of sight in the car park of East London Rugby Club. In July 2015, Johnson was publicly rebuked in Parliament by the Home Secretary who cited a detailed Home Office assessment that found 67 faults and concerns with these vehicles. The Home Secretary concluded her rebuke by affirming that the vehicles would never be used in the UK.[12] In the May 2015 General Election, Johnson, touted as a future Prime Minister, while retaining his job as Mayor of London, was elected as Member of Parliament for the constituency of Uxbridge and Ruislip South, some 30 miles west of Newham.

The post-Olympic policing culture was marked by a palpable despondency. By the end of March 2013 senior police in Newham admitted to 'seeing the glass half empty', and feeling like 'giving up', as central diktats piled up in their in-boxes; resources were being pared back, and there was a feeling that career prospects were diminishing. Decisions were imposed without consultation, and the relatively new office of MOPAC was blamed for much of the reduction of local police autonomy as individual police divisions lost their ability to manage resources in accord with the needs of local communities. For instance, Newham, with an official population of 308,000 experienced just under 33,000 crimes in 2012, and consequently should have received significantly more resources than a borough like Richmond upon Thames with a population of 187,000 and under 12,000 reported crimes. Yet Newham were informed by MOPAC that they were to lose two police stations in comparison to Richmond who experienced no closures. In addition, police intelligence officers were relocated from local police stations to two East London hubs covering the MPS's six North Eastern boroughs.

The UK general election of May 2015 returned a majority Conservative government intent on imposing further cuts on public services, and the Home Secretary Theresa May resumed her campaign to drastically reduce the cost of policing. When the police highlighted the possible consequences of these cuts,[13] May accused the force of 'crying wolf' over the potential risks.[14] The working environment of London's police officers was best summed up in an article written by an MPS officer who had resigned in frustration:

> Against a backdrop of fiscal austerity, the looming threat of terrorism – in some instances directed at police officers themselves – the shakeup of pay, conditions and recruitment proposed by the Winsor review, and the lingering impact of scandal that taints both previous and present management in London's main police service, the Met is losing excellent police officers hand over fist.[15]

Meanwhile, as we detail in Chapter 4, Westfield had created a series of crime-related problems that inspired complex interagency responses, and Newham MPS had also to police the newly-titled Queen Elizabeth Olympic Park (QEOP). The various commercial and public entities located within the QEOP would produce inevitable disputes between public- and private-sector interests, which in turn could have significant implications for the governance of this new space. One of the first post-Olympic Special Events on the Park was a rap concert that attracted a crowd of 10,000; there were just two stabbings and no one in the MPS was sure if they were 'gang-related'.

Revisiting the Olympic threat: gangs and terror

In this book we have emphasized the importance of terrorism and youth gangs in the construction of the 'Olympic threat'. Of these two threats, terrorism is relatively intangible, difficult to locate and residing in alcoves dominated by a difficult to define 'other'. As we discuss in previous chapters, this made it crucial to raise violent youth groups to the level of national threat, for its proponents are highly visible traditional deviant entities, who under the convenient, now seldom questioned umbrella of the 'gang', have, along with terrorism, proved resilient threats that have outlasted the Games.

Post-Olympic terror

The fact that the Games did not produce a terrorist incident should not detract from the huge effort that was expended to prevent such an occurrence (Fussey, 2014). Although some of the prospects for Olympic terror may well have resided in a knowledge-bubble floating some way above our security clearance, as we have highlighted throughout this book, we could not ignore the fact that a significant portion of Newham's population endured, both in the build-up to the Games and during Games Time itself, an existence under the cloud of suspected terrorism.

Following the 2005 London bombings, allegiance to Islam had come to indicate potential terrorism, and suspicion of Muslim communities had heightened (Pantazis & Pemberton, 2009). The counter terrorist momentum that had built up before the Games had not subsided in the wake of a terror-free Olympics, and the stereotypical virtues of Asians, such as tight-knit communities, family structure, and religion were now considered as suspect and nurturing crime (Hudson, 2007). The surveillance of Muslim residents in Newham that was enabled by the Olympics had established a precedent (Spalek, El Awa & MacDonald, 2008), and in 2014/15 Newham was second only to Westminster in generating CT activity.[16] As one Newham officer explained, 'In the months before the Olympics we'd get an average of three taskings (jobs) a week, we're now dealing with an average of 90 a month'. By 2015, the matrix that calculated the terrorist threat to London was 'severe', just one below the pinnacle of 'critical', the prime targets remained American and Jewish interests, next were British military personnel and institutions, followed by police officers. Within its boundaries the borough had one building belonging to the military, and three police stations. The QEOP with its array of prestigious businesses and sites combined with the Westfield Mall, Stratford Centre and the new and extensive transport hub, contrived, in the eyes of specialist CT officers, to produce a considerable portfolio of potential targets.

As a result of the post-Olympic assessment, Newham police officers were instructed not to travel to and from work on public transport while wearing uniform, and transport routes frequented by police personnel received extra uniformed police attention. By 2015, Newham still had three police stations. East Ham had been closed shortly after the Games, and public access to two of the remaining Games stations had been severely restricted due to financial cutbacks. Knowing that police may well be terrorist targets, the 'bomb car' paid special attention to police stations. Dual uniform patrolling had been abandoned as a result of cutbacks, and officers on single patrol and making inquiries alone were asked to give frequent updates via radio communication as to their whereabouts.

Although we were informed, perhaps not unsurprisingly, that the primary threat was now ISIS,[17] in 2013 adherents of the Al Qaeda linked *Al-Shabab* militant group killed 63 people in the Nairobi Westgate Mall, and in February 2015 the group made a statement directing its followers to attack a number of western targets including London's two Westfield Malls.[18] In addition, Newham, as with many other areas of the UK, had a number of its residents travelling to Syria in order to fight with ISIS.[19] [20] This was all in addition to the more orthodox demands made upon specialized CT officers in the form of centrally generated, intelligence-led operations.

Terrorism is similar to organized crime in that within the police organization it is shrouded in mystique and commands a specialist response from the police. Consequently, this area of policing becomes a terrain owned by special operatives with carefully defined, at times dangerous, knowledge (Hobbs, 2013: Chapter 2). However, apart from the fact that potential new targets were now in existence, we have no reason to link Newham and terrorism any more than we would link any other part of the UK. The threat of terror had criminalized large portions of urban Britain, and combined with attempts to protect borders (Bowling, 2013), this has huge implications for the prospects for civil life in Newham. CT work in the post-Olympic borough now included continuous education for shop staff and security personnel. For instance *Stratford One,* the vast student residence built adjacent to Westfield, required specialist CT officers to train security guards regarding the 'suspicious behaviour' displayed by its residents. Teachers may express alarm at the suspected radicalization of their pupils. Personal motivations triggered a CT response as local men invoked branded terrorism as a way of threatening local police. A Newham CT officer explained, 'We'll get called to a domestic violence (incident), the aggressor gets nicked. He's furious at this affront and will trot out to the arresting officer something along the lines of "Al Qaeda will come for you"'.[21] The most innocuous of police stops could result in CT activity: 'We got one where a stop and search saw the officer do a search of the suspect's i-phone . . . and we find images of him in a desert holding a Kalashnikov . . . obviously we have to delve further into who he is and what that image represents'.

However, we would caution against conflating police activity with actual terrorism. We do not know the full extent of potential terrorism in Newham, and frankly we suspect that neither do the police. For terrorism has become an 'instrument and a modality of the incorporation of the local into the global' (Diouf, 2000: 680–681), which illuminates the dazzling transnationalism (Beck & Sznaider, 2006: 9), of Newham as an unco-ordinated set of global practices rather than as an exterior, hostile, and essentially alien threat. The very notion of assessing a 'terror threat', which is usually covert and shrouded in ideas, opinions, gossip and rumour, not to mention a measure, no matter how small, of actual intent within a borough typified by a 'vernacular cosmopolitanism', steeped 'in marginality' (Bhabha, 1996: 195–196), is no simple task. Indeed, it remains as complex and perhaps as impossible as it did before the Olympics. This is unlike the borough's other major Olympic threat, which in the post-Games era remains hidden in plain sight.

The post-Olympic gang

In the years immediately following the 2012 Olympics, the policing of Newham's gangs was shaped by intelligence-based recommendations from the MPS Centre, as well as by policy positions held by Newham Council that retained some of the conflicts and ambiguities of the pre-Olympic era described earlier in this book. Police strategies were intended to be shaped by gang-focused data that derived from the MPS's 'Gang Matrix', and just two weeks after the Games, the matrix claimed the existence in London of 224 gangs and 3,574 gang members, of whom 557 were in custody. The matrix estimated that '20 per cent of the MPS Gang Matrix nominals [members] are aged under 18 and one in four gang members have mental health issues'. A multi-agency response was recommended. The matrix also classified different categories of gang criminal activity, including gun discharges, robbery, and serious youth violence. However, some Newham officers criticized the continued absence of drug-related activity in these categories, and as one DCI commented, 'Drugs fuel the gangs. If you live outside family, employment and education you do so by drug-selling or robbing drug dealers . . . So, an integral category of gang activity is disregarded by the matrix'.

Crucially, and echoing our scepticism in Chapter 3, the matrix report recognized that only a small minority of recorded crime was 'gang-flagged', and in Newham less than 10 per cent of SYV, and only around one quarter of gun discharges were classified as 'gang related'.

Two months after the Games, Newham Council and police were commended in a Home Office inspection for their 'strong leadership and effective partnerships', but communication was raised as an issue to be addressed, while more work was seen as desirable around girls in gangs, post-prison counselling, and restorative justice methods. A year later, the Olympic-gang project Operation Massachusetts (see Chapter 3) won silver at the Home Office sponsored Problem Oriented Partnerships Awards. The project withdrew 60 gang-related videos from YouTube, and claimed a 75 per cent reduction in youth violence in the borough. However, Operation Nulfuss in June 2013, led by Newham Gangs and Firearms Unit (GFU), with backing from MPS TSG units and Newham Council's Enforcement and Safety officers, focussing on stopping gang-related drug markets in the Stratford/Maryland area, suggested that Operation Massachusetts had not entirely cleared up youth-related problems in the borough.

Post-Olympics, the Mayor of Newham and many Newham councillors continued publicly to refuse to recognize officially the existence of gangs in the borough. As a Newham Council communications officer put it during one post-Olympics Gang meeting, 'We'd get a very negative response from the Mayor's office if we spoke of Newham's "gang problem"'. A council official, who co-chaired a Newham Forum on SYV and gangs, added that Newham councillors 'are split on whether LBN has a gang problem or not. Some admit privately that there is one, but that's an opinion they don't want to admit publically'. One GFU officer later complained about the irony of this situation stating, 'We've got to go cap-in-hand to LBN to get funding for an issue the Mayor doesn't want to acknowledge exists in his borough'.

The resulting ambiguity regarding the council's attitude to gangs was compounded by the Mayor's financial support for anti-gang activity, which enabled council personnel to work alongside the police gangs unit assisting in their intervention work. The full-time council-funded post of 'Gangs Coordinator' was retained, and in 2013 the council established a 'Gang Security Committee', comprising of eight councillors who met with police and other agencies to discuss gang-related issues. In 2014, this committee produced *The Report of the Crime and Disorder Commission into Youth Violence and Gang Crime in Newham*, and while failing to explain the nature of Newham gangs, the document did seek to reassure residents that the local council was on their side, and set out generalized recommendations for action, such as restricting social housing tenancies for known offenders, and showing a commitment to conflict resolution measures (London Borough of Newham Crime and Disorder Scrutiny Commission, 2014).

In an extraordinary few days in Newham in mid-2013, a machine gun was discharged, seven youths were stabbed and one murdered. In addition, the practice of 'riding out' (trespassing *en masse*) into adjacent 'territories' and attacking rivals remained a popular and enduring feature of the lives of a significant minority of Newham's youth. The main rivalries centred on Custom House, Stratford, Woodgrange and Beckton. But in terms of the holy grail of 'Intel', policing strategies and priorities would change when approaches to data-gathering for the Gang Matrix were amended by an increasingly influential corporate Centre.[22] For example, in mid-2013, all 32 MPS boroughs were required to input their intelligence so that the Centre could produce a list of the top identified gang members. The new metrics prioritized specific offences (suspected or known) relating to violence and rape, and demoted those with involvement in drugs. The adjusted matrix highlighted how individuals could shift rapidly up and down the rankings through the reclassification of the seriousness of their activities. In turn, officers examined individual cases and reflected critically on whether a 'gang member' classification was really warranted: for example, for one youth whose home windows had been shot out, or for a 16 year old who had brandished a machete in a local altercation. Of the latter, the Head of the GFU commented, 'I don't want to badge him as a gangster . . . That would give him extra kudos'. Subsequently, the GFU found that it was hard for individuals to drop off the matrix ranking, even if they had given up on crime or left the locality entirely.

By August 2013, a year after the Olympics, 189 Newham residents were on the gang matrix, including 8 of the 'top' 20 gang members in London. Adjustments to the matrix saw association or 'hanging out' with gangs, and sexual assault being added to the score-list in early 2014: the 'gang' goalposts constantly shifted. Police anti-gang activity centred on monitoring changes within named youth groups, and the profiles and practices of gangs were understood to change significantly when individuals were arrested or released from prison, opening up new feuds with neighbouring groups, while younger associates sought status and influence. But, the structured hierarchical version of these groups, so central to the notion of a gang, once interrogated is so often lacking, revealing a group of young men whose focus is violence. As a TAG (Teaching Against Gangs) worker discussing the 'Woodgrange gang' explained to a Tactical Gang Forum meeting in March 2013, 'There's no Elders to talk with . . . It's crowded with the young and impulsive who want to prove themselves. One 14 year old holds sway and says he can get "straps" [guns]'. However, by that point, serious youth violence was down by 44 per cent; discharge of firearms down by 64 per cent; and knife attacks involving the under 25s down by 35 per cent.[23]

Yet many Newham officers were not convinced that interventions could really negate the local gangs. In late 2013, one GFU Sergeant admitted to a Tactical Gang Forum that they, the wider MPS, and various other agencies, might disrupt gang activity, but would not ultimately be decisive in dealing with gangs. Indeed it seemed that some social problems just disappear when they are no longer useful.

The PGM: the most suitable Olympic enemy

The PGM were, as we explain in Chapter 3, never a gang, but this occasionally violent collection of individuals included a number of young men with a penchant for street robbery, which along with their particularly resonant sobriquet, situated them at the very eye of Olympic anxiety. Rumour-mongering with regard to the strength, power and cohesion of the PGM had spread beyond the environs of local police culture, becoming embedded in the Metropolitan Police to the extent that they were cited by influential officers at the MPS Centre as a viable threat to the Olympics. As we have explained in Chapter 9, aided by some extraordinary 'Intel' reports from both the Centre and from local analysts, the PGM were utilized as a particularly useful symbol of threat when briefing provincial police providing Mutual Aid during the Olympics, and the threat of the PGM became a general racialized menace. Yet rumour-running through every level of the MPS lay at the core of this Intel. After the riots of 2011, the MPS found themselves attempting to facilitate social control in an uncertain milieu where order was believed to be in jeopardy (Siegel, 2008), and as Shibutani (1966) indicates, rumour is an essential part of group problem solving. Given the anxious void that existed after the 2011 London riots, 'improvised news' concerning the depth, organization and potency of the PGM alleviated uncertainty and ambiguity in an environment where 'grounds for suspicion and sinister hypotheses are never lacking' (Schneider, & Schneider, 2003: 91).

The PGM, that prime threat to the 2012 Games, continued to find themselves the target of police action in the months immediately following the Games. The

Robbery Task Force gained some moderate success with regard to young men associated with the PGM brand who were involved in gold-chain snatches in East Ham. Some associated with the PGM had returned to Stratford and were engaged in low-level street drug dealing and found themselves confronted by the Crime Squad. During 2012–2013 one especially notorious PGM member, a young man of Anglo-Caribbean heritage, had been on the *Safe and Secure* scheme in an attempt to leave the gang life, his meals were cooked, and his washing done by GFU officers. However, he dropped out of the scheme, and completed a prison sentence for three counts of robbery, during which time he was assaulted by a group of incarcerated Newham youths and as a consequence spent three weeks on the hospital wing. On his release he was jailed for a further six years in early 2015 as a result of his involvement in a robbery in West London.

The PGM were targeted by the municipal enforcement officers who patrolled Stratford Park handing out fines for littering, spitting, smoking and damaging the park furniture. They also conducted searches of the bushes and general foliage of the park to find wraps of cannabis that had been hidden by the youths. As a consequence of this consistent but effective harassment by council officials, some members of the notorious PGM, who just months before had been considered to be a major threat to a global sporting event, left Newham.

The PGM had never constituted a coherent group, and the demise of this loose-knit collective can be attributed largely to a set of distinctly non-law-enforcement-related circumstances. Some youths found employment, and so found themselves outside of the considerable spotlight that had been cast upon them by police and council officials. Others became homeless and moved out of the borough when the E15 Foyer was closed down in 2013. Some associated with the PGM made the mistake of robbing the wrong people. Retribution followed, and as they were not members of a gang themselves were unable to call upon fellow gang members for protection, and so fled the area. Others left because, like most local youths of the pre-gang industrial era, they matured, found partners, and became fathers, and as a consequence wanted more than a smoke in the park and a room in a hostel. There were no 'youngers' waiting to step into their footsteps. There were no succession issues regarding the PGM. When these young men departed Newham, they left no legacy. As explained in Chapter 9 in relation to public order and the Olympics, the emphasis on the PGM was associated with an attempt to provide institutional rather than public reassurance. There was a need for a 'policeable' enemy, and the PGM fitted the bill. But post-Olympics, they had served their purpose, they were no longer needed. They had no communal identity, and were now scattered, refugees once more.

Despite the understandable scepticism of LBN and some police officers, the 2012 Olympics established gangs in Newham as a major threat. The subtleties that we referred to in Chapter 3, and in particular our emphasis on the inappropriateness of the term in relation to the PGM, have now been largely cast aside in favour of expensive initiatives that have confirmed the emergence of gangs as a key focus of public policy.

In June 2014, courts were given civil powers to ban people from entering specific areas with certain individuals, or from wearing certain colours in public places. These injunctions required a lower burden of proof than criminal law, and meant that a person could face injunctions if they were 'one of at least three whose conduct is characteristic of gang behaviour'. A gang injunction is granted on the balance of probabilities that the respondent has engaged in, or has encouraged or assisted, gang-related violence. A Government Minister was quoted as saying that such legislation was needed because 'gangs do not always use a name, emblem or colours and might not be linked to a particular area'.[24] It is clear that these injunctions are little more than what the police used to call a 'ways and means Act': a somewhat bogus yet flexible tool that valorizes police discretion.

In January 2015, London's Mayor Boris Johnson unveiled the *Shield* initiative, where known gang members would suffer civil or criminal sanctions if any of the gang they were associated with carried out an assault, stabbing or any other serious crime. The scheme also invoked recalls to prison, gang injunctions, mandatory employment training and ejection from council housing.[25] The proposal from Johnson came two months after his office announced a 90 per cent cut to London's youth service. The gang genie, like its terrorist counterpart, will not be going back into the bottle.

Notes

1 See the BBC website, '2012 Olympics transport strategy hailed a success' (BBC, 13 August 2012).
2 Protest Liaison Officers (PLOs) have become a feature at demonstrations and marches in the UK since the 2009 G20 protests and the death of Ian Tomlinson (see Chapter 1). Easily identified by their sky blue tabards, these officers have been given the public task of improving dialogue with protesters. (See http://www.justiceinspectorates.gov.uk/ hmic/media/adapting-to-protest-nurturing-the-british-model-of-policing-20091125. pdf). However, a more critical perspective on the role of PLOs considers their role in intelligence gathering and covert observations (see https://netpol.org/).
3 A constant refrain during the Games concerned the 'Heathrow airport crime phenomenon', where a crime is reported to the police when it is discovered, and not where the crime has been committed, which could be many miles away. The refrain can often be heard around the MPS with regard visitors to London who become victims of theft.
4 A total of 18,200 military personnel were used in the Games.
5 Throughout the duration of the Olympic and Paralympic Games, only one police officer suffered the threat of assault in the Olympic Park. An off-duty police Inspector from a provincial force had been over-imbibing during the hospitality afforded to him by corporate sponsors, and he subsequently threatened an MPS officer on Olympic Park duties. He was arrested and charged with public-order offences.
6 Discussions around intelligence were absent from the debrief report, and no one from the Olympic Command Team were willing to discuss the omission.
7 For a discussion of the tensions between police, council and private enterprise, particularly with regard to the issue of tasking, see Hobbs et al. (2003).
8 Between February 2011 and May 2012, 142 FPN's were issued in Newham for false allegations of robbery.
9 Although there may be more, we could locate only one Newham-based police officer who lived in the borough.
10 Indeed, Newham MPS had problems finding individuals to constitute a neighbourhood forum, never mind one that claimed to be 'representative' of the local community.
11 https://www.london.gov.uk/press-releases/mayoral/new-maps-to-show-londoners-confidence-in-police.

12 'May rejects Boris's unsafe water cannon' (*The Times*, 16 July 2015).
13 'Police warn big budget cuts will lead to "paramilitary" force' (the *Guardian*, 18 May 2015).
14 (the *Guardian*, 20 May 2015).
15 'Why I quit the thin blue line: a former Met police officer on a service in crisis', (the *Guardian*, 23 May 2015).
16 Some officers expressed to us concerns that the post-Olympics attack on a serving British soldier outside a South East London barracks was accomplished by weaponry bought the day before from a DIY outlet, and required no long-term planning or extensive networking of the kind that would be susceptible to surveillance-based intelligence gathering. At a more mundane level, the strategic tolerance shown towards religious groups in Newham during the Olympics did not have a long-term 'legacy'. Anyone preaching violent fundamentalism in a public place, even if they were careful not to breach the law, would be managed by council officials, who invoked local bye-laws regarding obstruction.
17 'British anti-terror police arrest suspect with links to Isis', the *Guardian,* 14 February 2015.
18 'Al-Shabaab video calls for attacks on London shopping centres including Oxford Street and Westfield', the *Independent*, 22 February 2015.
19 'Six on charges linked to terrorism after arrests at Dover and raids in London', *Newham Recorder,* 16 December 2014.
20 For an important discussion concerning the recruitment of foreign fighters into a militant Islamic movement see Joosse et al. (2015).
21 Not much had changed over the years. In a previous era favoured responses to arresting officers included: 'I know where you live/drink', and 'I hope your children die of cancer'.
22 A further way in which the Centre impacted on local policing related to a radical shift in policy on the use of 'section 60' stop and searches which did not carry 'reasonable suspicion' in relation to a possible offence. In 2011, Newham had accounted for 35 per cent of all 'section 60s' across London. The MPS elected to cut these searches by more than 90 per cent. See http://researchbriefings.files.parliament.uk/documents/SN03878/SN03878.pdf.
23 However, some of Newham's violent young men were taken off the streets as a result of being found guilty of crimes that did not feature on the Gang Matrix. In 2014, two of the boroughs highest profile 'gangsters' were jailed, one received a five-year custodial sentence for a burglary in the Home Counties, while another received the same sentence for breaking his mother's arm in a domestic dispute.
24 Injunctions that could be obtained on the basis of police intelligence and without witness testimony were introduced in 2014 (*Evening Standard*, 6 June 2014). In January 2015, legislation passed through Parliament which removed the need to prove that a gang member wore any apparel that signified gang allegiance (*Evening Standard*, 19 January 2015).
25 By September 2015, two of the three London boroughs piloting *Shield* had rejected the scheme. 'Boris Johnson plan to tackle gang crime rejected by two of three pilot councils: People of Haringey and Lambeth refuse to accept Operation Shield amid fears its punitive measures risk worsening relations with police', (the *Guardian,* 11 September 2015).

References

Barrett, D. (2014) '"Get Medieval" on Rioters, Says Boris Johnson', the *Telegraph*, January 29.
Beck, U. & Sznaider, N. (2006) 'Unpacking Cosmopolitanism for the Social Sciences: A Research Agenda', *British Journal of Sociology, 57*: 1.
Bhabha, H. (1996) 'Unsatisfied: Notes on Vernacular Cosmopolitanism', in L. Garcia-Moreno & P.C. Pfeifer (eds) *Text and Nation.* London: Camden House.

Bowling, B. (2013) 'Epilogue', in K. Aas & M. Bosworth (eds) *The Borders of Punishment: Criminal Justice, Citizenship and Social Exclusion*. Oxford: Oxford University Press.

Diouf, M. (2000) 'The Senegalese Murid Trade Diaspora and the Making of a Vernacular Cosmopolitanism', *Public Culture 12*(3): 679–702.

Douglas, M. (1966) *Purity and Danger: An Analysis of Concepts of Pollution and Taboo*. New York: Praeger.

Evans, M. (2014) 'Plebgate: Andrew Mitchell did Call Policemen "plebs", Judge Rules', the *Telegraph*, November 27.

Fussey, P. (2014) 'Command, Control and Contestation: Negotiating Security at the London 2012 Olympics', *The Geographical Journal*, advance publication DOI: 10.1111/geoj.12058.

Hobbs, D., Hadfield, P. Lister, S. & Winlow, S. (2003) *Bouncers: Violence, Governance and the Night-time Economy*. Oxford: Oxford University Press.

Hobbs, D. (2013) *Lush Life: Constructing Organised Crime in the UK*. Oxford: Oxford University Press.

Hudson, B. (2007) 'Diversity, Crime and Criminal Justice', in M. Maguire, R. Morgan & R. Reiner (eds) *The Oxford Handbook of Criminology* (4th edition). Oxford: Oxford University Press.

Joosse, P., Bucerius, S. & Thompson, S. (2015) 'Narratives and Counter-narratives: Somali-Canadians on Recruitment as Foreign Fighters to Al-Shabaab', *British Journal of Criminology*, doi: 10.1093/bjc/azu103.

Kettle, M. (2014) 'Theresa May has Ripped up the Tory Pact with the Police', the *Guardian*, May 21.

London Borough of Newham Crime and Disorder Scrutiny Commission (2014) *The Report of the Crime and Disorder Commission into Youth Violence and Gang Crime in Newham*. London: Newham Council.

Pantazis, C. & Pemberton, S. (2009) 'From the "Old" to the "New" Suspect Community', *British Journal of Criminology 49*(5): 646–666.

Raine, R. (2014) 'Reflections on Security at the 2012 Olympics', *Intelligence and National Security, 30*(4):422–433.

Schneider J.T. & Schneider, P.T. (2003) *Reversible Destiny: Mafia, Antimafia, and the Struggle for Palermo*. Berkeley: University of California Press.

Shibutani, T. (1966) *Improvised News: A Sociological Study of Rumor*. New York: Irvington.

Siddique, H. (2013) 'Met Failure to Conclude "Plebgate" Inquiry is Quite Outrageous, Says Ex-DPP', the *Guardian*, September 18.

Siegel, D. (2008) 'Conversations with Russian Mafiosi', *Trends in Organised Crime, 11*: 21–29.

Spalek, B, El-Awa, S, McDonald L. Z. & Lambert, R. (2008) *Summary and Full Report: Policy-Muslim Engagement and Partnerships for the Purposes of Counter-Terrorism: An Examination*. Birmingham: University of Birmingham.

Stanko, E.A. J Jackson, J. Bradford, B., & Hohl, K. (2012) 'A Golden Thread, a Presence Amongst Uniforms, and a Good Deal of Data: studying Public Confidence in the London Metropolitan Police', *Policing and Society, 22*(3): 317–331.

Van Wynsberghe, R., Derom, I. & Maurer, E. (2012) 'Social Leveraging of the 2010 Olympic Games: Sustainability in a city of Vancouver Initiative', *Journal of Policy Research in Tourism, Leisure and Events, 4*(2): 185–205.

Winnett, R. (2012) 'Police Log Reveals Details of Andrew Mitchell's "Pleb" Rant', the *Telegraph*, September 24. Available at: http://www.telegraph.co.uk/news/politics/conservative/9563847/Police-log-reveals-details-of-Andrew-Mitchells-pleb-rant.html.

11 Post-Olympic Newham

A postscript

So given the promises, pledges, fears and hyperbole, was 'Newham's sports day' worth it? The 2012 Olympics marked the demise of the last vestige of Newham's industrial heritage. Its industrial past and concomitant production-based industrial cultures were concreted over by globally based consumerism in the shape of the Westfield Mall, and the corralled and choreographed leisure options of Queen Elizabeth Olympic Park (QEOP). After nearly half a century of decline, the political inheritance of Newham's culture in the shape of a municipal government grounded securely in trade unionism and its related programmes of communality was finally swept aside by non-democratic quasi-commercial agencies such as LOCOG, the London Legacy Development Corporation (LLDC), and the extra ordinary assemblage of governance that contrived to impose the Olympics and its legacy onto the London Borough of Newham. Yet three years after the borough hosted the Olympic Games, if one chooses to venture beyond the magic garden of Westfield and the QEOP, little has changed. Indeed, generally London remains a city of extremes, with the polarization between rich and poor becoming even more pronounced in recent years.[1]

Most importantly, the borough inherited the vast expanse of the Queen Elizabeth Olympic Park, (QEOP), an inheritance which along with the Thames Gateway project in the south of the borough collectively constituted an 'Arc of Opportunity',[2] promising, as we discuss below, the arrival of a new prosperous demographic. Inward investment promoted by the Games, and in particular the new housing that would accompany it, was seen as an opportunity to reverse a century and a half of poverty and population churn. Middle-class incomers would impact upon all aspects of life in Newham, including education, as they settled in new sites on what had been the Olympic Park. For it was also hoped, particularly by Newham council officials, that this transplantation of a bourgeois population into the 'gash' would have the knock-on effect of gentrifying the existing Victorian and Edwardian housing stock, as the borough became more attractive to middle class home buyers, who would settle in the borough to raise families.

In the midst of national austerity, Olympic *apparatchiks* and British politicians promoted an event that promised huge dividends for corporate investors and aspiring speculators (Cohen, 2013), particularly in relation to the Games legacy, a concept discussed in Chapter 1, whose very imprecision makes it a powerful political instrument (ibid: 344). The focus for the legacy of the 2012 Games, as we will discuss below, is the QEOP, whose future lay in the hands of the London Legacy Development Corporation (LLDC), an unelected quango who speak authoritatively of 'legacy' in terms of buildings and infrastructure; while the soft legacies measured in socio-cultural terms are by definition less tangible, and their financial benefits less easy to quantify. As we will suggest below, under the LLDC umbrella, most of London's Olympic assets were sold off to the private sector, and its key beneficiaries are international investors (Cohen, 2013: 158–160).

Fixed odds: the post-Olympic sporting dividend

As we discuss in Chapter 2, in a 2013 deal orchestrated by Conservative Party doyen Baroness Brady of Knightsbridge, West Ham United's Vice Chairman, the club will leave their Upton Park home of 100 years and move into the Olympic Stadium in Stratford. The football club will be the anchor tenant on a 99-year lease, and rent the stadium for an annual fee of around £2.5 million per year, and a share of the catering income. The stadium is to be re-fitted and refurbished to meet the demands of a specialist football stadium at a cost to taxpayers of £150 million; a further £40 million was loaned to the club by Newham Council. In the autumn of 2014, the refurbishment was not going to plan and a request was made by the club to the Council for a further £35 million. The building contractor Balfour Beatty requested a further £50 million to help the conversion, and received £25 million from the Dept. of Communities and Local Government.[3]

Only one politician broke ranks regarding this and related projects. In late December 2014, Andrew Boff, the Conservative Leader of the Greater London Authority, told the media that the reluctance of anyone to criticize Olympic-related projects was a product of too many political reputations being invested in the 2012 Games. His outburst came partly in response to the request from Balfour Beatty for another £35 million from the LLDC to assist the conversion of the Olympic Stadium to a football stadium, thereby making the then-estimated cost of the conversion some £200 million. Boff pointed out that the taxpayer was effectively propping up an English Premier League football club and that the developments on the park did not link with the rest of the area. He described the funding as: 'the biggest financial scandal of this century, but because it was the Games and the Games delivered a positive message, people have accepted it . . . Now there are too many political reputations invested in the Olympic Park . . . it's embarrassing to admit they got it wrong'.[4] Worse financial news was to follow. In June 2015, the LLDC announced that the conversion costs had risen to a final sum of £272 million, taking the total bill for the construction and adaptation of the Olympic Stadium to £701 million, almost all of it paid for by the taxpayer, and almost three times higher than the initial price of £280 million (Gibson, 2015a). In September 2015, and amongst growing criticism of Boris Johnson, the Information Commissioner ruled that the full details of West Ham's rental agreement for the stadium should be made public (Gibson, 2015b).

Newham was a particularly ripe target for the betting industry, and in the post-Olympic years this interest appears to have accelerated. In Newham in 2013 there were 87 bookmakers: six for each square mile – the third highest in any of the London boroughs.[5] These betting shops contained a total of 348 terminals, enticing punters to gamble up to £100 every 20 seconds.[6] Many MPs, councillors and council officials opposed this proliferation of betting shops, believing that they acted as a magnet for crime and antisocial behaviour: harming rather than benefitting economic growth on the high streets.[7] Newham's Mayor sought to prevent further businesses from opening,[8] and in April 2013 rejected a licensing application from high street bookies *Paddy Power* for a shop in Upton Park because its 'primary activity' would be from fixed odds betting terminals; *Paddy Power* sought to open a further 18 betting shops in Newham. The council also objected to *Betfred's* plan to increase the late-night opening hours of four of its Newham shops, leading it to drop its application.[9] However in June 2013, *Paddy Power* won its appeal at Thames Magistrates against the borough's refusal to allow it to open another shop. Whilst Newham had argued that the new branch would attract crime and antisocial behaviour and thus breach the 2005 Gambling Act, *Paddy Power* prevailed by arguing that the company made a positive contribution to the community, via preventing crime and operating in all required safety measures (BBC News, 2013).

A major legacy objective of the London 2012 Games had been to inspire a generation to play sport, which would be reflected in increased levels of sport participation among young people in the UK.[10] However, post-Games surveys revealed that participation in sport had failed to take off, and in some key areas had declined significantly. Former UK Olympics Minister, Tessa Jowell, argued that this legacy opportunity had been 'squandered', in part due to government cutbacks on sport programmes such as the 'School Sports Partnership' (Merrill, 2015). In September 2005 a publication produced by Conservatives sitting on the London Assembly reported a decline in the number of disabled Londoners participating in sport, with two-thirds of the Capital's 1.5 million disabled people unable to access sport (Tracey, 2015). In the six Olympic boroughs, the promotion of participation in sport was largely sacrificed through funding cuts to a variety of programmes (Aaron, 2013). In April 2014, the Newham 10K Fun Run, which was routed through the Olympic Park, was cancelled in the same week that the park was re-opened to massive media fanfare by Prince Harry. The organizers' spokesperson, former Team GB Olympic medallist Tessa Sanderson, explained that Newham Council had doubled its fees for managing and marshalling the event, which had begun in 2009. Officials from both LOCOG and Newham Council had participated in the pre-Olympic event. However, the PR capital to be gained from pre-Olympic enthusiasm was now worthless.

A further blow to sport in Newham came in February 2013 when funding for basketball from UK Sport was cut from £7 million per annum to nothing. The funding body's 'No Compromise' philosophy around investing only in sports that would return an Olympic medal meant that basketball, with little to no hope of such success for Team GB, was not considered worth funding. Yet, with an estimated 280,000 people in the UK aged 14 and over playing basketball weekly, the sport had a larger grass-roots base than any other Olympic team sport. Played in low-income neighbourhoods in many UK inner-cities, the game was second only to football in terms of participation in Newham, and in a subsequent 2015 report detailing a drastic decline in general sporting participation in England, basketball was one of the few sports to show an increase, 'especially among young people in school and further education' (Sport England, 2015). The decision to cut funding brought anger from the All-Parliamentary Group on Basketball who spoke of the 'inadvertent disenfranchising of a whole segment of UK society'. In response, UK Sport said that basketball had never qualified 'by right' for any Olympic Games. The logic of financial support – centred on medals not participation – was illustrated further in the public funding of sports that had few social roots in Newham or other inner-city areas in the UK, such as the modern pentathlon (£7 million), canoeing (£20 million), snowboarding (£4.8 million) and the skeleton bobsleigh (£6.5 million).

Work and shelter: a very basic legacy

The Olympic Bid promised to transform East London. The legacy would be some 30 years in the making and aimed to one day make living in Newham a similar experience to living in affluent West London.[11] A month after the Games ended, in the reception area of Newham Town Hall, the borough was being hyped as home to the 'Last Great Development Opportunity in London' and was intended to become, over the next 15 years, 'a young city within a capital city' with 75 per cent of residents aged under 45 and 42 per cent under 24. To house them, 35,000 new homes (10,000 described as 'high quality', no mention of the quality of the remaining 25,000) were being built, and 100,000 new jobs created. The Olympics were not mentioned. The investment required for this transformation was estimated at £22 billion, but this metamorphosis was not likely to be trouble-free. In 2014, the population was calculated at 328,000, with 24,000 names on the council's housing waiting list. In 2012 rent arrears in the borough's council and housing association properties were estimated at 43 per cent. Despite the huge investment that accompanied the Games, a large proportion of the borough's population still desperately needed decent affordable homes and meaningful employment prospects.

Work: the employment legacy

Much of the discourse surrounding the legacy of the 2012 Games focussed on job creation for local people. This had proved to be contentious. To be classed as a 'local' worker for Olympic-related construction, one only required an address in one of the host boroughs, and Newham had the highest proportion of new National Insurance registrations for adult overseas nationals in the UK across consecutive pre-Olympic years. The Host Boroughs Skills and Employment project with a budget of £11.4 million (DCMS, 2012), targeted 5,000 people for work, yet was delayed as the project did not hit targets which were subsequently deemed too 'challenging' (Hughes, 2012: 18). As Mean et al. (2004: 139) suggest, even if residents gained the necessary skills to apply for a job, they were at risk of being 'out-competed' for places, as they did not possess the necessary experience. Most construction jobs required specialist training and these jobs went to qualified workers from outside of the host boroughs (Kornblatt, 2006). The Skills and Employment project sought to increase employment opportunities for 'workless individuals' from disadvantaged groups (DCMS, 2012: 100) by increasing labour and business links for job opportunities within and around the Olympic Park, and establishing a training programme in construction and other sectors to prepare for suitable opportunities' (London Assembly, 2007: 25). Figures presented by the now defunct London Development Agency (2010) showed that 2,300 residents obtained work in the Olympic Park, and 6,200 were receiving 'employment support'. The majority of Olympic-related employment initiatives were short term, and the DCMS Meta-Evaluation (2012) revealed that only 3 per cent of residents in the host boroughs secured Olympic-related employment.

However, post-Games reports outlined how the six host boroughs' jobless rate had fallen by just 0.6 per cent (Hughes, 2012), while the DCMS Meta-Evaluation (2012) highlighted that only two projects carried out evaluations, and only one initiative in the Host Borough Skills and Employment Project had an end date that stretched beyond the Games. International migration and population churn continued and these factors often imported unemployment as new arrivals took time to assimilate and find work (Sissons et al., 2010: 56). A year after the Olympics, unemployment in Newham was almost identical to its pre-Olympic rate, and was the second highest of any London borough. In an overview of key poverty indicators Newham was unchanged from the pre-Olympic period, with the third highest child poverty rate in London (32 per cent), and the highest proportion of residents in low paid work – a third of working people living in Newham were in the category of low paid.[12] Thus, in short, the legacy of the 2012 Olympics has done virtually nothing to lift Newham residents out of unemployment and poorly remunerated work.

Shelter: the housing legacy

Post-Olympic Newham had the highest residential overcrowding rate in the country at 25 per cent, affecting over a third of households. In addition, 2,500 Newham residents were living in temporary accommodation, and, according to the London Poverty Profile, one home in four in the borough was overcrowded, rising to one in three in wards close to West Ham United's old stadium at Upton Park. The Boleyn Ground was set to be redeveloped as a 'village' of 838 homes of which just 6 per cent were earmarked as 'affordable'. The planning application lodged by the builders Galliard – who paid between £30 million and £50 million for the site (Prynn, 2014) – makes no mention of any social housing, in spite of a requirement in Newham council's core strategy that big developments must deliver 35 per cent to 50 per cent affordable homes, of which 60 per cent should be social housing. It is clear that the redevelopment of the Boleyn Ground, facilitated directly by West Ham United's move to the Olympic Stadium, will be yet another private development in Newham that creates homes which local residents cannot afford. In Olympic legacy terms, the attempted gentrification of Newham continues to gather pace.

London's landlords experienced a post-Olympic bonanza. The average London rent rose at 2.8 times the rate of the average salary in 2013; in Newham, that rate was doubled, at 5.6 times. In November 2008, at a conference hosted by the Notting Hill Housing Association at City Hall, Newham Mayor Sir Robin Wales had rejected the suggestion that he should increase the borough's social housing stock on the grounds that 'I don't want to import poverty into Newham'.[13] However, just before the Olympics he showed his enthusiasm for exporting poverty, and along the way gained considerable notoriety by writing to 1,179 housing associations around the country, including one 160 miles away in Stoke-on-Trent, in an attempt to find accommodation for some of the 32,000 families on the Newham housing waiting list.

In April 2013, a benefit cap on social housing costs across the UK came into play, and an exodus from the more expensive London boroughs to cheaper housing on the periphery began. Between July and September 2014, 306 homeless placements were received by Newham Council, while during the same period 323 homeless were moved out of the borough:[14] these developments have contributed considerably to the churn discussed in Chapter 2. The Head of St Antony's primary school in Upton Park explained the impact of this brutal strategy on some of her pupils: 'Social housing is a real concern for our school. A few of our families have been relocated overnight, often to homes outside London where they have no support network, severely disrupting children's education and undermining the social resilience of families' (Gould, 2015).

In the post-Olympic years, hundreds of Newham landlords were still renting 'beds in sheds' to immigrants (Robinson, 2014), and the lifting of immigration restrictions on Romanians and Bulgarians on 1 January 2013 led to concerns that more of this primitive accommodation would be provided by 'slum landlords'. Vowing to deal with the situation, the Mayor of Newham stated that private-sector rentals were to be well managed and of a high standard, as assured by Newham's Planning and Enforcement team (Duell, 2013; Raslah, 2014). Newham became the first council in the country to attempt to license every privately-owned rental property, and a council database was to be created with a view to acting against criminal landlords who disregarded the London Letting Standards and Office of Fair Trading guidelines. By mid-2014 Newham was seeking to prosecute 134 landlords for breaches of the Housing Act. By mid-2015, the highest fine imposed was £12,000, and three 'notorious portfolio' landlords had been refused licenses for over 100 properties. The Mayor also hoped that the government would consider withdrawing the 'four-year rule' whereby a building that has existed for four years without attracting complaints becomes eligible for properties being rented (Gentleman, 2012).

In October 2012, Sir Robin Wales announced that with the prospect of Newham's brave new post-Olympic world, the borough would change its social housing allocation policies so that members of the armed services and people in employment would be given priority by Newham Council. Explaining his logic, Wales stated 'This decision shows Newham is leading the country when it comes to progressive housing policy. By prioritising those who have seen active service in defence of our nation, we can recognise their achievement and help support their future. There are currently 30,797 names on our housing waiting list and these measures will help ensure priority is given to those who contribute to society ... These changes will also help to drive aspiration and form a stable community where people choose to live, work and stay'.[15]

This was a plaintiff cry for traditional Labourist principles rooted in an era which, as we describe in Chapter 2, saw industrial workers in full employment, and reimbursed at rates negotiated by trade unions who were represented in local politics and who had acquired a voice in key areas such as local housing policy. However, Newham is no longer dominated by such a demographic as it was in the 1960s, and this is not a traditional industrial-era Labour-voting population. For, as we also discuss in Chapter 2, a significant portion of Newham's population are, for a wide range of poverty-related reasons, unable to 'contribute to society' by way of paid employment, and many of those in work are not sufficiently reimbursed for their labours to pay their way in the contemporary rental housing market. The Olympics have not assisted their plight.

The Mayor's dilemma was exemplified when the E15 Foyer became a national symbol of the Coalition government's austerity policies. In August 2013, 29 young or expectant mothers from the Focus E15 Foyer were served notices to leave after Newham council cut funding for the hostel. On learning that accommodation was available for them elsewhere in the country in places such as Hastings, Manchester and Birmingham, the evicted women, determined to stay in their borough, started a campaign. They occupied four flats on the nearby Carpenters estate, and in doing so highlighted the fact that the estate had been left empty while awaiting demolition.[16] The two-week occupation ended when the mothers were offered affordable rented accommodation in London, and received an apology from the Mayor for their treatment, as well as a commitment to house 40 households in temporary accommodation on the Carpenters estate (Quinn, 2014).[17]

It would be all too easy to depict the Mayor of Newham as a pantomime villain working with corporate entities against the best interests of Newham's population. But this would be wrong. Among his many contributions to the borough, the Mayor made a £5 million investment in Workplace, the council's employment service, through which more than 22,000 people have found work, introduced a shared equity scheme to assist families get onto the property ladder, ensured that all local primary school pupils receive free school meals, and advanced a number of educational policies which yielded some impressive returns.[18] But poverty in Newham remains very high and a third of the borough's population is economically inactive. Consequently, the Mayor's prioritization of working families on the housing list, although understandable and in many ways commendable, will inevitably alienate large numbers of Newham residents, who like the excluded elsewhere in the capital, are vulnerable to attempts to decant them out of the zones of responsibility of cash-strapped London councils. Meanwhile, further fuel was added to London's red hot property market when the new Conservative government announced that they would extend 'right to buy' to 1.3 million housing association homes (Helm & Boffey, 2015).

The neo-liberal inspired context of the 2012 Olympics, consisting of global corporate drivers combined with central government philosophies relating to austerity, did nothing to assist those trying to manage a borough typified by a poor and disadvantaged population. Further, Wales' retro rhetoric on housing, displayed a misunderstanding of the nature of social exclusion in the post-industrial context, and alongside the MPS's demonization of transgressive local youth, succeeded in demarcating the borough's Games and post-Games population into vagabonds and tourists (Bauman, 1998). This is a particularly ideal dualism for both the Queen Elizabeth Olympic Park and the housing developments in what used to be the docks: the very location that had inspired the kind of pragmatically-based communality that Wales had sourced for his policy on the prioritization of local housing resources.

The notion of mixed housing economies is problematic, and the experiences of residents in other parts of the borough, notably Beckton, suggest that once tensions begin between the public and private housing residents, it can be very difficult to reverse (cf. Lindsay, 2014). One way around this predicament is to exclude the working classes completely from any new developments. The process of regenerating and rebranding East London had begun in the 1980's, with the deregulation of the financial sector and the subsequent development of Canary Wharf on the River Thames in the London Borough of Tower Hamlets. Post-Games, plans were advanced to connect Canary Wharf to Newham via 'London City Island' opposite the O2 at the mouth of the river Lea. This 12-acre development would feature 1,706 new homes, and be supplemented by a new HQ for the English National Ballet (Bryant, 2015). This project would be additional to a further £9.5 billion development over the next 15 years on 130 acres of 'docklands', which includes a plan for a mini-theme park for global corporate and consumer brands, and 3,000 homes centred on Millennium Mills, the last surviving disused flour mill on the Thames. Barry Jessup, a director of London housing developers First Base, said the mill would be attractive to 'people who can't afford to be in Clerkenwell or King's Cross anymore because it is too expensive' (Alwakeel, 2014). In Newham, these new residential developments on the Thames, along with those on the QEOP, appear likely to exist as island sites disconnected from any local context, and possessing few identifying characteristics other than their proximity to transport and shopping centres.

As we can see above, the Olympics were clearly just part of a property-driven transformation of Newham. This suggests that if we are willing to enquire beyond the press releases of the property developers, estate agents, and corporate predators who are currently enjoying a feeding frenzy in the borough, from the point of view of existing residents, the legacy of the 2012 Games is remarkably similar to Olympics held elsewhere (Garcia-Ramon & Albert 2000; Lenskyj, 2000:227–231).

Summer 2015: walking in the park

> Then close your eyes and tap your heels together three times. And think to
> yourself, there's no place like home.
>
> (L. Frank Baum, *The Wonderful Wizard of Oz*)

Stratford Broadway is still messy, chaotic and infused with a visceral threat/
promise that has only been enhanced by the Porsche dealership opposite Pudding
Mill Station on the High Street, and the purple 43-storey shaft of the Stratford
Halo, whose one-bedroom flats were mostly sold to overseas investors for
buy-to-let. Entering the Stratford Centre shopping hall one sees the same cluster
of pre-Olympic, lairy teenagers swarming outside of McDonalds. Once inside
the centre, the stalls, those persistent ghosts of the old Angel Lane market, are
still overseen by a roster of the usual suspects of chain stores. Walk through and
exit the shopping centre, and you effectively leave the borough on crossing the
A118. The options are to escape into the station and travel on an overground
train to Essex, Norfolk or Suffolk, or take a curved trip around North London
into the well-preserved glow of Newham's antithesis – the London Borough of
Richmond. Alternatively you may take the underground into the City or West End,
or the Docklands Light Railway for an alternative route into both the new and old
financial centres, or to the once remote and only recently renamed 'Docklands', or
even into some previously unreachable parts of South London.[19] Or walk into the
Westfield Mall and onward onto the Queen Elizabeth Olympic Park. Whatever
way the traveller decides to leave Newham, of all these possible destinations,
the 60 acres of land encompassing the 6.5km of waterways and the 15 acres of
woodlands of the QEOP, are the most alien. For while the E20 postcode is both
physically and culturally removed from Newham's past and present, it may well
be its future.

Newham remains a chaotic churning urban space riddled with long-term
poverty and all of its attendant maladies. The Olympics resembled a lifeline, and it
would be naïve to criticize the Mayor of Newham and those charged with running
the borough for grasping it with two hands. However, the Mayor of London, Boris
Johnson, proved to be a far more powerful Olympic player. In November 2012,
control of the Olympic Park passed from LOCOG to the LLDC, which became
the site's planning authority, renting large portions of the park on long-term leases
to development partners. The self-appointed chair of the legacy corporation is
London's Mayor, who has overseen on the QEOP the foundations of a fantasy of
private ownership, enhanced by bastions of body and mind self-improvement[20]
such as the Lee Valley Velo Park, the Copperbox, the London Aquatics Centre,
the Hockey and Tennis Centres, and of course the Olympic Stadium, along with
high-end shopping, all well connected by a state of the art twenty-first century
transport hub to the financial districts of the City and Canary Wharf.

It is clear that it was always the aim to use the London Olympics to attract
a new demographic to Newham rather than as a means to elevate the existing
population, and the proposed Olympicopolis makes this profoundly explicit

(Ellis-Petersen, 2014). Funded by £141 million of central government investment, this 'cultural quarter' of the QEOP will eventually house campuses of University College London, Loughborough University and the London College of Fashion. In addition, a 500-seat theatre of the Sadlers' Wells company has been promised, and the US government-funded Smithsonian Institute of American History and Life has accepted an invitation to establish a branch. A dance school and 'hip-hop' academy are also planned to open in 2018. The LLDC has promised that Olympicopolis alone will create 10,000 new jobs. In addition, Here East, a new creative and digital hub in the former 2012 Press and Broadcast Centres, is already home to BT Sport, and is expected to attract further broadcast media to the park.

The QEOP will provide a series of distinct neighbourhoods or, 'legacy communities',[21] which the LLDC promise will eventually contain 20,000 new homes. East Wick will be in the north-west of the park, and will be the responsibility of Hackney Council. Sweetwater will be in the south-west of the park, near Old Ford, and will be the responsibility of Tower Hamlets Council. The International Quarter, consisting of a commercial zone that will house 25,000 office workers and create 330 homes to be completed in 2016, and mixed development is planned around Pudding Mill Lane. On Chobham Manor potential buyers camped out overnight in January 2015 in an effort to secure a property on a development of 828 homes priced at £375,000 for a one-bedroomed property, with two-bedroomed properties being sold for £700,000. The development proved popular amongst both British and foreign investors, and, at the time of writing, the first residents will move in at the end of 2015.

The first residents of the QEOP moved into the refurbished Athletes Village in 2013. Consisting of 2,818 private homes and owned by Delancey/Qatari Diar, who paid £557 million for the site, East Village[22] is the UK's first private-sector residential development of over 1,000 homes to be owned and directly managed as an investment.[23] With an appearance and general ambiance not dissimilar to a high-rise Spanish holiday resort, with the exception of just over 350 of the apartments which were made available for shared ownerships, the properties on East Village are rental only with a private/social housing split of 60:40.

Private renters live in separate blocks to social housing tenants, most of whom come from Newham council lists and properties. Although we cannot substantiate further, we were told informally that these tenants had been heavily vetted by Newham Council, constituting 'the cream of the housing list', favouring 'those in work or actively seeking work or employment'. However, it was also suspected by Newham police, who have responsibility for QEOP, that the neighboring 'Olympic boroughs' which do not have a serious stake in the QEOP, but who were allowed to house some of their residents on the site, were not as stringent in their selection procedures, and as a consequence some 'problem tenants' may have found their way onto the QEOP. Whether or not this is true, it is interesting that at this very early stage in the history of East Village, where, as we discuss below, crime is extraordinarily low, and in the absence of an established criminal 'threat' such as the Portuguese Mafia, Newham police still need to identify a problematic 'other', and allegedly unruly tenants from Waltham Forest, Hackney, and Tower Hamlets conveniently serve this purpose.

East Village expects to soon boast a Saturday morning Farmers Market.

Bespoke policing: park life

On a sunny day the park's 27 acres of cycle paths and green spaces welcomes thousands of visitors: parents pushing buggies, tourists, joggers and cyclists. The absence of shelter from the elements also means that during the winter there are days when no more than a handful of people visit. The QEOP is privately-owned territory. The East Village management pay private security staff to patrol the neighbourhood, whilst the LLDC employ security officers to patrol the entire park. Newham police have a police station on the park to accommodate one Inspector, two Sergeants and 20 PCs. Although most of these officers are from Newham, one officer is seconded from each of the three neighbouring boroughs. The cost of the MPS presence is £1 million per annum, which is currently split three ways between the MPS, LLDC and Delancey. This arrangement has already produced what one supervisory officer described as 'constant' strain, as funders with a stake in this experiment in plural policing pressurize the public police. One recent example was the apprehension of three young people who had entered the Olympic stadium at night. Unsure if they were just curious students or urban explorers[24] the police released them without charge. The LLDC head of security wanted them charged as an example to others. The MPS refused.

The park and its residents are carefully watched. CCTV is a major feature of the QEOP and has proved effective in providing an early warning for identifying unwelcome youths in particular. Groups of young black men 'known' to the police are particularly unwelcome, and are informed by the QEOP police upon entering the area that they are being monitored by CCTV. Already *persona non grata* in Westfield, at this early stage in the park's existence, a combination of police attention and electronic surveillance appears to be sufficient in deterring these residents of Old Newham from venturing into E20.

All of the crime statistics generated by the QEOP currently, certainly until further Olympic neighborhoods are built and populated, 'belong' to the borough of Newham. So far these statistics are stunningly low, standing at around 20 crimes per month, mainly for criminal damage (graffiti), mild antisocial behavior, and bicycle theft. In 2015, police duty on the QEOP is pleasant, and if the sun is shining, a shift spent cycling around the paths and waterways of the park is clearly preferable to dealing with the stressful chaotic streets of Stratford, Plaistow, Canning Town and East Ham. For back in Old Newham officers are, according to a uniformed Sergeant, 'run ragged' on a daily basis with a workload of '20 crimes (each) week to deal with', which if correct, is a figure that is approximately the monthly crime rate for the entire QEOP. The low crime statistics suit the park's PR-conscious commercial partners, and its residents can rest assured that they live in an area where crime is virtually non-existent.

The LLDC are keen to keep it this way for as long as possible, pushing any crime generators onto the borough profile. One building, a privately owned residential complex for over 2,000 university students, is marketed as being on the Olympic Park, but actually sits at the boundary of the Westfield complex. When an entirely predictable amount of crime became associated with this building, for instance, drunkenness, drug use and assault, it threatened to pollute the QEOP's near pristine crime profile. Pressure from the LLDC resulted in the student residence being assigned to the Newham Borough police statistics, with borough officers now attending calls to the building and recording the crime statistics as theirs rather than being the QEOP team's responsibility. In neo-liberal society, market sensitivities are always to the forefront, and territory is an eminently flexible concept.

In Newham's post-Olympic milieu, the fresh territory of the QEOP is the site of 'plural policing' *par excellence* (Melossi, 1997; Crawford et al. 2005; Jones and Newburn, 2006), comprising of public and private police personnel, which with the pre-Olympic emergence of municipal policing should be considered as a principle legacy of the 2012 Olympics. As we discuss in Chapter 4, increasingly in Newham, the police are but one node in a network of security providers, and at times they will steer and at other times remain at arms-length (Crawford et al. 2005, Crawford, 2006). They face a future that may well see them competing for business with other agencies in a value-for-money culture of managerialism, metrics and customer-orientation (O'Malley and Palmer 1996, Johnston 1999). The commodification of policing which has gained a particular purchase in the unique spaces of Westfield and the QEOP will ensure the recalibration of state policing resources. Both collaboration and competition among commercial and possibly municipal providers, promise to reallocate policing services at the expense of the disadvantaged (Shearing, 1992). Consequently, divisions will emerge between different consumers, some of whom are well placed to manage risk, while other more 'at-risk' groups may find that the security market has little interest in satisfying their needs (Loader, 2000: 331). In addition, demarcation between responsive and preventative roles may well be contested as will the nature of co-ordination and collaboration (cf. Ayling & Shearing, 2008). Security tasks are likely to evolve as combined and symbiotic (cf. Sarre & Prenzler, 2000,) or pluralized (Crawford & Lister, 2006) as both strategy and implementation are negotiated as part of a security quilt (Ericson, 1994. Crawford & Lister, 2004) that is likely to gain in complexity as the park's various developments and its concomitant populations and workforces emerge.

Outside of the QEOP, Newham is largely policed by a workforce pressured by unrealistic and ever-shifting targets and fiscal restraints, and as a result of these unprecedented pressures, policing in Newham will change. Although history teaches us that officers will rapidly adapt to these pressures and find both legal and quasi-legal means of putting 'meat on the table', in order to 'keep the numbers up' (Manning, 2015) targets will inevitably be achieved at the expense of the borough's residents, whose fragmented cultures often exist in circumstances besieged by poverty and exclusion. These two qualities are as central to everyday life in post-Olympic Newham as they were in 2009, when Altman slighted East London with his 'gash' slur. Altman probably had the area that now constitutes the QEOP to the forefront of his mind when he made this comment, and it was here rather than in the rest of Newham that every public and private body with a stake in the 2012 Olympics has laboured to provide a legacy that is above all lucrative. The money-spinner of the QEOP constitutes one of contemporary UK neo-liberalism's most remarkable products. This marketizing of ex-industrial space represents a bizarre experiment in heavily regulated housing within a theme park that combines nature walks with shopping, where a sporting venue devoid of any historical context or communal memory sits alongside the branch of a world-class museum exhibiting a selection of its 137 million artefacts, such as Dorothy's ruby red slippers in the Wizard of Oz.[25]

The 2012 neo-liberal Olympics

The assemblage of control that emerged in the build up to the Olympics, and which matured during the Games and in its aftermath, particularly with reference to Westfield and the QEOP, featured some remarkably complex funding and resource arrangements. These arrangements blurred distinctions between the public, private and municipal, and involved competing concerns of visceral and reputational risk that confounded simplistic notions of policing (Garland, 1996: 453). The fragmented, disorganized, often opportunistic and cynical agencies of liberal democratic government sometimes battled, and at other times co-operated with business interests via a complex series of interlocking relationships that flowed through 'a network of open circuits' (Rose, 2000: 188) across various commercial and civic institutions. The 2012 local policing assemblage was 'hesitant, incomplete, fragmentary, contradictory and contested' (Rose, 2000: 183). While the local police attempted a business-as-usual approach, commercial concerns, particularly in the case of Westfield, were always on the front foot; the demands of the Games required extensive recalibration of roles, responsibilities and manpower, creating 'multiple and diverse organisational and coercive ambitions that, when taken together, combine into uneasy coalitions of control' (Fussey, 2014: 11). For as new threats morphed, old problems were rebranded, and powerful players from outside of the borough had their own fears, worries and interests to promote. Often with one eye on the post-Games environment, the emergent assemblage of control is a prime example of 'domain expansion' (Best, 1990), the process through which a, 'previously accepted social problem', represented here for instance by local youth, 'is enabled to expand' (Loseke, 1999: 82).

As we conclude this book in the Summer of 2015, the QEOP enjoys a small, carefully managed population, controlled and protected by an over-resourced police presence backed by several private security companies and an arsenal of CCTV cameras. How this hybrid system of social control will develop in an era of swingeing public service cuts is unclear, as at the time of writing there are no long-term contracts for the policing, safety and security of the evolving populations of the park. Huge changes are imminent. In particular West Ham United are due to become tenants of the Olympic Stadium in 2016, and even if its 54,000 capacity is not reached, the public order, safety and security dilemmas that the new venue will pose will vary considerably from those experienced by both police and residents at the club's old Boleyn Ground over the previous 102 years. In addition to the stadium, many of the new venues and attractions designated for the park will pose security and policing problems, the permanent population of the park will increase, and the anticipated enterprises and businesses therein will result in an increased footfall as jobs are created and visitors arrive. All of these changes will generate dilemmas for which the current hybrid arrangements are unlikely to be suitable. New security players, some with venue-specific briefs, are likely to emerge into an increasingly complex assemblage of control that will render the police-dominated arrangements (Crawford, 2006) of the past utterly redundant.

Unhindered by the restrictions and restraints of democratic government that cling on just the other side of the A118 in Old Newham, private security will be commercially obliged to step into spaces created not only by the park's rapid development, but crucially by the almost inevitable recall of officers from the QEOP due to a combination of cuts to public services and the demands of an administratively-bound, target-dominated institution and its political paymasters. Further, if a gap is created by the inevitable retreat of the public police from its current high profile on the QEOP, we also predict that Newham's municipal police will be summoned, at a price, onto the park, with inevitable consequences for the enforcement brief targeting rogue businesses and landlords that has been successfully developed by Newham Council. In this environment, where neo-liberal governance has ensured that every aspect of social life is marketized and privatized, the QEOP will almost inevitably see the public police succumb to cuts and retreat back to policing an increasingly fractious and chaotic population suffering from a toxic blend of benefit cuts and market forces.[26]

Newham is of course a far from isolated case, and neo-liberal pressures have impacted hugely on all UK local government administrations. However, the borough, with high property prices and spiralling rents, has been hit especially hard, and the effects of marketization, privatization, and an increase in private activity and responsibility (Drakeford, 2000:19) can be observed across its entire spectrum of social and economic life.[27] In particular, policing and housing (Birney, 2009. Matthews & Pitt, 2001: 5; Millie, 2009: 20–33) are in the process of being transformed through neo-liberal logic into interdependent nodes of social control.[28] This was noted by one of Newham's more experienced political players, who explained that ultimately it was market forces that would change the borough's demographics: 'The legislation we're throwing at private landlords will require them to be licensed to rent out places. This will put rents up. We'll get wealthier renters living in nicer places. Those who can't afford the property will go further east where there's places they can. The Olympics will take credit ten years down the line for transforming parts of Newham but it's fuck all to do with them'.

Old Newham: fortunes always hiding

Oh! it really is a very pretty garden
And Chingford to the Eastward could be seen
With a ladder and some glasses
You could see to Hackney Marshes
If it wasn't for the houses in between
    (Edgar Bateman/George LeBrunn, 1899)

While urban regeneration associated with major sporting events has focused on destigmatizing or rebranding poor neighborhoods, late modernity has witnessed a myriad of attempts by urban authorities to systematically exclude its less economically viable citizens. These strategies aim to reassure both visiting spectators and potential new residents that they will be safe (Ward, 2003). Concomitantly, the notion of the local 'community' being beneficiaries of Olympic-led transformation remains dubious. The post-Olympic residential enclosures on the QEOP reinforce existing socio-economic segregation (Poynter, 2009) and will be accompanied by symbolic economies that facilitate social stratification (Harvey, 2000), and in doing so render the culture of industrial-era Newham retrospectively fantastic. Gentrified enclaves will bring further demands from new residents for greater levels of security (Lindsey, 2014), exacerbating bordering processes and enabling 'spatial purification' typified by expensive housing and 'cathedrals of consumption' (Ritzer, 2005). Newham was never defined by its places of worship; its sacred sites, which were pubs, sporting venues, street markets, work places and other essentially communal spaces, are now sanctified commercial zones with guardianship given to security guards and other agents of social control (Sibley, 1995: 72).

The plan was always to use the Olympics in conjunction with the Thames Gateway project to introduce to Newham a middle-class population with its accompanying demands and services. Faced with vicious cuts from central government, Newham Council hoped to use the Games to radically alter the borough's demographic, encouraging young professionals to buy houses, deposit their children in local schools and place heavy expectations on local teachers to raise standards. Along the way, the demands of the bourgeoisie would clean the streets of dumped mattresses, and remove or marginalize everyday noise, nuisance and incivilities. But all of this would come at a cost that would push the current population either out of the borough or, for those not already 'decanted' to Stoke-On-Trent and all places in-between, still further into tightly constricted spaces of ethnically defined social marginality accompanied by high profile surveillance.

Politicians of all major parties have expressed their desire for Newham to change, and aided and abetted by the 2012 Olympics the housing market will over a period of time ensure that many of its current population will be priced out of the borough. In this way all of the key metrics upon which local services are judged, for instance policing, health and education, will improve as Newham gradually acquires a very different demographic and accompanying culture. Much of the population of Old Newham will find themselves excluded from the QEOP by a whole arsenal of social control factors, most of which relate to the housing and consumer markets that have been created in and around this new space. Policing is not irrelevant here, but unlike in Old Newham, the public police 'no longer aspire to be the guarantor and ultimate provider' (Rose, 2000: 186). In the QEOP, public policing is performed alongside the employees of key stakeholders to ensure the continued viability of this new territory, which is, above all, an enterprise zone whose commercial *raison d'être* stands in stark contrast to the warts-and all-social democratic governance of Old Newham.[29] Old Newham is but one battlefield upon which the UK's attritional welfare wars are fought, and many of its civilian combatants, locked into 'circuits of insecurity' (Rose, 2000: 187), are largely irrelevant to the glossy future of E20: it simply has no use for them (Winlow & Hall, 2013).

Newham police will carry on regardless. They will both repress and rescue the borough's population as required, reaching some targets set by their increasingly metric-minded masters, and (until next time) missing others. New public and private partners will emerge, and the churning population that the police are to serve will alternate between eye-avoiding apparent subservience, and fierce in-your-face resistance. Meanwhile, within their own ranks, local police must contend with diktats from a progressively remote, corporate-orientated Centre that is gaining increasing influence over everyday tasks, while the erosion of working conditions serves to disorientate a workforce which had thought itself immune to the wrath of punitive marketeers. More widely across Newham, for the police, the borough's multiple churning communities, the council and everyone working in Newham, the outlook is uncertain. The Games, its attendant property boom and the rest of the 'legacy' were rigged, and the market took all of the gold.

Notes

1 Over the past three decades, the capital has seen an 80 per cent increase in poor households. Approximately 36 per cent of London households are now classified as poor (up from 20 per cent in 1980), and in Newham, almost one in two households is now poor. See http://www.londonmapper.org.uk/analysis/poverty-and-wealth-1980-2010/.
2 See http://www.newham.gov.uk/documents/environment%20and%20planning/corestrategy2004-13.pdf.
3 See *Construction Enquirer*, October 2014.
4 See 'Scandal of the Wasted Millions spent on Games Legacy Projects', the *Times*, 31 December 2014.
5 See 'Newham Council to face Paddy Power in Court over Betting shop Application', *Newham Recorder*, 9 April 2013.
6 http://www.newham.gov.uk/Pages/News/Council-turns-down-bookies-application.aspx.
7 See'Labour Promises to Let Councils Ban Fixed-odds Betting Terminals', the *Guardian*, 20 December 2013.
8 'Newham Mayor Sir Robin Wales is Fighting to Stop the Betting Shop Industry Blighting our Streets', *Newham Recorder*, 15 January 2014.
9 However, the borough has an ambivalent attitude towards gambling, and the Council were willing to manipulate public opinion in order to enjoy the revenues to be gleaned

from the three casinos granted licenses in early 2011. One elected member claimed that: 'We have 'consultation exercises' . . . Usually approval for anything is around the 30% mark. This time it was different. We took an invited 100 members of the public to the ExCel Centre where they watched a presentation about the benefit of Casinos. They got a three-course meal, which the Council paid for and all got a £75 shopping voucher to spend in Galleon's Reach Mall . . . the approval rating was 72% in favour of Casinos . . .'

10 See https://www.gov.uk/government/uploads/system/uploads/attachment_data/file/78316/Taking_Part_Olympic_Report.pdf.

11 Host Boroughs Unit (2009), *Convergence, Strategic Regeneration Framework: An Olympic Legacy for the Host Boroughs.*

12 http://www.londonspovertyprofile.org.uk/key-facts/overview-of-london-boroughs/. The research was carried out by the New Policy Institute (NPI) and commissioned by the Trust for London.

13 In 2010, while coping with £28 million of coalition cuts to the borough's budget, Newham Council spent more than £111 million on a new purpose-built headquarters, including more than £10,000 on designer chandeliers.

14 See 'Revealed: London's Secret Exodus of the Poor', the *Independent*, 30 April 2015.

15 http://www.localgovernmentexecutive.co.uk/news/newham-council-give-armed-services-and-employed-people-priority-social-housing.

16 The estate was built in 1967 and includes three tower blocks as well as homes with gardens, smaller blocks of flats, and a school. The cost of refurbishing the entire Carpenters estate was estimated at £70 million, but was complicated by a number of factors including the use of asbestos in the original build.

However, the major reason that large parts of Carpenters estate had been vacant for eight years is that a deal with University College London, who had planned to build a £1 billion campus, had fallen through. The sociologist Ruth Glass worked at UCL when she first coined the term 'gentrification'.

17 In February 2015 Robin Wales was found guilty of breaching the council's Members Code of Conduct as a result of his response to Focus E15 supporters at the Newham Mayor's Show in July 2014.

18 http://www.newham.gov.uk/pages/News/Newham-schools-deliver-strong-GCSE-results-in-line-with-national-trend.aspx.

19 However, contrary to planners' hopes and expectations, Eurostar does not stop at Stratford International Station.

20 The 114.5-metre high Arcelor Mittal Orbit Tower, which cost £19.1 million, with £16 million coming from Britain's richest man, the steel tycoon Lakshmi Mittal, and the balance of £3.1 million coming from the the public purse, is the tallest structure on the QEOP. Post-Olympics the structure hosts various functions including one-hour early morning yoga classes on the viewing platform at a cost of £17 per person. Alternatively, the platform can be hired for weddings at a cost of £10,000. In the financial year 2014/2015 the Tower lost £520,000, or £10,000 a week (the *Guardian*, 21 October 2015). In a 2010 press release Mayor Johnson described the sculpture as 'the perfect iconic cultural legacy'.

21 http://queenelizabetholympicpark.co.uk/our-story/transforming-east-london/legacy-communities-scheme.

22 Chobham Manor and East Village are two separate areas. The LLDC is the planning authority for East Village but has no land holdings whereas at Chobham Manor the LLDC is the freeholder.

23 See http://www.e-architect.co.uk/london/london-olympics-village (e-architect.co.uk, 15 August 2011).

24 Urban explorers are hobbyists who explore, usually illegally, buildings, ruins, and other components of the man-made environment.

25 See 'Smithsonian Considers London Outpost in Olympic Park', *BBC News*, 27 January 2015.
26 See 'Tenant Evictions Reach Six-year High Amid Rising Rents and Benefit Cuts', the *Guardian*, 14 May 2015.
27 The various dimensions of privatization indicated by Vickers and Wright (1989: 3) are highly relevant to understanding all aspects of life and work in 2012 Olympic era Newham:

- '(A)bolishing or severely curtailing public services on the assumption that private provision will fill the gap'. At the 2012 Games we can see this being played out in the policing of the Games and in its aftermath on the new territory of the QEOP. This can also be observed in the increased role of private landlords providing accommodation in the wake of local authorities selling their housing stock.
- '(S)queezing the financial resources of publicly-funded bodies in the hope of inducing them to seek compensating private funding'. Councils such as LBN hit by severe budgetary constraints are forced to rely on private developers for large housing projects, for example on the QEOP and in the attempts to sell off the Carpenters estate.
- '(I)ncreasing the financial contribution of consumers for public goods and services – a policy partly inspired by the desire to reduce the role of the State as purchaser'. This can be observed for example in the slashing of benefits, in particular housing, and driving up the contribution of recipients, as well as pressing those recipients to seek out markets commensurate with their incomes, wherever those markets are and regardless of established social networks.
- '(T)ransferring to the private sector public policy responsibilities'. For example the Olympic driven commercialization of security and the replacement of public policing by private security companies, as well as hybrids such as municipal police.
- '(E)ncouraging private finance to build and operate public works and infrastructure'. As evidenced in the case of Westfield and the shopping centres subsequent clout regarding policing and transport in particular, as well as the complex arrangements that we have described on the QEOP.
- '(I)ntroducing notions of efficiency and of management techniques into the public sector'. This has clearly impacted on every aspect of the administration of LBN but in particular in terms of the metric driven measures of New Public Managerialism designed to impose business principles of economy, effectiveness and efficiency within Newham MPS, and the MPS Centre in the hope of imparting a greater 'commercial orientation' into its ethos and functioning.
- '(S)elling land and publicly-owned housing stock'. This first impacted significantly upon the housing market in Newham, as we explain in Chapter 2 with the onset of buy to let and has continued apace as the value of land in Newham rose significantly as a result of the Olympics.

28 https://www.gov.uk/government/policies/improving-the-rented-housing-sector—2/supporting-pages/anti-social-behaviour-in-housing.
29 The neo-liberal ethos of the QEOP is entirely consistent. Even its school – Chobham Academy, part of the Harris Federation, a charity whose founder, Lord Harris, is a self-made businessman – has formal Academy status, and so is entirely independent of direct control by democratically elected local government. (http://www.publications.parliament.uk/pa/cm201415/cmselect/cmeduc/258/258.pdf).

References

Aaron, C. (2013) 'Measuring the Legacy', *Journal of the International Centre for Sports Security, 1*:100.
Alwakeel, R. (2014) 'East London's £3.5bn Plan for "Meatpacking District" in Docklands Gets Go-ahead'#, *Evening Standard*, 27 April 2014.

Ayling, J. & Shearing, C. (2008) 'Taking Care of Business: Police and Commercial Security Vendors', *Criminology and Criminal Justice*, 8(1): 27–50.

Bauman, Z. (1998) *Globalization: The Human Consequences*. Cambridge: Polity.

BBC News (2013) 'Paddy Power Wins Licence Refusal Appeal', 17 June 2013.

Best, J. (1990) *Threatened Children, Rhetoric and Concern About Child-Victims*. Chicago: University of Chicago Press.

Birney, E. (2009) *Making People Behave: Anti-social Behaviour, Politics and Policy* (2nd ed). Cullompton: Willan.

Bryant, M. (2015) 'New East London Home for Leading Ballet Company', *Evening Standard*, 27 May 2015.

Cohen, P. (2013) *On the Wrong Side of the Track? East London and the Post-Olympics*. London: Lawrence & Wishart.

Crawford, A. (2006) 'Networked Governance and the Post-regulatory Ptate? Steering, Rowing and Anchoring the Provision of Policing and Security', *Theoretical Criminology, 10*(4): 449–479.

Crawford, A., & Lister, S. (2004) 'The Patchwork Shape of Reassurance Policing in England and Wales: Integrated Local Security Quilts or Frayed, Fragmented and Fragile Tangled Webs?', *Policing* 5(3): 41–430.

Crawford, A. & Lister, S. (2006) 'Additional Security Patrols in Residential Areas: Notes From the Marketplace', *Policing and Society, 16*(2): 164–188.

Crawford, A., Lister, S., Blackburn, S., & Burnett, J. (2005) *Plural Policing: The Mixed Economy of Visible Patrols in England and Wales*. Bristol: Policy Press.

DCMS (2012) 'Meta-Evaluation of the Impacts of the Legacy of the London 2012 Olympics and Paralympic Games. Report 4: Interim Evaluation'. London: Department for Culture, Media and Sport.

Drakeford, M. (2000) *Privatisation and Social Policy*. Harlow: Longman.

Duell, M. (2013) 'Return of the East End Slums: Rogue Landlords Create "Sheds with Beds" to Illegally House Migrant Families in one of Country's Poorest Areas', *Daily Mail*, February 12.

Ellis-Petersen, H. (2014) 'London Olympicopolis Culture Hub Plan gets £141m Funding', the *Guardian*, 2 December 2014.

Ericson, R. (1994) 'The Division of Expert Knowledge in Policing and Security', *British Journal of Sociology, 42*(2): 149–175.

Fussey, P. (2014) 'Command, Control and Contestation: Negotiating Security at the London 2012 Olympics', *The Geographical Journal*, advance publication DOI: 10.1111/geoj.12058.

Garcia-Ramon, M. & Albert, A. (2000) 'Pre-olympic and Post-olympic Barcelona, a Model for Urban Regeneration To-day?', *Environment and Planning A, 32*(8): 1331–1334, 2000.

Garland, D. (1996) 'The Limits of the Sovereign State: Strategies of Crime Control in Contemporary Society', *British Journal of Criminology, 36*(4): 445–471.

Gentleman, A. (2012) 'The Woman who Lives in a Shed: How London Landlords are Cashing in', the *Guardian*, May 9.

Gibson, O. (2015a) 'Olympic Stadium Cost Rises to £701m From Initial £280m Estimate', the *Guardian*, 19 June 2015.

Gibson, O. (2015b) 'Details of West Ham's Olympic Stadium Deal Must be Made Public', the *Guardian*, 15 September 2015.

Gould, M. (2015) 'Local Residents Angry at Lack of Social Housing at West Ham's Ground', the *Guardian,* 24 February 2015.Harvey, D. (2000) *Spaces of Hope.* Edinburgh: Edinburgh University Press.

Helm, T. & Boffey, D. (2015) 'Ex-Whitehall Chief Criticises Right-to-buy Housing Policy', the *Observer*, 31 May 2015.

Hughes, D. (2012) 'The Long-term Legacy for the UK from the Olympic and Paralympic Games', House of Lords: Library Note, retrieved from: www.parliament.uk/ briefing-papers/LLN-2012-037.pdf.

Johnston, L. (1999) 'Private Policing in Context', *European Journal on Criminal Policy and Research, 7*(2): 175–196.

Jones, T & Newburn, T. (eds) (2006) *Plural Policing: A Comparative Perspective*. London: Routledge.

Kornblatt, T. (2006) 'Setting the Bar: Preparing for London's Olympic Legacy'. London: Centre for Cities.

Lenskyj, H.J. (2000) *Inside the Olympic industry: Power, politics, and activism*. New York: SUNY Press.

Lindsay, I. (2014) *Living with London's Olympics: An Ethnography*. London: Palgrave Macmillan.

Loader, I (2000) 'Policing and Governance', *Social Legal Studies, 9*(3): 323–345.

London Assembly (2007) *A Lasting Legacy for London? Assessing the Legacy of the Olympic Games and Paralympic Games*. London: greater Londn Authority/London East Research Institute.

London Development Agency (LDA) (2010) *Creating a Legacy: Socio-economic Benefits from the 2012 Olympic and Paralympic Games*. London Development Agency: London.

Loseke, D. (1999) *Thinking about Social Problems.* New York: Aldine de Gruyter.

Manning, P. (2015) 'Researching policing using qualitative methods', in Copes, H. & Miller, M. (eds) *The Routledge Handbook of Qualitative Criminology*. Abingdon: Routledge.

Matthews, R. & Pitt, J. (2001) *Crime Disorder and Community Safety*. London: Routledge.

Mean, A., Vigor, M. & Tims, C. (2004) 'Conclusion: Minding the Gap', in *After the Gold Rush: a sustainable Olympics for London*. London: Institute for Public Policy Research.

Melossi, D. (1997) 'State and Social Control *à la Fin de Siècle*: From the New World to the Constitution of the New Europe', in R. Bergalli & C. Sumner (eds) *Social Control and Political Order: European Perspectives at the End of the Century*. London: Sage.

Merrill, J (2015) 'Huge drop in Women and Disabled People Participating in Sport After the Olympics', the *Independent*, 29 January 2015.

Millie, A. (2009) *Anti-Social Behaviour*. Maidenhead: Open University Press.

O'Malley, P. & Palmer, D. (1996) 'Post-Keynesian Policing', *Economy and Society 25*: 137–155.

Poynter, G. (2009) 'London 2012 and the Reshaping of East London', in Imrie R., L. Lees & M. Raco (eds) *Regenerating London*. London: Routledge.

Prynn, J. (2014) 'Upton Park to be Redeveloped into a 700-home East End "Village" when West Ham Complete Move to the Olympic Stadium', the *Independent,* 10 February 2014.

Quinn, B. (2014) 'Newham Mayor says Sorry for Treatment of E15 Housing Campaigners', the *Guardian*, 6 October 2014.

Raslah, J. (2014) 'Tackling Newham's Beds in Sheds', *Newham Recorder*, January 7.

Ritzer, G. (2005) *Enchanting a Disenchanted World: Revolutionizing the Means of Consumption*. London: SAGE.

Robinson, M. (2014) 'Thermal Imaging Camera Reveals Shocking Extent of Illegal "Beds in Sheds" Housing for Immigrants Built by Rogue Landlords', *Daily Mail,* March 4.

Rose, N. (2000) 'Government and Control', *British Journal of Criminology, 40*: 321–339.

Sarre, R., & Prenzler, T. (2000) 'The Relationship Between Police and Private Security: Models and Future Directions', *International Journal of Applied Criminal Justice, 24*(1): 91– 113.

Shearing, C. (1992) 'The Relation Between Public and Private Policing', in M. Tony & N. Morris (eds) *Modern Policing.* Chicago: Chicago University Press.

Sibley, D. (1995) *Geographies of Exclusion.* London: Routledge.

Sissons, P., Dewson, S., Rose, N., Martin, R, & Carta, E. (2010) *Understanding Worklessness in Newham: Final Report.* Brighton: Institute of Employment Studies.

Sport England (2015) *Active People Survey 9Q2 April 2014 – March 2015.* Loughborough: Sport England.

Tracey, R. (2015) *Sporting Chance: Increasing Disability to Sport.* London: London Assembly, Greater London Authority.

Vickers, J. & Wright, V. (1989) 'The Politics of Industrial Privatisation in Western Europe', in J.Vickers & V. Wright (eds) *The Politics of Privatization in Western Europe.* London: Frank Cass.

Ward, K. (2003) 'Entrepreneurial Urbanism, State Restructuring and Civilizing "New" East Manchester', *Area, 35*: 116–127.

Winlow, S., & Hall, S. (2013) *Rethinking Social Exclusion.* London: Sage.

Index